GETTING TO THE BUBBLE

ALSO BY MIKE McCARDELL

Chasing the Story God
Back Alley Reporter
The Blue Flames That Keep Us Warm

GETTING TO THE BUBBLE

Finding Magic Amid the Urban Roar

Mike McCardell

HARBOUR PUBLISHING

Harbour Publishing Co. Ltd.
P.O. Box 219
Madeira Park, BC
V0N 2H0
www.harbourpublishing.com

THE CANADA COUNCIL | LE CONSEIL DES ARTS
FOR THE ARTS | DU CANADA
SINCE 1957 | DEPUIS 1957

Cover design by Anna Comfort, photographs
by Nick Didlick
Printed and bound in Canada

BRITISH
COLUMBIA
ARTS COUNCIL
Supported by the Province of British Columbia

Harbour Publishing acknowledges financial support from the Government of Canada through the Book Publishing Industry Development Program and the Canada Council for the Arts, and from the Province of British Columbia through the British Columbia Arts Council and the Book Publisher's Tax Credit through the Ministry of Provincial Revenue.

Sales of this book help support Variety—the Children's Charity.

Library and Archives Canada Cataloguing in Publication

McCardell, Mike, 1944–
   Getting to the bubble : finding magic amid the urban roar / Mike McCardell.

ISBN 978-1-55017-443-4

   1. Vancouver (B.C.)—Anecdotes. 2. Vancouver (B.C.)—Biography.
I. Title.
FC3847.36.M443 2008   971.1'33   C2008-904850-4

This is dedicated to everyone I have ever met, you have all helped me.
But especially to Reilly.
You changed my life.

CONTENTS

BOOK FOUR

You may have seen the story. Two brothers working in the same Vancouver coffee shop, rooting for different English league soccer teams. One for Manchester United, the other for Liverpool. They were East Indians who were born in England and now living in Canada. Perfect demographics for the new world. Nice, exciting guys. They each thought the other was nuts.

But I did not know any of that when we walked into the shop. We only wanted coffee.

We ordered two small dark roasts before we saw the soccer game on a TV in a corner. And we only noticed that when a guy in front of the screen suddenly jumped out of his seat and was yelling.

"We're gonna win! We're gonna win!"

That's enough to get my notice.

"Can we take a picture of him?" I ask the woman behind the counter.

She smiled, nodded, and cameraman John Chant turned on his camera and pointed it at the screamer.

"I can't stand it. I can't. If we hold on for three more minutes I win, —I mean WE win!" said the fellow in front of the TV. No he didn't say it. He shouted it.

I immediately liked him. He changed the "I" to "we." He was a good guy.

"Who you rooting for?" I asked.

"Liverpool, of course." He looked at me like that was a stupid question. He had an English accent.

John and I think this is wonderful. What more could we hope for? A fanatical fan makes good television.

Then from behind the counter someone was loudly saying that he was "crazy, and a nutcase."

I turn with the microphone to talk to him. This is conflict, at least on the level I like.

Cameraman John Chant is pulling on my arm.

"Are *you* crazy? The action is here by the TV."

But the man behind the counter is still yelling: "He's crazy."

"Why you saying that?" I shout. I drop a word in the question to save time.

"He's my brother, and he's crazy."

A brother mocking a brother over sports? What more could I hope for? And then the brother behind the counter let loose with the worse insult of all: "He's cheering for the wrong team."

Two brothers, different teams; one screaming, the other critiquing. Can my heart stand any more joy?

John turns back to the game just in time to hear "HE SCORES!!!" And he films the guy in front of the TV trying to jump through the roof.

"Two minutes to go," shouts the Liverpool brother. "I'm trembling."

That was the Liverpool brother saying that of course. But I am trembling, too.

There is nothing better, at least not for me. Five minutes earlier I was considering changing jobs and had lost faith in the most important secret I had learned in my entire life. And now, everything was okay again. In fact, better than okay.

Nothing could beat this.

"It's insane at home," said the woman we had ordered the coffee from.

"What do you mean?" I ask.

"He's my brother-in-law," she said, while pointing to the Liverpool guy.

Oh, my jumping heart.

"That means obviously . . ." I am trying to think of who's related to who, but I hear screaming from the Liverpool section. ". . . you are his wife?" I am pointing to the brother behind the counter.

"Yes, we are Manchester United fans."

John is filming the Liverpool guy.

"Thirty seconds to go. Got to shoot the end of the game," John shouts at me.

I am thinking we've got to shoot the brother and sister-in-law's reaction to the Liverpool relation's reaction to the end of the game, which of course is impossible. That would take two cameras.

"We won!" shouts Liverpool brother.

"Loser," shout the Man U fans.

John spins around. This is the challenge of instant real life happenings. They instantly happen all at once.

The brothers laugh, they argue, then John sees them secretly shaking hands behind the counter. "Don't tell anyone," they say.

In trying to get the shot John leans across the counter and knocks over the donuts.

"Don't worry," says the woman who grabs the donuts and points to her belly. "Twins coming soon, and they will be Manchester United fans." John gets that on camera and I am secretly saying thank you to many heavenly coaches.

Then we get our coffee, which we paid for before we learned about the game.

Total amount of time in the coffee shop, Bean Around the World, on Mainland in Yaletown, which the family owns, twelve minutes. And most of that was spent getting the spelling of everyone's names and joking with them about the game and their special way of watching it and putting the lids on our coffee cups.

How did all that happen?

That is what this book is about. How was that story found? How is anything you want found? How do you get what you want? I can tell you because the secret was shared with me by a boy named Reilly, who some might say was a little slow. But after listening to him my life changed. I found basically that all things are possible. And that is true.

I know there are thousands of positive thinking books out there, and they are all good, and they all work, and they all seem to be written by Oprah.

Reilly will probably never write a book. He was nine years old when I met him and he had the mental capacity of someone who was six, or maybe a wise sixty-year-old.

I wrote about him in the last book and include him in every talk that I give. It is a funny story on one level. He was fishing at Trout Lake using a stick as a pole. There were still a few twigs and leaves sticking out of it. A string was attached to the tip and at the end of the string was a paper clip pulled open to make a hook, with bread as bait.

The story that I always tell is that he believed that he would catch a fish, someday. But while he told me that he sniffed. He sniffed like any nine-year-old.

"I believe that if you really, really (*sniff*) believe in something (*sniff*), it will happen." (*Sniff.*)

His foster mother told us he had never caught a fish, but he said he believed he would, someday. She also said the lake had a calming influence on him.

"Have you caught anything?" I asked him.

"No, but I believe (*sniff*) that I will."

"Have you ever got a nibble?"

"No, but I believe . . . (*sniff*) that I will (*sniff*) get a nibble."

With each sniff a glob of green mucus was sliding out of his nose and reaching his top lip. Then he stopped talking for an instant and sucked it back up through his nostril.

"And I believe you get whatever you want . . . (*sniff*) if you believe it enough and really want it enough. (*Sniff.*) If you believe you will get it . . . (*sniff*) . . . you will." (*Sniff.*)

I was getting sick. My stomach was turning. I was going to throw up. The mucus was slimy and bright and, ugh, I hate even now to think about it.

"I believe you can be anything . . . (*sniff*) . . . you want to be."

But how could I stop this kid from speaking? You don't do that when you are listening to beautiful eternal truths that could change lives.

You don't say: "Hey, kid, forget about saving humanity and blow your nose."

Also it is forbidden in my trade to interfere with reality, even if I was thinking: "Please, blow your nose before you go on with the wisdom of Socrates."

When he finished talking I turned to the cameraman and said, "Did you see that?"

"What?"

"Did you see the nose?"

"What are you talking about? I saw a beautiful child talking about universal truths."

"You didn't see the nose?"

He looked at me like I was weird.

Thank you story god, or lucky stones, or whatever majesty kept the camera from moving a half-inch to the left, which then would have seen the mucus.

Then it would have been a story about a kid not blowing his nose. It would have been a joke. Instead, it became a lesson in living.

At first it made me think how closely united are comedy and tragedy. You laugh at someone else's dandelion-covered lawn, and curse if a kid blows the seeds your way. But it was more than that.

Time passed and Reilly remained in my head.

"You get what you want, if you believe you will get it."

That's nice, I thought. But you don't get what you want. You are what nature and the world and your family threw at you.

"You get what you want, if you believe you will get it."

What I want are stories about ordinary people doing extraordinary things that we just happen to stumble across.

Five years after meeting Reilly, John Chant and I had been looking for something, anything, for three hours. I was falling asleep in his van.

"Which way do you want to go now?" he asked my nodding head with the closing eyes.

"I guess that means straight," he said.

The truth is it did not matter which way he turned. Our destination is always somewhere where there is something that is worth stopping for, but we do not know where or what it is.

He turned left. Then right on the next block.

Then he hit the brakes to wake me up.

"I need potato chips," he said.

"Please, God," I said. "We will find something. Help us to find something. I am convinced we will find something."

"I still want potato chips," said John.

We will find something, I said to myself. We will. I am convinced we will. Reilly said all I have to do is believe. That had become my mantra. I am convinced we will find a story. I do not hope we will. I do not dream or wish we will. I am convinced we will.

But I am starting to doubt because it has been three hours and it is raining and no one is out.

For five years since I met Reilly, one thousand consecutive working days, there had been no day without a new story about some wonderful, wacky or touching person. I hate to write that because I fear I will put a curse on it. But on the other hand, Reilly taught me how to believe.

He does not change reality, but he changes the way we see reality.

Also since I met Reilly I do not only *hope* to have a good day, I *expect* a good day. And I do not hope to be healthy, I expect I will feel good. I guess I have been lucky. I have not been sick for five years, and I have not had a bad day.

Of course Reilly is only human. It can't go on forever and this day of the story of the Soccer Brothers would be the time when I found even Reilly was not perfect.

At 3 p.m. I thought for sure that the hitting streak was over. John and I were getting tired, and depressed. Is there a day when there is nothing out there? At least nothing that I can see?

We are on Mainland Street and I see an elderly woman carrying flowers. Suddenly the world is wonderful and Reilly is right.

"Stop."

But John cannot stop because we are in traffic and we will be rear-ended.

"Can we go around the block and I'll jump out. Maybe she's bringing them to someone or home for herself."

Obviously she is bringing them to someone or home for herself. My brilliance sometimes astounds me.

John turns the corner and the little old lady is gone. *Poof,* vanished. I get out and start looking in the stores, but it is useless. She is gone. How does a little old lady with a bunch of flowers disappear? I don't know, but I do know I have lost a slow-walking woman with bright flowers. That is not easy.

"Please," I say to a hole in the clouds. But honestly I am thinking, "I can't handle this. I can't do this job."

But Reilly said you get what you want. You get what you expect.

I want to find a story. I expect to find a story. It is not as profound as I want to get off skid row or I want to win a lottery. All I want is to see somebody doing something.

And suddenly, I expect we will find something. I expect it, EXPECT, we will find something.

We see a tiny coffee shop

"Maybe they have chips in that store," says John.

And maybe there will be a story in there, I think.

They have organic coffee. John said he'd buy. But then, suddenly, "let's leave," he said.

"Why?"

"They have Styrofoam cups. That's not right to have organic coffee in Styrofoam."

This guy has principles.

Outside the store I say, let's go to the left, there is a place that looks like it might have chips. And maybe there will be a story that way, I think.

He sees a Starbucks to the right. He wants Starbucks. He loves Starbucks. Coffee wins over chips. On the way to Starbucks we pass Bean Around the World, which we didn't see earlier.

"Okay," said John. "For a change I'll try this."

Once we drink coffee, I think, we will be refreshed and find a story.

And then we ordered the two small dark roasts and saw the soccer game.

How did we find that story? How do you find anything you want? Fluke? Luck? Coincidence? The story god? All I know is that night a funny, fantastic tale of conflict and snide remarks and laughter about two brothers and one soccer game was on the air.

Thanks to Reilly. (*Sniff.*)

GETTING TO THE BUBBLE

There are many stories for which you can give credit to Reilly.

It would seem so easy. At least if I were looking at it, it would seem so easy. A story about a four-year-old teaching a two-year-old how to blow bubbles should not be hard to do.

But we were heading for the eagle before we got to the bubbles. You see, the producer of the *Newshour*, who is a knowledgeable birdwatcher, told me that he had heard that a worker in the North Vancouver transfer station shared his lunch every day with an eagle.

When I met the cameraman, Tony Clark, I said this is going to be an easy day. We just watch a guy feeding an eagle.

We drove to the dump.

"Well, that's not quite the real story," a guy told us.

The truth was that a fellow who had a trained hawk was hired occasionally to scare away the seagulls. It was not an eagle and it was returning to the man because it had been trained to do that after it terrified the other birds.

Since some viewers might not think that was a kind thing to do it would be better not to share that story with us, the fellow at the dump said.

Well that is a good thing, I think, because when we almost get a story, but miss it by just a little bit like the facts are wrong, the next one is usually better.

We are driving by train tracks and see a guy taking pictures of graffiti on the side of a grain car. That reminds me of the man who takes pictures of freighters and his friend who takes pictures of smoke stacks of freighters. This will be easy.

"No, thank you," says the photographer who has tattoos going up and down his neck and a large dog in his car. "I'd rather keep this private."

Well, this is a better thing, I say, because two stories that go bad mean the next will be super.

We pass by a woman digging up her garden. She has the whole thing dug up. This will be lovely, a hard-working woman improving the world.

I don't understand a word she says.

Things are getting better, I think. The next story will be outstandingly super.

A man with a very large cowboy hat is sitting on the seawall with a friend. There might be a character under the hat.

I walk by just close enough to barely hear what they are talking about without actually snooping. It is a deep, serious conversation, not the kind you interrupt.

The next story will be much, much better.

We see some people taking pictures of crocuses in Stanley Park, but they are standing above the flowers and bending over like a bunch of upside down L's with their cameras pointing straight down. Now that is funny and just what we are waiting for.

We get out and they walk away.

We cannot say, "Hey, stop, and would you bend over like an upside down L again so we can take a picture of you?" because asking someone to do something is acting and not news and so it is against the rules.

The next story better be good, I think. Or else.

We are passing a bathroom. Please, stop, I ask Tony. I am getting old and need more frequent draining.

I get out and pass a hard hat who is clearing away more of the storm devastation. He says he does not believe what has just happened. I think those are the first words of a great story.

He tells me I did a story about him six years ago and was telling his co-workers about it a minute before we pulled up and I got out of the camera truck. It must be karma, he says.

I say it makes for very large goose pimples, but not a story for television.

We are both still wondering about how the world works as I go on with my hunt.

The next story will be incredible. I just know it.

Tony tells me he has found it while I was in the bathroom. A guy with a stepladder and a camera overlooking the water. Whatever he is doing will be good. How could a guy with a camera and a stepladder not be good?

We walk to where he is. He is the man who photographs freighters, photographing more freighters, and he has already been on television.

The next story will be very, very, very good.

We pass a guy planting trees in the park.

Hello, hello. All the usual stuff. It turns out he ran a head shop on East Hastings until apparently the forces of law and order shut him down. He grew marijuana. Now he plants trees. Wow. You don't find stories like that in your average media.

Sorry, he says. He prefers not to talk publicly about that.

The *next* story will be beyond belief.

We have circled the park and now we are going around again. I am getting dizzy. I am getting frustrated. I am starting to wonder if this is the way stories are really found.

We go to the old, empty, abandoned bear pit and I tell Tony stories about the last bears that lived and died there and the one that rescued a kitten that some rotten kids had thrown into the pit.

And then we hear a little kid with his mother and aunt talking about the lions and the tigers in the woods. Oh, story god, thank you.

We run to catch up. Hello, etc. May we talk with him? Etc.

"We heard you talking about the lions and tigers, and I am thinking it is such a nice story about a child's imagination."

"I don't really believe that," he said. "I was just pretending."

Mother and aunt are urging him to pretend again because they know that will get him on television, but the kid is adamant. There are no lions and tigers in the woods of Stanley Park.

The next story will be . . . etc. You get the picture by now.

Another kid is riding a stick like a horse. Imagination again. The same story, but replace the tigers with a stallion.

He has a pretend horse at home, says the mother, but this is just a stick. She does not want him on television riding just a stick.

I am about to quit. I am not thinking how good the next story will be, I am thinking nothing, at least nothing good.

And then in front of the Vancouver Aquarium we see bubbles floating over the heads of a couple of kids.

A four-year-old girl is blowing them. Her two-year-old sister, who is sitting in a stroller, is trying to blow them.

We meet them and their mother. The girls are Imogen, four, and Genevieve, two. Their mother is Sharon and she tells us that her Imogen remembered the last time they went to the aquarium they got bubbles in the gift shop and that is what she could not wait to get this time. Fish are fine, but bubbles, now that is something you can do.

I watched as her breath gave birth to balls of soap and water.

I watched as Genevieve had the problems of being two. She held the plastic hoop in front of her lips and inhaled.

"No, sweetheart," said her mother. "You have to blow out, like this." She showed her.

But the in and out part can be confusing. Just try to get a two-year-old to blow a stuffed-up nose while you are holding a tissue paper around it.

"No, blow out."

But out is hard. In is more secure. So the tissue stays dry and the nose wet.

"Try like this," said Imogen. She held the soapy hoop in front of her sister's lips and then Imogen put her face alongside her sister's cheek and blew.

Bubbles.

"Wow," said Genevieve.

The four-year-old was teaching the two-year-old.

Imogen dipped the hoop in the jar and held it again in front of Genevieve. A two-year-old breath came out and one bubble burst out and took flight.

"Wonderful, beautiful," said her mother.

On the tape you could hear clapping, coming from near the camera.

She did it again and more bubbles were born.

Genevieve's head was being rubbed by her mother and Imogen went back to blowing her own bubbles.

As we left, both sisters were filling the world with balls of floating translucent soap.

"Wow," Genevieve said again.

Wow, I thought.
It took four hours of looking and fifteen minutes to shoot.
And it was the best story of the day.

A FLAT SANTA AND A SMALL TREE

Cameraman John McCarron and I are in his van driving up and down back alleys and finding nothing. Literally, nothing. We went down by the Fraser River where I have done a few stories about Bert, the ninety-five-year-old guy who runs Northern Building Supply. He started the lumberyard seventy years ago when he needed a job.

But poor Bert's wife had died just a few days ago. They had been married more than 60 years. We did not want to bother him.

Then we dropped in on Walter the mechanic, up the street. He is greasy and tough and strong as always, but his oil-smeared coveralls said "John" on them, not Walter.

Walter, who was now John, said he got too big to wear his Walter coveralls, so he borrowed John's. That would have made a story, except Walter said, "Are you kidding? My wife would put me on a diet, and I don't want that no how, no way, nowhere."

So John the cameraman and I went to New Westminster where Diana, the woman who sweeps the streets, wears a different hat for each season. We found her in the works yard, with a winter hat. But she had a doctor's appointment.

It was then past 3 p.m. and this story has to be on the air in three hours, and we do not have a story. And John has a new company van and an appointment to have cabinets for his equipment put in in forty-five minutes.

This will be a challenge.

We drive by a deflated Santa. Thank you story god. One is funny. But one does not make a story. Try finding more deflated Santas when you are on deadline. It would be easier to find the meaning of life.

Then just before the sun goes to sleep we find three more. Now we have four deflated Santas.

Is that what makes a story?

Well, it's better than one Santa, and four is a trend, a pattern, a way of life. If there are four deflated Santas because the power air pumps get turned off during the day then there must be four thousand of them.

Four thousand deflated Santas? The town is swarming with flat St. Nicks. This is a story that needs telling.

"Hello, boss. Ecology has stolen Christmas. Saving electricity is taking the stuffing out of the season."

"Is this a Christmas disaster?" he asks.

News is made of disasters and this is a dismal disaster with a holiday angle.

"Great story," he says.

It is so easy to please a news editor. Just tell him everything is bad and he will think that everything is good.

John drives to the cabinetmaker with his new truck, I take a cab back to my car and then get to work and hear the words of doom from a producer. "You have ten minutes to make your spot. And there is no spot after it."

"I can only find one picture of a deflated Santa," says the editor, because we are in very much of a hurry and the tape is flying by quickly.

"Hurry, find the other ones."

"Where?"

"Somewhere on the tape."

"Forward or back?"

"Yes."

"Two minutes left."

"There, see, right there. Tons of flat Santas, well at least three more."

We put them into the story and say, "Christmas unplugged is not like the old Styrofoam Santas that kept standing through power failures."

But it is Christmas and we have to avert disaster. With thirty seconds to go, add "Santa is just sleeping, a nap during the day so he can work all night."

Say it into the microphone, and presto, the truth is alive again that Christmas is crazy and magical and you believe everything.

The story of the flat Santas was on the air. It is not news, but it keeps me going and for that I am thankful.

Is that all you do for a living? Don't you wash windows, or something? Many ask that.

And Tuesday, I was with cameraman Karl Casselman, who is very, very strong and energetic and eats a great deal to keep going. Hours went by and all we have managed is for Karl to get a bagel and cream cheese at Seigels' Bagels on Cornwall. We go on looking. We find nothing. An hour later Karl said he was hungry, again, and so we went to his favourite pizza place on Commercial Drive. He got two large slices and offered me a bite of his pepperoni while he chewed on the pineapple.

Then walking down the sidewalk is a couple with a baby and so therefore it must be the child's first Christmas. The father is carrying a tiny tree, so small it seems like it must be the tree's first Christmas also. There might be some connection.

"Stop."

Karl stops in the middle of the street, I jump out and talk to them. "Excuse me, hate to bother you, but is this his first tree by any chance?"

I am taking a chance that the baby is a "he." You don't want to get that wrong. But if you get it right most new parents like you more.

"Yes."

Thank you story god.

The little one is Nicholas, we are told, a year old.

Karl parks somewhere. I don't know where. He runs up with his camera.

"You have pizza on your chin," I say.

He wipes it off and we talk to the couple and Karl takes pictures of the tree and the family and I am in heaven.

As we leave, Karl tells me something obvious, which I missed. Nicholas is another name for Santa Claus.

I go back the station and put the story together and ponder and ponder over the closing line. Nothing seems right.

It comes to me, "Nicholas is another name for Santa Claus."

I think it's the pepperoni that makes him so smart.

COFFEE BREAKS

John Chant bought me coffee. It was at 14th and Main, where there are two coffee shops. Starbucks on one corner, JJ Bean on the other. JJ Bean used to be a bank. It was only a year or two ago that people deposited money there. Then it became a coffee shop. Coffee is where the money is.

I once did a story on the coffee shops between 12th and 28th on Main. I ran out of fingers, and toes, and ears. We all should have invested in coffee.

So John bought me coffee and said since he had done that, it was my job to find the story. John has spent thirty-five years helping me find stories. He found the single one best story of my life. It was about litterbugs. You may know it.

We were driving on Main Street when he said, "That ticks me off." He does not use profanity. He is a hard-nosed street-level cameraman but his speech is clean.

"What? The price of coffee?"

"No," he said. "That does." He pointed to some paper flying out of the window of a luxury car parked in front of the train station at Main and Terminal.

We looked at each other. "You think we could?" we both asked at the same time.

As we watched more paper come out, we both nodded.

"We can."

He wheeled his van across Main Street through traffic like it was his finger weaving through his other fingers. He is a conservative family man, strongly connected with his wife and his church, but what he really wanted to be in life was a race-car driver. His dream is to be on a German autobahn without a speed limit. He moves his camera van through the city like he's on roller blades.

He parked near the offending carload of inconsiderate idiots and started recording the events through the windshield. Let me tell you, if we had more John Chants working on police surveillance we would have less crime.

He filmed the next load of hamburger wrappings sailing out of the window. And then he shot another flying gift to the city—used napkins.

We stepped outside and confronted the litter low-lifes. There were two guys and two women in the car, all very well-dressed.

We asked why they were throwing their garbage out.

"Excuse me," said the driver with a heavy accent of indignation. "What gives you the right to speak to us?"

I was looking at his gold watch, which was on the same hand that was holding another gift of ketchup-smeared litter.

I ignored the question. I couldn't answer it anyway, so I just said, "Why are you throwing this garbage out?"

He turned his back on us.

"Ok, we'll try again," I said. "Why are you throwing this on the ground?"

He pushed a button and the window went up.

I raised my voice. "Why are you—?"

Before I could finish he put his car, which was running the whole time we were talking, into reverse and stomped on the gas.

I grabbed his garbage from the ground while the car was still backing up. He jammed it into drive.

But the back window was still open. Oh, lord let my aim be good. He stomped on the gas. I tried chasing him. In less than a second he would be out of range, so I threw the ketchup-covered napkins and greasy papers at the open back window.

His foot was faster than my arm, but at least one glob of smeared paper went in, just where the fancy suit was sitting.

Now talk about reaction to a story. Because of John I was a momentary poster boy for those who hate littering.

And because of John some litter-throwers are now on the run.

But that was then, and now we were looking for Christmas. And not just any Christmas. It had to be a different Christmas story or why would you watch?

And we had been going for hours, too many hours to count. Even my granddaughter would get sick of me after that many hours. But where do we find a different Christmas story? I had been in and out of the van countless times asking a guy in a backhoe if he had any decorations in his cab, or if they had a Christmas tree in the impound lot of Busters. But no tree grows in Busters.

Meanwhile John is lifting weights while he waits for me. He has an eight-pound rubber-coated steel dumbbell he uses to keep healthy since they cut open his chest to fix his heart. Cameramen are very entertaining.

And then we went to Trout Lake, to use the bathroom because of the coffee he had bought. Before we got to the bathroom we passed a couple raking leaves. "Nice couple," John said.

That's good enough for me.

Hello, hello.

The man, Peter Snoeck, was ninety-one and his wife, Nel Snoeck, was eighty-three and they were nearly newlyweds. He had proposed sixteen years ago on Christmas Day. Thank you, story god.

"He called me when I was away visiting my daughter," said Nel.

"She didn't believe me when I asked her," said Peter. "She asked me to hold on."

Nel said she thought that getting married when they were both past any sensible age for doing such a thing was silly.

"So I asked my daughter and she said, 'Do it.'"

Life's stories are like life itself, with endless turns, and if you keep going you'll almost always find a surprise, and occasionally, a prize at the end.

The husband and wife were beautiful. They were in love. Nothing goes wrong when you are in love. Nothing.

And then I ran to the bathroom in the park. Nothing makes life as exciting as too much coffee. Nothing.

A CHRISTMAS WISH

The rain will probably fall. The teakettle will be whistling and it will be 6 a.m. and your eyes will be full of dust because you went to bed at 5 a.m. You were up wrapping presents and writing tags that give credit to someone else for giving them.

And then seemingly a minute after you close your eyes you hear a stammering voice by your pillow.

"Mommy, Mommy, Santa came, just like you said, Mommy, wake up."

The dewy-eyed little one woke you after going into the living room and discovering against all odds that Santa had really come. The little feet ran back to your bedroom because this news was the greatest thing that had ever happened in the entire history of the world.

"Wake up, wake up, Mommy. Daddy, Daddy. Santa came."

This was something you had to see. It could not wait until 7 or 8 a.m. Those were times for the rest of the year when the day came like it always comes and getting up was an intrusion to a dream. But not today. Today was Christmas and Santa had come and, "Mommy he left a pile of presents, just like you said."

And with small fingers wrapped around your finger you are lead to this discovery. You step into the room with the tree and there are gifts that were not there the night before.

You say, "You are right, child. Santa did come. Check the hot chocolate and see if he drank it."

And the little eyes look into the cup left by the tree.

"Mommy, he drank it! And he ate the cookies, and look, the carrots left for the reindeer are gone. Mommy. He came!"

It is a moment of joy, pure with no disbelief. Santa came.

It may never happen again, at least not like this. But it almost always happens at least once.

The presents are not nearly as important as this moment. The discovery that Santa did really come, just like you said he would, gives the gift of belief that will be remembered by both the giver and the receiver for the rest of time.

"Santa came, just like you said, Mommy."

Tragedies will come, as they always do. The presents inside the boxes will be forgotten. The toys will break. The lives will break, although we pray the lives will have a chance to fade before they end.

But for one moment in each child's life they will shake you out of your dream, and whisper into your ear, "Mommy, Mommy, Santa came, Mommy. Just like you said. Santa did come. Come and look."

Add religion? With or without it, the gift is in the reality that the unbelievable happens, which is the basis of all religions.

Merry Christmas.

OLD FOLKS

It's not vitamin pills or diet or exercise. I'm sure they help, but it's something more than that.

Old folks are now a whole new breed. I've told you about the hundred-year-old who went bowling on his birthday. He also lives alone, climbs a ladder to clean out his gutters and is nearly blind.

And the hundred-year-old woman who got a tattoo on her birthday, and she plans on another one for her one-hundred-and-first.

And the hundred-year-old who went to the Army, Navy and Air Force club on Main Street to celebrate his birthday because they had cheap beer that day.

And there is the ninety-eight-year-old woman who has lived in Lynn Valley ninety-seven years and was the subject of a photo exhibit. She made everyone laugh. You would swear she was a standup comic as well as a sweetheart. Her story is a few pages ahead, called "Nan and Stan." She makes everyone happy. It is not how she stays alive, but how she keeps those around her alive that is amazing.

But there is this other guy I recently met. Harold Wolverton. He is only in his ninetieth year, and so a youngster in comparison. He wrote a letter to me asking if it was okay if he recorded stories out of my books for his friend who is ninety-three and blind.

Yes, of course, I wrote back. You are the nicest guy in the world to do that, I said. And then I offered to record some myself.

That led to us having coffee and I learned he was in the Canadian Air Force during the war as a radar operator in Mosquito bombers. That was scary. Then surviving the bombing of London was scary. But his stories are funny, even though they often concern death.

I called him and said I had a CD of some stories I had made and would mail them to him.

No need, he said. He would pick it up from my home. He was out driving and would be there in twenty minutes. I stepped outside to see if I could see him driving down the block. I think it is wonderful that someone who is ninety is still driving a car. I am guessing he has an old Oldsmobile or a full-sized Chevy, which he would have bought new twenty years ago.

I see nothing but a motorcycle coming my way. I hope the biker does not scare away old Harold.

The motorcycle keeps coming, then stops in front of me and the biker pulls off his helmet and says hello.

I am looking at ninety-year-old Harold straddling his rumbling steed.

"It's only a 250," he said apologetically, because the bigger bikes are too heavy to pick up. He used to drive a Harley.

Ninety years old and dropping his gloves into his helmet.

"They are just garden gloves," he said. "The leather ones cost too much."

Ninety years old and driving from North Vancouver to Maple Ridge to visit his friend and deliver the CDs. Driving on his motorcycle with the CDs tucked inside his shirt like a teenager.

Ninety years old and saying riding is way too much fun to give it up just because he is ninety.

And then he laughed. The same as the old bowler, he laughed. And the tattooed hundred-year-old woman, she laughed. And the guy getting cheap beer, he laughed. And the oldest resident of Lynn Valley, she laughed, and made others laugh.

I know healthy foods and exercise help, but doing something that is fun, like laughing, is what really is keeping these folks alive, and the way they live, not just the fact that they are alive, is probably the best medicine for the rest of us.

More on Harold . . .

Stories about good people are like wine: if you wait they get better. And like wine, tasting their stories and their company is intoxicating.

When Harold got out of the Air Force he wanted to be a dentist. But he had only $1,900 that he and his brother had saved in war bonds during his four years of service, dedication and surviving.

The first year of dental school cost twice as much.

His older brother suggested that they take his money, build a house and sell it and use the profits for Harold to follow his dream.

Trouble was neither of them had ever built anything but a birdhouse when they were kids. However, they had a friend who did know how.

That was Frank Aicken, who was a few years older than Harold and he had just gotten out of the army. Before the war Frank built houses. After the war he went back to building houses.

Harold and his brother drove their beat-up car to Frank's house and knocked on the door.

"Frank, tell us how to build a house."

That was all there was to it, just the total self-confidence that if someone they trusted told them how to do something they would be able to do it. No schools, no tests, just faith in themselves.

Frank's wife, Audrey, made them sandwiches and coffee and Harold and his brother listened to the instructions for laying a foundation.

The next morning they started work on a tiny lot they had bought on the outskirts of Vancouver. They did what they were told.

That night they went back to Frank's and got more learning.

The next morning they put the learning to work.

That night, back at Frank's.

The next morning, back at work.

A week later the foundation was done. Audrey made more sandwiches and coffee and they learned how to frame.

Framing in the day, kitchen table learning at night.

Three months later, with instruction now every few days, the house was done and a for-sale sign was in the front yard.

"We sold it for $4,000," said Harold. "We doubled our money."

He did not bother to mention their salaries, because there was no salary. Other than food and building materials, all their profits went into the dentist fund.

Can you imagine someone today putting in three months of work to help someone else, even their brother, go to school?

"What? Are you crazy? You want me to give you money? Get another credit card. Get a loan. I've got my own problems."

But not Harold's brother, Newton. All the money went to Harold's education. And to keep paying tuition until he graduated they built four more houses, with Frank giving them kitchen table advice the whole time, and of course, for free. Meanwhile, to make a living Frank was building his own houses.

Can you imagine coming home from a day of swinging a hammer and cutting wood, but instead of relaxing you spend your nights telling someone else how to hammer and cut wood? That is more than friendship. That is dedication.

Harold's brother, Newton, died about ten years ago. But Frank is still around, except he is now blind.

And remember the earlier stuff about Harold?

He had written me a letter asking if he could record stories from my books to give to a blind friend of his. His blind friend is Frank.

I remember my feelings when reading: "I am 90, my friend is 94 and blind. Would it be okay to record your stories for him?" I remember feeling blessed that there are such good people still around.

More than sixty years after Harold sat at Frank's kitchen table listening to Frank, he is back sitting at the table, and Frank is listening.

JOE AND THE DOOR

He wanted to make things better. When they kicked in the door it was disaster. Inside they took so many treasured belongings: jewelry, mostly, but some elegant plates and the pictures that had nice frames.

They could have kept the frames if only they had left the pictures; those were irreplaceable, his family, his ancestors, his wife when she was his bride. But it was all gone. And what wasn't taken was smashed.

Why did they have to ruin so much? Taking it was painful. But sweeping up the ancient broken dishes was senseless.

When Joe Kamiya and his wife of many years returned home their home was ruined, once again.

The first time it was all taken away was 1941 in Vancouver. Joe was young and married only a few years when they were separated by the RCMP and sent off to prison camps to sit out the war.

Now they had just celebrated their sixty-ninth anniversary, and their door was smashed in.

But Joe wanted to make things better. He was that kind of guy.

One of his granddaughters, Brandy, was getting married. His sons were born in Canada and one of them had married a white Canadian. Now the daughter from that marriage was getting married and Joe wanted to give her something that was both from his heritage and something that would show her bad things can be made good, which would be the greatest gift of all.

When we saw him he was carrying a large hunk of wood down a driveway to his backyard in Lynn Valley.

"I'm making something for Brandy," he said.

Seeing someone who was ninety-three carrying a large piece of wood is reason enough to follow him. We might learn something.

"It is for her wedding," he said.

He put the slab of oak on a table saw and cut a thin slice about the length of a dinner knife and half the width of a pinky finger.

Then he cut another one, and another.

"How many are you cutting?" I asked.

"Maybe a thousand, maybe more. I want them to last as long as she lives."

"What are they?" I asked.

"Good things," he said.

After twenty minutes of cutting he took the rectangular pieces of oak inside his home and started shaping them with a small planer. His fingers wrapped around the tool with an intimacy of uncountable reunions, like a long affair of love.

"What are you making?" I asked.

"A turn in the road," he said, "from sad to happy."

Then he took one of the sticks and began sanding it. He had done this many, many times. You knew that because with each stroke his fingers tightened more at one end of the wood, then loosened at the other.

Up and down and up and down and a tapered stick was being born in his fingers. He put it down on a table and picked up another long rectangle and began sanding it.

His wife was sitting quietly in another room. She motioned to us to come.

In that room were row after row after row of chopsticks drying from light rubbings of varnish. She told us they were each paired in matching sets, so that the colour and grain of one looked like it belonged to the colour and grain of the other. Then each pair would be tied together.

"He wants them to be perfect," she said.

"How many pairs will he make?" I asked.

She smiled and shrugged. "When the door is gone he will stop," she said.

In the other room Joe was still sanding.

"This will really get rid of the bad?" I asked.

He looked up while his fingers were still changing the shape of the wood.

"When I am finished there will be no bad. There will be only chopsticks, and that is good."

The wedding was beautiful. And everyone ate with something that magically had become something else. The victim of violence was now daintily lifting rice and fish.

A year later Joe's wife died and Joe followed her soon after. But as Joe said, he left enough chopsticks, made from a door that had been smashed in during a robbery, to last a lifetime, and that is good.

NAN AND STAN

The bell in Ridgeway school was ringing. She would be late. She had to go up the trail and there were tree limbs lying across it and some of those were too big to climb over.

Doreen Cliffe (everyone called her Nan) was more than worried. This meant she would have to stay after school and she had promised her mother that she would be home on time to help with the family dinner.

One of the teachers was standing on the front steps of the school ringing the bell. Nan could picture her. And now she had only five minutes to get there but she could not make it.

"Can I give you a ride?"

It was shouted at her from across the road.

A young man on a milk wagon on Lynn Valley Road was leaning toward her from the seat on a buggy.

"Can I take you somewhere?" he shouted.

In 1925 it was not often you saw someone on these roads in North Vancouver.

There were almost no cars, just horses and buggies and wagons. Except for the streetcars on Lonsdale, people mostly walked when they wanted to go somewhere.

She didn't know the driver on the buggy, but she ran to him.

"I'm late for school."

"Well, climb up here and we'll try to get you there," said the handsome young man holding the reins. There were large milk jugs in the back of the wagon.

They raced up the road and she got to school and she spent the day thinking about the young man whose name was Stan. Stan and Nan. Nan and Stan. She liked that.

The next day they met again. Stan was delivering milk from his parents' dairy farm, but he went off his route, again, to take her to school.

They were married four years later and started their own trucking business. She became Nan Houlden. They stayed in love almost fifty years before he died.

When I met Nan she was the subject of a photo show at the Cedar Garden assisted living home in Lynn Valley. She was then ninety-eight and the longest continuous resident of North Vancouver.

I expected a little old lady when we arrived. We found a glib, funny, lively woman who said, while looking at one of the pictures of a group of women, "They were in my Stitch and Bitch Club."

"You can't say that," I said. "At least not on TV."

"You tell me why I can't," she admonished me. "They were my Stitch and Bitch Club. We could say it in the '40s and you're telling me I can't say that now on television?"

"I guess you can say anything you want," I said, humbly.

"I formed it after the men all went off to their men's clubs and left us women behind.

"But I wasn't going to be left behind," Nan went on. "So I formed this club and we would meet once a month and stitch clothes and bitch."

Just for my sake, she emphasized the word "bitch."

"And at each meeting each of us would put fifty cents into a jar. At the end of the year we went out for lunch and had a blast."

Her eyes twinkled when she was remembering.

There were about fifteen women in the photo.

"Which one is you?" I asked.

She pointed to a woman who had a big smile. The face had changed a bit, but not the glow.

"How many others are still around?" I asked.

"None of them. I am the only one left." She said she had good new friends in this home. "But all of those women, and the men in the other pictures who I knew back then, are all gone."

She has children and grandchildren and great-grandchildren. But of the friends who shared her youth, none are alive.

Still, she was happy and talkative and said she was looking forward to her one-hundredth birthday, "just because it would be nice to be here."

I told her about a woman who I met who got a tattoo on her one-hundredth.

"I have a tattoo, also," Nan said.

She did not look like the kind of woman who would do such a thing, but then what do you ever know of a person just by looking at them?

She started to unbutton her blouse. Whoops, I better not look. Then she opened the top until part of her left breast was showing.

"You can't do that," I said.

"Are you going to try that 'I can't' stuff again?"

I am thinking, *I love this woman.*

There on her left breast was one small red rose.

"Why?" I asked.

"I can't tell you or I'll cry."

"I don't want you to cry, but please, tell us."

She looked down at the rose, then up at us, at me and at a cameraman with a big machine with a large glass lens pointing at her, and she said, "I loved my husband so much."

There was a long pause after that. When you are entering someone's very private world you show respect and stay quiet. If they want to go on, they do. If they change their mind, you don't pry.

Tears were coming from her eyes.

It is hard to know when to turn away. You have been invited here, but on the other hand you have no right to cause pain. And on the other hand, this is the moment when a heart in need that may be watching later may be touched. It is a difficult balance.

"Every year on our anniversary he brought me a dozen roses, except when he could not afford them. Then he brought me just one. One long-stemmed rose."

"After he died I could almost not bear it. Then I had this tattooed over my heart, to stay close to him."

The tears were falling down her cheeks, but this is the moment when you know you are going to be moved with a power that you cannot find in movies or novels or the love stories of the young. This is the moment when you are looking into the face of devotion.

"I wanted the rose that he gave me to be mine forever, and when I die it will go to the grave with me."

She smiled, and lowered her head.

The story ended with a close-up picture of the rose and then a beautiful picture from the back of Nan while she was looking at the photos of her youth. That was the part that went on television.

What was not on television was a moment of beauty for me. It was me hugging Nan Houlden, and knowing that I was learning about love.

SANTA'S PROBLEM

Some guys have very good connections. Like my friend Rob Stuart. He used to perform in the old Georgia Hotel wearing a kilt and singing Scottish songs. He makes people cry with "Danny Boy" and raises goose-bumps with marching-off-to-war songs.

But most of all, he knows Santa Claus, which when he told me made me sit up and say, "What'd you say, brother? You know *who*?"

"Santa," said Rob.

"Like the real Santa Claus?" I asked.

Rob nodded.

It's not every day that you meet someone who is on speaking terms with the Big Guy of Christmas Eve. As far as I know, Santa has an adult phobia, so right away I was thinking that Rob must be a special guy.

"I spend time with him every Christmas," he told me, "and we share a lot of jokes and almost as many tears."

"Tears?" I ask. "What do you mean, poor kids who aren't getting gifts on Christmas morning?"

Rob shook his head. He has a white beard and a big smile, much like Santa's, which I guess is a reason that he and the Big Guy get along so well. When the two of them are talking it is like they are looking in a mirror.

"No, even poor kids get some toys," he said. "But there are some things Santa can't deliver."

42

He told me to come along and he would show me.

A cameraman and I followed Rob into a mall. It was the same in every mall right before Christmas. There was a line of kids waiting and a photographer who would take their picture when they sat on Santa's knee, and a lot of mothers who were waiting so they could get the pictures and then be able to send them to grandparents and friends, but they still had all that shopping to do, so please, Santa, hurry.

Rob introduced me to Santa but I was skeptical.

"Are you the real Santa?" I asked.

He smiled and somehow before he answered, I knew he was. He had a twinkle in his eyes and rosy cheeks. But most of all, he was nice.

"Yes," he said. "I am the real Santa."

"But how come if I go to another mall I will see you there too?"

"Ho, ho, ho."

That is his standard answer. And when I thought about it later, I knew that was the perfect answer. A most wonderful friend once told me the secret to life was simply to laugh more.

Santa spreads that secret everywhere. He keeps on laughing, no matter what.

"I am very fast," he said. "And I have magic. You can see me here, and you can see me there. You can close your eyes and see me. I especially like blind children, they see me best."

I was not going to argue with that. I have been to the children's Christmas parties at the Canadian National Institute for the Blind and when the little children sit on his lap and look up at his laughter, I know they see him.

"So what is it Rob wants me to know?" I asked Santa.

He smiled and asked if we had one of those remote microphones that he could hook onto his vest.

"I won't let you know anyone's names, but I will let you hear what I hear," he said.

We put on the microphone and went far to the other side of the mall. We could see kids on his lap, but could not get close enough to see their faces.

"Santa, I want a Barbie."

"Santa, I want a train set and a bike and a Nintendo and a Game Boy."

"Santa, I want a six-shooter but my mother won't let me have one. Can you get me one?"

To each one Santa replied, "We will see what we can do, but there are many boys and girls so we cannot make promises."

And then he added, "You should listen to your mother. She is a very smart woman."

A small girl climbed up on his lap.

"Have you been a good girl?" Santa asked.

"Yes."

"And what do you want for Christmas?"

There was a long pause.

"Do you want a doll?"

Another pause.

"Can you tell me what you want?"

A very small voice, so small Santa had to move his ear down closer, said, "Santa. Can you make my mommy and daddy stop fighting. They yell all the time and I am scared. And my little brother is even more scared."

"I am so sorry, my little angel," said Santa. "I can't promise you, but I will try."

And as she got off his lap he leaned forward and whispered to her, "Don't be afraid. You will be alright."

The little girl walked away toward her mother who rushed off.

As Santa straightened up and as the next child was walking toward him we could hear him say, "God help her."

And then, "Hello, little boy, have you been good this year?"

Over the next hour we hear:

"Can you get a new heart for my daddy?"

"Can you make Daddy stop hitting Mommy?"

"Can you make the scars go away from my brother's face?"

"Can you help my mommy and daddy find the money for rent? I don't know what rent is, Santa, but they are always worried about it."

And then Santa was gone. They had stopped the line a few minutes earlier and after the last child had spoken to him, Santa suddenly vanished, like magic. The last boy did not know if he wanted a soccer ball or a hockey stick or a baseball bat because he did not know which sport he wanted to become famous in.

Santa told him to go home and think about it really hard and Santa would know his decision, but he was not making any promises.

Rob joined us later and gave us the microphone. "Santa dropped it off before he left. Could you hear anything from way over there?"

The cameraman said he had heard it all. "Funny story about that soccer ball and hockey stick and baseball bat," he said.

"Anything else?"

The cameraman's eyes were almost wet.

"I hope Santa has a lot of magic," he said.

CHRISTMAS JADE

A strange thing happened just before last Christmas. A jade plant in my back room suddenly burst out with soft, white, delicate flowers. I guess I was not paying attention because the last time I looked it was all green with those fat leaves.

Then I thought, hey, plant. Can't you get it right? It's not spring, it's winter.

You know what a jade plant is. You probably have or had one in your house. I don't know how to describe it except it's a jade plant, the kind that survives living with people.

This one was given to me by my wife in 1973, the year we moved to Canada. She bought it for fifty-nine cents in Woolco, long before Wal-Mart took over. It was in a four-inch plastic pot and there was one skinny stem sticking out of it.

It was the first plant of my life. We did not have plants in New York, at least not when I was growing up.

I did not know anything about caring for plants, but this thing hung on and kept growing. I changed jobs from a newspaper to television. I had some problems, as we all do. I had some good stuff happen, as we all do. And the jade grew bigger and bigger and went into larger and larger pots. Give it a drink once a week and it is happy. The stem is now thicker than my forearm.

My kids were in kindergarten and the first grade when it was in its little plastic pot. Now my granddaughter, who came for a visit today, is lying on the floor drawing pictures beneath this big plant, with little white flowers covering its top.

We are both going out later to buy a Christmas tree because my granddaughter will pick out the most beautiful one in the lot. But I think on Christmas Eve, right before I go to bed, I will be looking at this jade plant with the little white flowers more than the lights on the tree, and thinking for half my life you have grown up with me, you big old friend.

There is nothing more to it than that. I just want to thank you, plant, for breaking the rules about when you should do things and looking so beautiful at Christmas. You know how to give a gift.

CHRISTMAS SOCKS

You know about The Cat In The Hat. Well? Well, this is the lesser-known story, which many men share, called The Year In The Socks.

It happens every Christmas. I get a new pair of socks.

"These are your new socks," says my wife, "so no one will see the holes in your old socks."

They come with instructions: "Save them. Don't wear them," says my wife, "unless we are going somewhere where you have to take off your shoes."

She tells me this so I do not wear holes in my new socks before I get a chance to show them in public. It is important, I am told, to let others know that I do not have holes in my socks.

Then came January. I shovelled snow. I wore my old socks. They kept me warm. One small hole does not let in much cold.

February, my roof is leaking. I put some tar on it. Old socks are working with me. New socks are safe in the drawer.

March: roof still leaking. More tar. Old socks are trying as hard as me to find the leak. Old socks have larger hole, much like roof.

April: my car with 600,000 kilometres gives up the ghost. I get new car. Old socks fall in love with new gas pedal. Hole is getting larger.

May: granddaughter is born. Beautiful girl. I wear old socks to greet new child because I will not have to take off shoes in hospital. Socks feel happy.

June: rear-ended in new car. Old socks feel sad. I sew up first and second holes in socks and get new rear end on car. New rear end and old socks are doing fine.

July: wife reminds me to wear new socks if we go somewhere that I have to take off my shoes. So far, no invitations.

August: rain starts again. Roof leaks again. More tar. Old socks feel like roof, full of holes.

September: finish two weeks of walking at the PNE looking for stories. No one looks at my socks.

October: roofers put on new roof. Still, no one looks at my socks.

November: granddaughter thinks toes sticking out of socks are funny.

December: Christmas morning. Get new pair of socks, with instructions. "These are your new socks, save them."

Boxing Day: start wearing last year's new socks.

DON'T MENTION THE "C" WORD

I have another message to everyone who says we should drop the word "Christmas" because it might offend someone. It is not an angry message, just a bit of history.

Tonight is the third night of Hanukkah and I should be getting a present. I got one when I was kid. That was because my friend's mother wasn't sure if I was Jewish or not and rather than make me feel like an outsider she gave me a toy. I came back on the fourth night and got another one.

Then on Christmas her son, his name was Hymie, would come to my house and Mother would have a present for him. She wasn't sure if he was Christian or not because Hymie sometimes changed his name to Henry and rather than make him feel like an outsider she gave him a toy.

Many of the people in my old neighbourhood were Jews, and many were Christians. Most of the kids were both, depending on who was giving out presents. I grew up with a yarmulke, a skullcap, on my head and a crucifix around my neck.

"Why are you putting on a clean shirt?" my mother would ask. "It's Saturday, you're supposed to clean the oven."

"Can't do it," I said. "I got to go to synagogue."

"You can't go to synagogue," said my mother. "You're not Jewish."

"But Henry is Hymie today and I want to go with him."

The next day Hymie, who had become Henry, walked to church with me. We were friends and friends stick together.

Outside the church we both pulled out our crucifixes and took off our yarmulkes and went inside and whispered jokes about the old people. Before going into the synagogue we put on our yarmulkes and buttoned up our shirts over the crosses, and went inside and whispered more jokes about the old people. For sure, we were never going to be old.

We were told to be quiet in both places. But beyond that I liked listening to the cantors chanting in Hebrew and he liked singing "Onward, Christian Soldiers."

Now, to all those who say we should not sing Christmas carols and not have Christmas pageants I would like them to explain to Hymie just how those things might upset him.

THE PORSCHE AND THE TREE

On my way home from work just before Christmas I passed by the Three Guidoes Christmas Tree Lot. They sell trees on East Hastings just across from the PNE.

"Why do you call yourselves the Three Guidoes?" I asked the first time I went there.

"Because I am Guido," said the first.

"And I am Guido," said the second.

"And . . ."

"Stop. I get it," I said to the third one, who was Guido too.

But only Guido-One came out to talk to me on this day several years after I met them. Guido-Two and Guido-Three were trying to help someone get a seven-foot tree into his two-passenger Porsche. He had asked for the best tree they had, paid for it, and they carried it out to his car.

"They're kidding," I said, looking at a tree almost as big as the car.

But Guido-One shook his head. "No joke."

"Big wallet, small brain," he said.

Guido-Two and Guido-Three said they could tie the tree on top, but the Porsche driver said it might scratch his car.

"If we cut it here," I heard Porsche man say, "I could get it inside then screw it together at home."

"You are now making a joke," said Guido-Three.

Porsche driver apparently had assumed that the tree was collapsible.

Guido-One told me that is not unusual. Some people are so accustomed to artificial trees that they think real ones can be folded up.

"It can be done," said Porsche man. "I believe in proactive management. Cut here."

Guido-One said no. Guido-Two said no. Guido-Three said something under his breath.

"Well, how the heck am I going to get this thing home?" said very annoyed Porsche man.

Guido-One picked up a small, humble, Charlie Brown tree.

"This looks like it's made for your car."

Porsche man stepped back. "You must be joking," he said.

He told them to give him his money back and burned rubber leaving the parking lot.

As we watched him go, Guido-One looked at the big tree and the little tree that had been left behind.

"You are both going to have a much better Christmas now," he said.

CANUCK PLACE

Pip was looking out through the second floor window of Canuck Place a few nights before Christmas. Down on the front steps the choir was singing "Silent Night."

The TV cameras were pointed at the lighting of the big tree, but Pip would not go downstairs to join the celebration.

She was with a sick kid, a really sick kid. The kid could not get out front to watch the singers so Pip stayed with her at the window.

Pip—her last name is Parr—is a young, pretty nurse.

At Christmas at Canuck Place they try to send all the kids home, at least for a while. It's good for them to be in a bed they have known before and surrounded by people they know.

Except for the kids who are really sick, the kids who have almost no time left to play with their toys.

The year before it was Will and Maddy, both five. On Christmas Day only Pip and one other nurse were on duty. They volunteered to stay because Will and Maddy could not go home.

Last year Pip turned on all the speakers in the nearly empty Canuck Place. The music filled rooms and hallways that had no one in them. Only the two children were still inside on that Christmas Eve.

In one room Will and his parents were listening to the music. In another, Maddy's parents were sitting quietly, holding their daughter.

Pip and the other nurse brought in small trees, one for each room. And they served turkey dinners, and the kids had presents and they tore off the paper and "they had the best Christmas you could ever imagine," said Pip.

It was easier for the kids. For the parents it was hard, very, very hard. Will and Maddy's parents will always remember that Christmas, and hug each other.

Canuck Place is amazing. They take the worst pain in the world, a kid who is dying of cancer, and they make the end almost border on happy. They wrap their arms around the parents of the dying kids and smile and are cheerful and make it almost bearable. That is as close to a miracle as you can get.

They do not know until a week before Christmas if a kid will be strong enough to go home one more time. If they are not, they will be like Will and Maddy. Neither one made it to kindergarten.

Pip was upstairs watching the choir with the one girl left in the house. She was in Pip's arms.

"Do you have kids?" I asked Pip.

"No," she said. "These are my children."

She looked out the window. The young girl in her arms looked up at Pip's face. She almost smiled, then closed her eyes. Her parents were on their way.

It was different than the first Christmas Eve, I was thinking. This was not a beginning. But there was a child in a bed which was almost a manger, and there was an angel, named Pip. And now outside they were singing, "Silent night, holy night."

Pip rocked the child in her arms. Maybe I was wrong. Maybe it was like the first night.

PUCK LUCK

"Why's that guy avoiding us?"

"He doesn't want to tell you his secret."

"Which is?" I asked, begging, pleading.

We were outside Eight Rinks watching folks go in for hockey games. They carried those incredibly large bags full of stinky equipment before they started flying at each other in one of the scariest, fastest games on earth.

"It's a teddy bear."

"Are you kidding me?"

No, he wasn't kidding. That guy over there, who slipped in the door before we could get to him, had a teddy bear in his bag for good luck.

Others had their older brother's T-shirt, or a necklace, or a coin.

We were on the hunt for lucky things.

Back in the days when we were able to talk to the actual players without making a formal request in writing, I had asked the Canucks what their lucky charms were.

We were behind their bench during a practice. It was fun to see they were normal people who believed in lucky socks or lucky buttons. They were humans back then, but that was in the '70s and they were not surrounded by media-protecting public relations Plexiglass and they were not making $10,000 per shot. They were also scoring more, but that is another matter.

Thirty years later I thought we could do that again, but in humbler surroundings: Eight Rinks, where the famous practise but the real people play.

"Your lucky thing?" I asked a young woman.

She held up a picture of her boyfriend.

That is sweet. But that does not make a story.

"You should talk to Sid, but don't get too close."

Sid Jones. He was goalie for the VIA Rail team. His record was an amazing fifteen wins, five losses and three ties.

Million-dollar players in the NHL don't have records like that.

"How'd you do it?" I asked.

"My lucky charm," he said.

I backed off. It was true what they said. Don't get too close.

"My boxer shorts," he said. "They bring me luck, so long as I don't wash them."

"How long?" I gagged. I stepped back. It was hard for the microphone to catch his words, but it was a powerful whiff that came from him.

"Seventeen years," said Sid.

I took another step back. The cameraman, who was further back behind me, stepped back. I followed.

"Are you kidding?" I was having trouble hearing him now.

"No, I haven't washed my shorts for seventeen years. And they work."

I backed off further. Hearing was not that important.

"Are you ever going to . . .?"

And then I thought of the futility of my question. He probably could not even hear it, but of course not. He would never. Not as long as he was winning and he was winning as long as he did not wash his underwear.

We left the ice.

Belief kills and belief cures, I heard a long time ago. You get what you believe you will get.

But sometimes you can tip the scales in your favour. Just ask anyone who tries to get in for a close shot on Sid. He won't try it twice.

FROM THE SIDELINES

"**Y**ou got what?" I asked my friend Ken, who knows everything there is to know about hockey.

He held up a puck painted with blue images of hockey players skating across the ice under the Olympic rings.

"Is that for real?"

He nodded. He had a puck from the Torino Winter Olympics of 2006. They only made three hundred of them and they were kept under lock and tight security. These were the actual game pucks and they went only to VIPs and a few star players.

"How'd you get it? And how'd you get that welt?" I asked.

The welt was across his forehead and was ugly now, a week after he came back from the games.

He held up the puck. Ouch.

Ken and I used to work together when he was a news cameraman. We were both almost killed doing a story about blasting on the Sea-to-Sky Highway. We worked together during forest fires near Cranbrook and got close enough to be told to make sure our four-wheel-drive truck was parked facing away from the fire with the doors wide open and the motor running. Fires in forests move quickly.

But nothing was as exciting or dangerous as covering a hockey game in the Olympics.

He held a camera on his shoulder through thirty-one games in fourteen days. There was little time for sightseeing. The Olympics are exhausting to cover.

He left news because it was too mundane. He preferred sports, so now he travels the world shooting Ironman races in Brazil and cross-country skiing in Norway and hockey in the Olympics. When he is in Vancouver he shoots the Canucks. It is always the same: he is one of the photographers on the sidelines waiting to shoot three seconds of close-up as a player rockets past him spraying up ice and trying to hold onto the puck.

He has seen probably a thousand hockey games. He can read what is in the minds of players, and he, like a veteran player, can tell where they are going to be four seconds ahead of them arriving there.

Wayne Gretzky had that talent while he was skating. Ken Oreskovich has it on the sidelines. His lens is there waiting for them. That's how you get those incredible close-ups of players whizzing by.

Then came Torino. Which teams were playing on the day of the puck doesn't matter. It was early in the elimination and Ken was standing on the sidelines where he had been so many times before. Italy, Vancouver, Moscow, it was always the cold, narrow space that he paced between the boards and the fans.

Then what happened?

"*Bam*," he said. "The puck was fired over the glass, hit something, ricocheted off, then *smack*." He put his hand to his forehead.

A hard rubber puck was going a hundred and fifty or two hundred kilometres an hour when it hit the "something." Lucky for him it hit the whatever-it-was first. And then it slowed down to only about one hundred clicks an hour when its next collision was with his head.

He was knocked out, immediately, instantly.

"Then this doctor came to treat me and he . . ." Ken paused. The next line is not supposed to be said because who would believe it? "The doctor swiped the puck."

He only knew this because the other cameramen who rushed to his aid saw that the medical doctor who was sworn to preserve life was preserving his own memorabilia. The doctor had slipped the puck into his own pocket while he was applying ice packs to Ken's head.

The other cameramen were shouting at the doctor, "Give him back the puck," when Ken's eyes opened again.

The doctor apparently felt the exposure would not be good for his practice and took the puck out and dropped it on Ken's chest and then left.

"And then this weird thing happened," said Ken. "I was awake and could hear the crowd saying, 'Hey, cameraman, I'll give you fifty euros for the puck.' Then someone else shouted, 'I'll give you eighty.' They were coming down out of the stands offering me ninety, a hundred euros."

He said his head was splitting and his eyes were foggy, but he felt the puck in his fingers and said no.

Back in Vancouver he took the puck out of his jacket pocket and showed it to me. We were outside Eight Rinks in Burnaby. Some amateur players spotted it from twenty steps away.

"Hey, that's an Olympic puck, man. Is that real? Where'd you get that? Can we see it? Can I hold it?"

He showed them. Then he put it back into his pocket.

"Some day my grandson will have it," he said. "And no one is going to top that show and tell."

News editors in TV and newspapers try to tie stories together, so that after two or three related looks at something you get to see the connections, and maybe see something larger. Here are three stories on Main and Hastings. If we put the pieces together there may be some hope for that hopeless intersection.

THE PROBLEM WITH COMING HOME

I have just returned from vacation and here is the problem.

There is no Main and Hastings in New York.

In a city with eight million people, which is more living souls than all of British Columbia and Alberta combined, they cannot find enough drug dealers and drug addicts and poor homeless folks to take over even one little corner. When it comes to sleaze, the folks in the Big Apple could sure learn a lesson from the village of Vancouver.

You walk anywhere in New York, even in the parts of the city where there is little money and none of the glamour or the sky scrapers that make the city famous, there is not even one itsy bitsy street that looks like Main and Hastings. They have congested, noisy streets and on the sidewalks music from CDs, and laughter and shouting and arguing and vendors hawking, and kids playing, and mothers talking, but not one visible drug dealer. Where did they go wrong?

It once had plenty of ugliness to flaunt. In the 1970s and 1980s it was so dangerous and dirty that Hollywood made a fortune filming movies about the crime and litter and graffiti-covered subways and police corruption. There were vast areas of the city in which no one knew how many people lived there because the census takers would not go into them.

That has all changed. Now it has the official reputation of being the safest large city in North America.

Many things have created the change. We will mention a few of them later. But the question is always asked when someone looks at Main and Hastings: "If you clean it up, where will all these lost, drug-addicted souls and all those unpleasant criminals go?"

The answer is the same as what happened in New York, and the answer is a question: Where were all those wasted souls before New York hit the skids and before Main and Hastings got to be Shame and Wastings?

The answer: they did not exist. Of course there were drug addicts, and of course there were drug dealers and criminals. But they were miniscule in numbers compared to now, and they took their drugs in private and in hiding. And since there were fewer of them they committed their crimes less frequently, and more sporadically. It was possible for the police to keep up with them and they did not take over entire areas of the city.

The same was true in New York before crime and drugs started infecting the city like a giant sickness in the early 1970s. It was so bad that a million people left the city during that decade, including my wife and I to protect our children. By the mid-1980s it got worse with an epidemic of crack cocaine.

It seems so simple to say, but before drugs and crime started sweeping through the city there were fewer addicts and criminals. That is obvious. And just as obvious, when the epidemic swept the city many were infected. Very simply, stop the disease and there are fewer who will be sick.

When it started to be cleaned up the older addicts and criminals, those in their thirties and forties, had only a short time to go on this earth. But what was most important was that new, younger ones did not replace them. In time, they were not there.

Most of the people who hang out at Main and Hastings do not have long life expectancies. That is sad, but true. And what is more sad, but clear to anyone who looks at that corner, when the old ones die now they are replaced by young ones, more and more young ones, who quickly grow old.

Most of those there now will not live long enough to see the area cleaned up. But if it were transformed into a good part of town instead of a magnet for youth seeking something, the romance of drugs and poverty, the young ones would not be attracted. They would not go there. They might get a job. Amazing.

It would take a long time. You would hardly notice it at first.

No one noticed in New York as litter slowly disappeared and graffiti faded. But then it seemed suddenly you could look at the new New York, where even on the poorest streets with people selling meat roasted in barbeques in cut-in-half oil barrels, there are no groups of nasties selling drugs. These are not the fancy streets of Manhattan, where the teriyaki shish kebabs are barbequed in pushcarts that tourists take pictures of. These are the poor streets with no tourists, and no drug dealers.

And that brings us back to New York not being hip, not like Vancouver. It does not remember how to create even one measly, slimy, ugly intersection infested with street rats who openly sell illegal chemicals to lifeless, desperate addicts who shoot up without trying to hide. Who would bother to sneak away into the shadows when lighting a crack pipe in plain view has no one in authority saying, "Hey you can't do that."

That is one of the charms of Vancouver. New York has lost that old-time romance of drugs and crime and depravity.

I also travelled to four cities in Florida, none of which have managed to do what Vancouver does so well. In each of those cities, plus New York, I counted the homeless on my fingers, and did not use up both hands. Those who I did see were obviously not able to deal with life as easily as most of us. None were young, none were in their twenties, none were walking up and down between cars holding signs saying: "Hungry, Homeless, Travelling, God Bless."

None, like our own creative and youthful Vancouver homeless, were travelling in the same spot with the same sign for years.

The ones I saw in New York and Florida were actually homeless, and sad, and in the entire city numbered fewer than you see on any one street in Vancouver on any day, most of whom are in their twenties and if not walking between cars are begging while sitting underneath signs in windows saying "Help Wanted."

What's wrong with America? It lost the knack of making parts of beautiful cities too ugly and embarrassing to even drive through, and so scary that tourists go away with only one awful story.

We manage to do it, why can't they?

That's the problem with going away, you forget about the power of Main and Hastings, which has grown from Main and Hastings to Columbia and Hastings to Carrall and Hastings to Abbott and Hastings to Cambie and Hastings. And when you come back from other cities you say, "Wow, we've done something beyond belief, we've accomplished something large. We probably hold a world record in 'ugly.'"

We could teach those American cities a thing or two about creating a distinctive lifestyle without lifting a finger, just by not caring about it and turning our backs. What could be easier?

But somehow they think they can get along without a Main and Hastings. Losers.

I told someone in Vancouver this story. She got angry and said she almost wanted to tell me that if it was so good there why don't I go back?

I don't want to. Vancouver is my home. I just want it to become what my birthplace has become. I want someone to make a perversely bad joke that Vancouver is so beautiful—all of Vancouver—it has lost its knack of being ugly.

IT STARTED WITH A LEAK

The drop squeezed through the crack in the roof and fell out of the black ceiling.

It fell past the blackened windows. It fell past the peeling billboards. It gathered speed as it fell more than thirteen stories and then hit a sleeping man lying on the floor.

Another drop followed. The sleeping man rolled over, but the floor was wet. He crawled to another part of the floor and went back to sleep.

Another drop followed.

"We got to fix the leak," said the maintenance man.

"Why?" asked the new owners.

"Because it's going to rot away and the whole thing will fall down."

"Well, just fix the leak, but nothing else."

But you have done something like this, and you know what happened. You have had a renovation project that started with a leak and you wound up with a new bathroom. Or you simply wanted to fix a loose board on the stairs but when you were finished you had a whole new deck.

The same happened with the leak in the black ceiling and millions say, thank God.

The leak was in the roof of Grand Central Station in New York.

I was on a tour of the station because I am on a search to learn what happened in the city where I was born and grew up in and that in many ways shaped me. How did it go from being almost unlivable to most desirable?

My wife and I left New York in 1973 because crime was so bad we could not in any stretch of good faith think of raising our children there. We went to sleep with the sound of gunfire outside our apartment building.

My wife covered our children with her body in a concrete playground while the cops on one side of the playground and bad guys on the other had a gunfight. My wife and children lay under the bullets.

My father-in-law had a gun put to his head. My mother was mugged. My wife fought off youths who were beating up an old man in our apartment lobby. I had a sawed-off shotgun pressed into my stomach.

It was not a good place to live.

"In the 1970s," said the guide on the tour, "you got off a train in Grand Central and prayed you would make it to the sidewalk."

We saw the old clock that had been in the middle of the giant station. It had a bullet hole in it.

"This was a scary place in the '70s and '80s," said our guide. "Mostly it was empty, except for homeless and drug dealers and criminals. You would not go into the bathroom back then, even if you were dying to go because you would probably die inside."

I remembered the bathroom because it was worse than he described. And I remembered the inside of the grand terminal in the early '70s because I was a police reporter for the *New York Daily News*, which lived by crime stories.

I was young, I was tough, I was streetwise and I was terrified of going into Grand Central Station to cover yet another shooting or stabbing.

It was dark: the giant five-storey windows were painted black, the ceiling was black, and there were few working light bulbs in the walls. Most were either smashed or burned out.

It was the same in Times Square. It was frightening to go there. There were no tourists except the ones looking for drugs or peep shows. Most of the lights on the Great White Way were dark.

But in Grand Central the drip came down right after new owners had bought the station. The new landlord was the Metro-North Railroad, a large corporation that cared only about the bottom line, not about history or culture or preservation. They purchased the building because they needed a place to park their trains. They did not care about tourists or bathrooms. Bottom line: keep the building standing without spending.

It was just an old piece of junk, which now needed a tiny patch in the roof.

They fixed the hole and stopped the leak. But then underneath the hole while they were cleaning up, someone used a damp cloth on the ceiling and found, under the blackness, a star. It was a golden, painted star that was somewhere in the history books, but no one had seen or remembered it for three generations. It had faded from view and memory.

Just as a lark, some maintenance men scrubbed a bit more and found another star. It hit the newspapers. "There's a sky up there on the ceiling of Grand Central."

People got interested. Calls went to Metro-North. It would only cost a little bit to scrub a bit more.

The scaffolding was the most expensive part. With just soap and water and some brushes and elbow grease the blackness dissolved and under it was a constellation, no, under it was the entire heavens spread over one of the largest ceilings in the world.

But it was wrong. That's not the way the sky looks, it was backwards. And then they read more in the history books. This is the way God saw it, looking down.

Everyone thought it was the diesel smoke from the trains that had blackened the stars until someone else read that there were no diesel engines in the trains, ever. Right from the beginning in 1912 all the trains ran on electricity.

The soot was analyzed. It was all from cigarettes, one little puff at a time floating up and up until it covered the stars.

And then the renovation syndrome kicked in. You can't have such a good-looking ceiling over such a miserable-looking room below. Everyone takes the credit: the public, the newspapers, the company. It does not matter. What happened next was that the reno spread to the windows, which still were covered with paint left from World War II when they were blacked out in fear of air raids.

And then the reno went to the main large departure room that you see in pictures. By the time we left New York the corridors in the station were tunnels of plywood because of falling plaster and debris. We walked through wooden catacombs without seeing the walls or ceilings.

They removed the wood and fixed the plaster.

Then someone said the people hanging out in the terminal are not very nice. They sit on all the marble steps and sell drugs.

So the owners put up some inexpensive signs: No Sitting On Steps. And they asked the police to enforce it.

And then the landlord said such a nice-looking place should have somewhere to eat. They asked only local New York restaurants, no chains or franchises, to take a chance. Twenty-four amazing places to eat now operate in the vast waiting room that was empty when we left.

As happens in all renovations, it seemed like it would never end. There was always scaffolding up somewhere and workers everywhere. But the better things got, more commuters lingered and got coffee and lunch and looked up at the ceiling. It took twelve years.

Today half a million people will go into the station and look up at the stars. Yes, half a million, and yes, today. Just as half a million went yesterday and will go tomorrow: 150,000 commuters and 350,000 tourists. Half a million people go to Grand Central every day and marvel at a most incredibly beautiful building that not long ago looked like Main and Hastings under a leaky roof.

They all spend a little money, which has paid for the renovation.

And one thing more: there is no room left for the drug dealers.

And another thing: mayor Rudolph Giuliani came around after that, saw what was happening in Grand Central and said, "Why don't we try the same thing in Times Square?"

The lights are now back on there too. And as the guide told the story, it was clear the rejuvenation of the train station and the city did not come about from some large, complex plan. It all started with just a tiny leak.

NOW THE GOOD NEWS:
THE THIRD STORY

NEXT STOP, FABULOUS MAIN AND HASTINGS
      "Ladies and gentlemen, you can't imagine this, but this area used to
be the home of criminals and drug addicts. Now, it is one of the most trendy
spots in town."

Those were more or less the words of the guide who took us through
Grand Central Station. Once the ugly open sore, now could we just please
stay here a little longer, it is so beautiful.

That got me imagining about the near future on Main and Hastings in
Vancouver and an imaginary guided tour:

He is pointing out the spiffy Carnegie Library with a few well-dressed
people chatting outside, and the reopened Pantages Theatre, and the reno-
vated bars and coffee shops, and the narrow old hotels which have been con-
verted into condos in what is now the city's most desirable part of town.

I am convinced it will happen. And it will happen just as it happened
in New York, almost by accident. Just as the drip in the ceiling of the train
station started the clean-up of the entire terminal, and then Times Square,
and then the city, one small thing happened in Vancouver's skid row that will
change everything.

We were driving around looking for a story and the cameraman Tony

Clark, who is very good at spotting things, said, "There's a guy sitting on a table in a doorway reading a newspaper."

He said it looked like a shop, maybe a fix-it shop or a gift shop or something, but someone was reading a newspaper at a table and how many tables do you see at a doorway to a shop? Good enough to stop and ask.

Jerrod Tiffin was sipping his coffee at the table that was half on the sidewalk of East Cordova near Columbia. He said hello, and he said this was his patio to the world.

Across the street a young hooker with many tattoos and a half-unbuttoned blouse was screaming at a man who was either a pimp or a nonpaying customer. They used many bad words loudly to each other.

"It is all part of the show," said Jerrod.

A native artist in a wheelchair stopped and Jerrod said hello. They talked and the artist showed Jerrod a carving and Jerrod said no. The rejection did not matter. The two of them continued talking about the neighbourhood and the weather and politics. It was like a backyard in suburbia.

Jerrod bought the space in the old warehouse in 2006 for $400,000, which was half the price of a Yaletown condo where he moved from. Then he showed us inside.

Wow. That's what I said. Wow. The main room has a ceiling that ends seventeen feet above the spot where you are standing. That is almost two floors in Yaletown. He has two thousand square feet of space. You could fit three and a half average Yaletown condos into his living room and kitchen.

"How could I say no?" he asked.

He has one-way glass on his front windows. He can see out, no one can see in.

"I tell my friends I have a twenty-foot wide screen TV."

The scenery is fascinating, mostly passing drug addicts. Sometimes it is quiet, except for the sirens. He and his friends barbeque on the sidewalk.

It is not for everyone, he added. He is honest.

But it is the beginning. First Jerrod, then the Woodward's building, which will be a busy condo development not long after the ink in this book is dry. Then the old, tiny rooming houses that have been bought by the provincial government will be refurbished and one by one the vacant lots along Hastings will be filled with both high- and low-income housing.

Bit by bit, drop by drop, adventurous person by adventurous person will move in and the street will change.

It is like the cleaning of the ceiling in Grand Central Station. Scrub away the dirt and find one bright spot. Then scrub some more. Slowly, just as the brightness faded, it returns.

In New York it took more than a decade before anyone even noticed things were getting better. And then it seemed the sun was coming up every day. Suddenly newspapers were writing about the reduction in crime and the arrival of tourists and about the opening of restaurants and the improvement in the economy.

It was not like the old days of dirt and muggings and fear and hopelessness. How did it all happen? Just like how did it get bad? It just did, bit by bit, one drug dealer moving in brought with him a drug addict, and then another dealer followed and two or ten addicts moved in.

And to change for the better: one renovation. One guy named Jerrod buying a home one block from Pigeon Park. Woodward's with tax-paying people moving in.

And then, slowly, "Ladies and gentlemen, you can't imagine this, but this used to be filled with criminals and drug addicts. You wouldn't walk down the street. Now, we will stop for you to shop and take pictures."

Just wait. It will happen.

TENEMENT LIVING

One more New York story, because in one way or another it belongs to all of us.

There is a new must-see place in New York called the Lower East Side Tenement Museum. It was not there when I left. Back then in the early 1970s the Lower East Side was abandoned except for drug pushers, drug addicts and squatters.

If you had a job and paid your taxes and brushed your teeth you would not fit in. You would probably be robbed and then killed if you went there.

The Lower East Side is that bulge on the east side of Manhattan that you can see on a map. It was the home for basically all the immigrants who poured into New York for one hundred and fifty years, from the early 1800s to the mid-1900s.

All those stories of the Jews, the Germans, the Irish, the Blacks, the Poles, the whoever from wherever who went to America and then fanned out across the country and Canada, went through the Lower East Side of New York. It was the funnel for humanity.

All those pictures of the pushcarts on the crowded streets were on the Lower East Side.

All those stories of rags to riches were on the Lower East Side.

All those stories of rags to crime and poverty were on the Lower East Side.

And then in the late 1990s when New York was rapidly climbing out of civic chaos to a renaissance of beauty, the Lower East Side was rediscovered by a young and suddenly well-off generation. Now condemned apartments have been turned into upscale condos, and abandoned stores have become boutiques. Street after street of the old brick tenements have been knocked down and replaced by green spaces, narrow parks where human dirt and filth were stacked five stories high.

"We can't let this history die," said a group of do-gooders in the late 1990s.

They saved and borrowed and bought one of the tenements. It is on Orchard Street. Go there if you go to New York.

There are numerous tours. I will tell you about just one of them.

The nice young tour guide herded our small group inside the front door of the tenement. There were just six of us, because the rooms were not big enough to hold more.

"Please close the door behind you," she said.

We did. It was dark. It was the middle of the day and we could barely see each other.

"They did not put windows in the doors because it cost more," said the nice young guide.

We opened the door again. The guide was standing on the narrow stairway.

"Suppose you were the mother of five or six, average for 1870. You were carrying up your laundry that you washed in the back in the well. Coming down the stairs was someone carrying their bodily waste in a pot because there were no toilets. Behind him was someone carrying down the ashes from their coal stove and dropping those ashes all over the stairs.

"Coming up behind you was a young woman with groceries. And up and down the stairs were countless kids, because there were four families per floor and there were five floors.

"And there was no light."

The bedroom upstairs held a bed, what we would now consider a single bed. It was the only bed. Also in the room was a dresser that looked like it belonged in a child's room, and one chair. There were no windows and no light other than candles.

The next room was the kitchen. There was a coal-burning stove, a small table with three chairs and again, no windows.

No running water. No toilet.

Everything happened in here, washing, cooking, eating, ironing, all without enough light to see.

The next room, the living room, had two windows and overlooked the street. The kids slept here. The small ones put two hardback chairs together and slept on those. The older kids slept on the floor.

They did not think they were suffering, most of the poor immigrants in 1870 lived this way.

Nathalie Gumperts moved into this apartment with her husband, Julius, and four daughters. They were from Germany. There were many Germans in New York then. In 1850 there were more German newspapers than English papers in the city.

Nathalie gave birth to a son in the dark back room. He died soon afterwards of dysentery. The well for their water around back was next to the outhouses. They did not make the connection.

In 1873 the United States went into a depression. Julius had breakfast one morning and left to look for work. He never came back.

Nathalie went to the police.

"Are you kidding, lady? We have five thousand people a day getting off boats and moving into this neighbourhood, and you want us to look for your husband? Good luck."

Nathalie had no money. She took in clothing to be mended and her daughters had to sew piecemeal work after school. They could not go out and play on the street.

The people at the museum know the family well. They have records of their names and the rent they paid.

Ten years later Nathalie received a letter from Germany telling her that her husband's uncle had died and left him $600. This was a great deal of money. Rent was $10 a month.

But the money was left to her husband, not to her. She spent five years writing letters and begging before she got the money.

"And the first thing she did," said the guide, "she moved the heck out of here."

She bought a house uptown, which would be way downtown now.

"And we know she did well because here is a picture of her," said the guide.

She showed us a black and white photo of a woman with a stern, tired face and the rest of her covered by a long, black dress.

"We know she did okay because she had a picture taken. There were not many pictures back then."

None of her daughters married until after she died.

The museum people traced her family to the next generation, and the next and the next and the next.

"Here is a picture of her great-great-grandson."

We saw a contemporary, nice-looking man with a beard.

"Ironically," she said, "he had breakfast one morning, left for work and never came back."

There was a pause. Crummy guy, we thought.

"September 11, 2001," she said. "He was in the North Tower."

Pause. Silence.

"The family had its memorial in this room," she said, "where Nathalie started their new life."

Whether it was in a ghetto in a big city or a tiny, frigid cabin in Saskatchewan, whether the father left or not, or was killed or not, or the mother had a photo or not, we all have the same family tree. It does not matter if it is a different family, it is still amazing to stand in a room like that and touch the walls and breathe the air.

We all have been there.

BAD HAND? THEN RAISE THE BET

He picked us up in his Porsche SUV. His Bentley was at home.

So what? I have met rich people before.

He got out of the Porsche and struggled to walk. One foot moved forward and the other dragged on the ground trying to catch up. Then the first foot moved again and his back arched and he threw himself forward for the next step.

This time it is not 'so what.' It is sad, but I have known others who have hard lives.

"Here," he said pulling out a bottle of Johnny Walker Gold Label, "We will have a drink later."

I have not known anyone who did that before.

His name is Winston Anderson and he is my wife's cousin and we visited him in Florida last summer along with a half dozen other relatives who we had to see because we have not seen them in a long time. What other reason would you need to visit relatives?

But before the Scotch he had to settle some business. He was leasing a warehouse to the school board and had to get his executive polished cherrywood desks moved to another of his warehouses.

"They pay me for the building and they pay the taxes," he said. "I like that kind of business."

He is from the West Indies and is of East Indian decent. He looks like a Vancouver cab driver. He has no advanced schooling. His sister says he doesn't really read much. But then she said, "He doesn't have to. He is very smart."

I heard about this cousin twenty years ago after he broke his neck in a motorcycle accident. He was in a hospital for a year and a half, in bed, and was told he probably would not walk again.

But some little fragments of nerve endings were still stretching out their frayed ends to each other, just barely holding together, and when he pulled himself to his feet it was not actually a walk. It was a triumph.

He moved to Florida to a town near his wife's parents. He could drive, so he used the last of his money to get an old pickup truck and bought shrimp from fishermen and tried to sell the shrimp to restaurants.

"The first guy told me to get out. He buys his shrimp from wholesalers. He could not trust a guy selling from an old pickup." Others did the same.

He failed in the shrimp business.

He was broken and broke.

He went back to his doctor for a checkup on his neck. His doctor told him to use what he had.

When Winston told me that I did not know what it meant. He had nothing.

He was getting around mostly on a walker.

He looked at his walker, the only thing he had. He said it might be better if there was a small change in it.

He made that change—a different handgrip.

Then he started producing walkers with his new handle. He got a patent and started a company. He looked at other medical equipment used by people who can't walk. He modified an electric scooter and got another patent.

Then he made improvements in other equipment and sent them to a factory to be made.

It happened slowly but two decades after his accident he drove us to his home at the edge of his city. It is on a two-hundred-acre ranch. The home is ten thousand square feet.

He drove us around town. He owns this mall, and that mall, and that one over there. All neat-as-a-pin small strip malls.

He adores his daughter, who, like all fourteen-year-old girls, fell in love with horses. So he bought her six of them. Then he built a barn in his back-yard to house them. Then he named one of the malls after his daughter.

We are not concerned with overindulgence. Winston does whatever Winston wants to do. We are only concerned with the man who had nothing and did something with what he had.

He has much money, probably more than much. According to his family and friends and my wife and me, he is friendly, generous, funny and humble.

The day after we had the Gold Label he took us out for a Chinese lunch. He did not want to go to the large smorgasbord place that he owns. He preferred a small, cozy restaurant nearby.

The cook who owns the restaurant is his friend. His English name is Sean and he is Chinese and from Malaysia. He owns the restaurant in the building owned by Winston.

He sat down at the table with us and Winston and Sean swapped a list of old, well-worn inside jokes. They laughed a lot.

Sean told us that Winston had helped bring his entire family to America.

Since we are from Vancouver, Sean told me that Vancouver has the best Chinese food in the world. He knows about the Chinese restaurants here.

He cooked us an extra special meal and it was wonderful.

Winston had a couple of glasses of wine with his lunch and when we left he handed me the keys to his Porsche. He is a smart man.

On the way back to his office he pointed back at the restaurant and said he owed that guy a lot.

"Why?"

"He's the one who would not buy my shrimp."

SOMETIMES IT IS BETTER
NOT TO KNOW

It was written in flowers: "I'm Sorry."

When you say something with flowers you mean it. Flowers are expensive.

The stems and buds and petals were wrapped around each other to make long ropes of colour and fragrance and then they were woven into a chain-link fence around a vacant lot at Twelfth and Main. Each rope became a letter and each letter was about the size of a small child.

When they were put together the words were the size of a universe of atonement.

"I'm Sorry."

We stopped an old man.

"Have you ever apologized for something, something really bad?"

"Yes," he said, then walked on.

In that moment you knew it was something. What it was we did not know, and we had no right to know. But it was something.

We stopped a little old lady. All the old ladies seem to be little.

"Have you ever apologized for—" We did not get to finish.

She looked at the words in flowers on the fence, bending her head a bit so she could read them and nodded as the large letters came together in an old memory.

"Once," she said.

And then she walked away. Again, we had no right to know, but it was something never to be forgotten.

Wrongs and apologies are seldom forgotten.

The letters in the fence were hard to read unless you backed off and stood near the curb.

Then they were a billboard: "I'm Sorry."

In seven characters they held all the pain and begging in life.

"Someone gave me roses, once," said a woman. "He was very sorry."

"Did you forgive him?" I asked.

She smiled. That was a turning point. "Yes," she said. Then her smile grew. It must have been a good turning point, an apology that changed everything.

"Someone once pleaded with me," said another woman.

"Did you forgive?"

"No," she said, and left.

Some things you just don't forgive.

These were the stories of reality: begging, pleading to undo something that cannot be undone, being forgiven and not being forgiven.

We did not need to know what was behind the apologies. That is the stuff of the check-out aisle tabloids. They sell very well, but it is not the sleaze that changes lives, it is the sincerity behind the "forgive me."

We did not know anything about why the flowers were speaking from the fence. Someone said it was shortly after Valentine's Day, "so maybe, something or other, you know, Valentine's Day. That has to be the reason behind it."

I was glad he left. His reason was making my head hurt.

We checked to see if there had been a car accident at the corner. There was not.

That left the unknown, unanswerable, eternal questions of love and a broken heart.

We were about to leave when a man approached us and asked what we were asking. We told him and asked if he had ever apologized for anything.

He did not want to hear the question. He only wanted to tell us something. He pulled out of his shirt pocket a photo of a baby.

"My son was born yesterday. His name is John."

"Beautiful baby," we said, and he walked away happy in a way that is hard to explain. It is the way you are happy after a baby is born.

The TV story ended with him almost, but not quite, skipping down the sidewalk and the flowers behind him in the fence. We said in that picture are all the stories of love and life: mistakes and apologies, forgiveness and rejection, and most of all, endings and beginnings.

And we thought that was the end of it.

A month later I got a call from someone asking for a copy of the story. He had heard it was on TV but did not see it because he is an art student and what art student in the world would ever admit to watching TV?

The flowers were a school project to do some kind of public art.

Oh, darn. If we had known that in the beginning we would never have done the story. Or it would have been a story about the artist and why he chose that for a theme. But we would not have asked passersby about their inner feelings if the question was not from someone actually apologizing for something. It would be somehow cheapening the question to the people on the street.

I sent him the copy, and then I thought how lucky we were not to have known. Because if we did know and did not do the story we would have never seen that woman's smile when she remembered what forgiveness gave to her. And we would not have wondered how life changed, maybe for the better, for the woman who did not accept the apology.

But most of all, we would not have seen the picture of baby John. No matter how you get to it, learning about a birth starts the story all over again. And John's story will have love and heartache and mistakes and apologies and rejection and forgiveness and smiles, and then more love.

Even though it was just homework from the art teacher, we gave it an A-plus.

THE BLIND LEADING THE REST OF US

"It's just another art project," I said.

"But it's cool," said the cameraman. "And besides, it's a good picture."

You cannot argue with that. We look for pictures and see if the story grows from that.

It is what television is all about. Looking at something until your bottom hurts and your stomach is full of coffee. Looking for things is why God made our eyes.

We would not have space travel if we did not see the stars. We would not want new cars if we did not see those flashy hunks of gasoline-sucking boxes zooming down the street.

We live in a sighted world. We learn almost everything through our eyes. How they evolved is a miracle of amazement.

The sun was burning down on some sightless creepy crawly thing and somehow some cells in the skin said, "Hey, there might be something out there."

So they changed and presto, a million years later, someone said, "You look hot. Can I have a date?"

Eyes are what we open in the morning and stare in the mirror with and say, "Oh, heavens, why did you drink so much?"

Eyes teach us that roses are supposed to be there and dandelions are not. Eyes show us that old books are classics even if we don't open them while something recommended by Oprah is a must-read, until she denounces it.

And eyes spotted the flowers in a vacant lot a block east of Arbutus on Broadway.

"Cool. You got to do something with that," said the cameraman who was not going to be pried away from this spot because there, right in front of him, was a picture.

The flowers were in glass jars sitting in a row on a narrow wooden homemade table in the middle of the lot. Around them was rubble and weeds and seagulls trying to wedge open the tops of cans that once held beans or soup and were thrown into the lot by poor homeless folks.

"Beautiful," said the cameraman. "Find a story to go with it."

So I asked people how they imagined someone got into the lot.

"Climbed the fence," said one.

"Sneaked under the fence," said another.

"Broke through the fence," said a third.

Boring, I'm thinking. Utterly boring and unusable and wasted and what am I going to do and my job is coming to an end. I think that often at times like this. There is no hope to find anything useful about a bunch of flowers behind a chain-link fence.

And then I saw a man with a seeing-eye dog and a woman holding his arm coming our way.

Thank you.

"Excuse me," I say. "But we were wondering if—"

The man interrupts. "I know your voice."

"Me?"

"Who are you?"

I start to tell him. Yes, of course. It is like old friends. He cannot see me but he knows me.

I recognize him. He is Gil Hewlett, the former director of the Vancouver Aquarium.

Gil is totally blind. Diabetes.

"I know you can't see them," I said. "But there's a bunch of flowers in glass jars on a table in the middle of a vacant lot. They are behind a chain-link fence. What do you think?"

That is an unfair question. What fence? What vacant lot? What flowers?

"That is such a beautiful thing someone has done," Gil said.

"How do you think they got there?" I said.

"Doesn't matter," he said. "If someone has put flowers in a vacant lot, it is beautiful."

The probability that it was done to get marks in school did not enter his mind. Someone doing something beautiful was good enough.

We were asking a question that connected the eyes with the brain. His answer connected the eyes with the heart. We saw the subterfuge, he saw the flowers.

Thanks, Gil, for showing us what was there.

IT'S NOT NEWS WHEN YOU KNOW
THE NEIGHBOURS

6 6 **T**here was a fire overnight in Surrey," said Wayne.

"So?" I asked. It was a Sunday morning. "We are looking for something uplifting."

"I just want to check it out," said Wayne. This is unusual. There is an overnight crew that chases fires and there are other cameramen who would be assigned if it was a big fire.

Wayne Decoff, the cameraman, started heading to 127th Street near 105th Avenue. I go along because he is driving. That's one of the laws of nature.

"Why?" I ask again.

"I just want to see," said Wayne.

Odd again. He knows our goal is the opposite of tragedy.

Over the Pattullo Bridge and I still do not want to go. Fires are a tragedy if you are in them, otherwise they are a few seconds of flames on the air and then forgotten.

"I just want to see where on that street it was," said Wayne.

He drives through the little bit of remaining bush in North Surrey and I can see this normally happy, friendly and talkative guy is serious and quiet. His eyes are moving left and right. He knows what he is seeing.

"I grew up around here," he said.

We saw the fire truck a few blocks ahead.

"That's my street," he said.

Suddenly he was not a news cameraman. He was someone who used to live there, next to where fire trucks were parked. The firemen were winding up their hoses.

"That's my house," he said, pointing to the one next to the still smoldering building.

Now it was personal, disconnected by twenty years but still feeling the connection.

Wayne got out of his van carrying his camera. He walked around looking at the stale smoke rising through the collapsed roof.

"They were nice people who used to live there," he said.

I took the camera from him. If you put it on wide angle and push the record button it works. You don't get the beautiful pictures that professional photographers make and find, but it is serviceable, and at this moment I knew that emotion was more important than art.

Wayne saw a woman across the street.

"Do you remember me?" he asked.

Eileen Magnall looked at him, twisted her lips, then, "Oh, my, gosh. You're one of the Decoff boys."

They laughed, then went right into talk of the fire. It was sudden, it was scary, everyone got out and no she did not know the people who lived there. They were not friendly like in the old days.

And then, without missing a beat, she said to Wayne, "Your mom just died. I'm sorry."

They hugged. Somehow news of old neighbours always gets around.

Wayne crossed the street to his old house.

"See those trees," he said, pointing to two large evergreens in the front yard, next to the house that had burned.

"Dad planted them. When they were small they were the perfect distance apart for a soccer goal."

A pleasant, white-haired man came out. Wayne told him he grew up in the house and they exchanged names. The new owner is Bob Selig, who said he loved the house but the flames last night came only an arm length's away from destroying it.

"The firemen saved my home," he said.

The two of them walked around the yard, with Wayne, who is probably twenty years younger than Bob, telling him memories of the past.

Then Wayne walked over to the firemen who were packing up. He has been at more than a hundred fires, and always he asks, "Do you know how it started? How many firemen were here? How long, how bad? Suspicious?" The usual questions.

This time he only said thanks for saving the house next door.

The story was not about a fire. It was about how you see things, and how the world changes when you are not watching or reading about someone else. It is very, very different from what you see on television or read in the newspapers.

THE BIG WHITE ROCK

When you are big, as in being an adult, it is still big. When you are small, it is even bigger.

And there is no way you can climb it. Every day around the calendar when it is not raining, and of course this is in White Rock where it never rains, someone is trying to climb it.

But it is impossible to climb because there is nothing to grab onto. The base goes in like a giant ball so your feet slip under it and then it bulges out in the middle. If you could get past the bulge there is nothing to grab onto to get to the top. So, it is impossible.

But many have done it, like other mountains that were impossible to get to the top of but now are tourist attractions.

It is the White Rock in White Rock, a city in which no one ever asks how did it get its name, although many ask which came first, the city or the rock.

Some have thought the rock was painted white after the city named itself White Rock. This of course is silly. It would be like Vancouver being named Vancouver before Captain George Vancouver sailed into the harbour.

The rock was white for centuries after a glacier left it behind millenniums ago. It was white back then because the seagulls living nearby ate shellfish, clams and oysters, and their guano came out the same colour as the bits of shells that were going in. And the birds would roost on the rock. And slowly it changed from grey to white, and it stayed that way.

In the nineteenth century, sailors used the gleaming white boulder as a daytime lighthouse so they would know where they were.

In the late twentieth century vandals started using it as a drawing board, so others would know where they had been. So now the white is all paint, because city officials are not going to let graffiti darken the name of the city and they cannot wait for the seagulls to do the work for them.

That is the history of the White Rock in White Rock.

I was looking at some little kids trying to climb it. The rock is ten times bigger than they are tall so their efforts were mainly running to it, hitting it with their feet and bouncing off. It is wonderful how little kids can bounce.

Some a little older, in the range of eight or nine years, were trying to put some driftwood up against it so they could climb on the wood and then somehow jump over the bulge and fly to the top. It is wonderful how eight- and nine-year-olds believe they can fly.

"I was up there once," said a kid with a crewcut. He was bigger. He was eleven and his name was Alex.

"How?" I asked.

He put his hand to his face so no one would see. This was a secret.

"We got a ladder," he said.

Whatever works, I thought.

He had the smile of an innocent, smiling child. It is wonderful how eleven-year-olds have the best times of their lives.

"How was it, standing up there?" I asked.

"Cool," he said. "I was on top of the world."

Except for the "cool," those are the same words Sir Edmund Hillary said after Everest, which was also impossible to climb.

THE SUPER FAN

"I can't believe I got my face into this."

He was in his late sixties and had added a few pounds since he was seventeen and his face had filled out but I could still see his eyes behind the steel bars of the old catcher's mask. They were twinkling.

"I got this glove from my parents in 1952," said another guy. It looked like 1952 vintage, small and five fingers.

Ray Gora reached up and snagged a ball that was thrown by a teammate on a team that was not going to play anyone else on this fine baseball day. Ray had started the move to get the guys together, one last time.

They were the Canadian Legion's Richmond Junior B League Champions from 1955, gathering for their fiftieth anniversary at Minoru Park.

"We played somewhere out here," said a beefy guy who was swinging a bat, "but it all looks different. No one cut the grass for us and that street over there," he pointed to a busy road, "there were never any cars on it."

Through phone calls and the Internet they had found eleven of the original fifteen guys. A couple had vanished and a couple had died.

The purpose of getting together this morning was just to say hello to each other, maybe get someone to take a picture of them, and then spend the rest of the day playing golf.

As a joke, and because we were there, they got together and started singing "Take Me Out to the Ball Game." That was thoughtful of them, because

I did not know how I was going to put a baseball team on television without playing baseball. Singing helped.

The rest of the time they had some infield practice, hitting, bunting, throwing. Some were still pretty good, some were a little stiff. One looked like he was still trying to impress the coach.

We finished and said goodbye and we were leaving when I saw, way over there in the stands, one woman sitting and watching. As we passed by I said hello and asked if she knew any of the players.

"A long time ago one of them caught a ball right near where I was sitting. I had been watching him," she said. Her name was Judy.

"Which one?"

She pointed at the one player, Bob, who was trying just a little harder than the others to hit and catch and throw.

"I went to every game," she said, "and watched him until I reached over and caught a foul ball that he was going for. I ran and he chased me. Then he dropped his glove and I ran back and grabbed it." She laughed. "Then I let him catch me."

That's the way baseball should be played, even if it's not in the rule books.

Judy and Bob became Mr. and Mrs. Chicalo.

"As long as she was watching a game I tried to impress her," he said. More than half a century later she was still watching and he was still trying to impress.

"Of course I remember that foul ball," Bob said. "It was the best catch of my life."

Then Bob left his teammates and sat alongside his wife.

She took his glove and held it in her lap. The same glove he wore fifty years ago.

We were halfway across the field but we could hear the other guys singing: "Buy me some peanuts and Cracker Jack, I don't care if I never get back."

They were singing for Judy and Bob.

THE ONLY DIFFERENCE WAS THE YEARS

In one day I met both of them and I could not believe how they were linked even though they are so incredibly different.

First was a young girl selling lemonade. She was at the edge of False Creek where new condos are going up across from Science World. It does not matter if you cannot picture it. The important thing is she was selling lemonade on a lonely stretch of asphalt, and she was reading a book.

Her lemonade was going for fifty cents a cup.

"How much have you made?" I asked.

"A dollar," she said.

"And what are you going to do with your money?"

"Buy books," she said.

Her name is Rukshana Begum and she said she was eleven, going on twelve. She had come from Bangladesh five years ago. She spoke no English. The written English word looked like lines going everywhere.

Like all kids, she learned the new language fairly quickly. Kids are lucky that they are so innocently brilliant.

And then she started to learn to read, like six-year-olds, one letter and one word at a time.

"Do you read a lot?" I asked.

She nodded, with her sun hat flopping up and down.

"How many books have you read?" I asked, expecting a high answer, maybe more than a hundred.

"Thousands," she said.

"Thousands is a lot of books, are you sure?" I said.

"Thousands," she said.

"What is your favourite?"

Without hesitation, "*Little House on the Prairie*, by Laura Ingalls Wilder."

I was more than surprised, I was amazed that she included the author's name.

I did not ask her what she wanted to do later in life. It was obvious, she wanted to read, and I knew some day she would grace this country by being a wonderful, bright and understanding woman. Canada got a lucky shake when she landed here. Some day folks will say she was always unforgettable.

Two bicycle riders bought lemonade. She was polite, she thanked them, and then she went back to reading her book.

An hour later I saw a guy pulling lawn mowers out of his beat-up old van. He looked as bad as the van. He had a scruffy white beard that covered most of his face and wore thick glasses.

But the reason I stopped to talk to him was the writing that covered the van's windows. It was poetry, in the rough.

I'm The Garden Fiesta,
Mowing And The Resta.
Michael's Besta.
No Garden Be Messta.

"That's brilliant," I said. "Are you Michael?"

He looked at me as though I was neither a student of the obvious nor poetry. Obviously he was Michael. It was his van and his poetry.

"I'm not here for the money," he said. "I just want people to feel good."

He started up his gas-powered lawn mower.

"I can't hear you with the motor going," I said.

He shut it off.

"You don't have to, just read my windows."

Then he started the mower again.

I read the windows. On one in the back was written in paint:

Lawn mowing
As knowing
It's the Neat
That's Showing.

And next to it:

If Your Garden's A Mess
Get Michael Who's
The BEST.

He passed close to me and shouted, "Poetry makes them laugh and brings me the work."

Here is the scoop on Michael Springford. He was in the Navy during World War II. He tried driving cabs after that but did not like sitting all day. He started cutting lawns and trimming bushes. He liked the exercise. That was in 1950. He was eighty-three when I met him. He was still cutting lawns, an average of five a day. And he was writing poetry on the windows of his van. What more could you hope for when you are near the end of life?

Rukshana was selling lemonade and reading a book every two days. What more could you hope for at the beginning of life?

Michael and Rukshana: different ages, different lives, different everything and yet links in a chain that is holding all of us together.

She may run the country some day. And if Michael is still around he would say:

If your kids don't like readin'
Rukshana is what they're needin'

REMEMBERING ONE DAY

In Flanders fields the poppies blow
Between the crosses, row on row

John McCrae wrote that sitting on the back of an ambulance. He was a doctor in the Canadian Army. He was in his seventeenth straight day of hell, trying to ease the pain of the screaming, dying men in an endless battle in France.

His best friend, who was also one of his students in medical school, had been killed the day before and McCrae buried him in the mud, without the aid of a chaplain.

He was staring at the grave in an almost totally destroyed, totally desolate place called Flanders when he started to write a poem to get his mind off the blood. A few straggling, wild poppies that had survived the shells and the boots were bending in the wind between the fresh graves. He wrote about them.

That mark our place; and in the sky
The larks, still bravely singing, fly
Scarce heard amid the guns below

It is the same in every war. Many die, and those who don't can never forget those who did.

Smokey Smith said very little as they wheeled him into the Lynn Valley Legion in 2004.

Someone was singing an adapted song with a World War II rhythm: "We love you Smokey, we do."

Everyone stood and applauded.

"It is an honour just to be here," said a woman.

"I didn't have to go to war because of him," said a young man.

They called him Smokey because he was fast. He "smoked" the other kids in races in high school in New Westminster.

He joined the army not for noble, patriotic reasons, but only because he needed a job. He was older than many soldiers. By the time he was in Northern Italy he was thirty and had won twelve medals for bravery and had been wounded twice.

He was not disciplined or obedient or controllable. The army loves "Yes, Sir" men. Smokey was an "Up your rump" man. He was promoted to corporal nine times, and then because of something he did that those in authority did not like, he was demoted back to private nine times.

And it was as a private that he faced those tanks and all those enemy soldiers on one night of heavy rain.

He was ordered to establish a beachhead on a river. It was pouring. The rain was gushing out of the sky. The river had risen six feet in five hours. He had to get across it. He had two men under his command.

He left one to protect part of the river bank.

Smokey and one man went on until, in the dark and the rain, they were attacked by three tanks, two self-propelled guns, which means rapid-firing cannons on wheels, and thirty soldiers.

Just Smokey and the one man now under his command were facing them. Impossible is a word we use when we know we cannot do anything, because, well, because they were two guys and there were tanks and guns and a small army facing them.

And this army was not just facing them, they were shooting. And the young soldier with Smokey was hit. So Smokey grabbed an anti-tank gun and fired at the steel giant coming straight at him.

He was not going to let them get to his wounded comrade.

He hit the tank and knocked it out. Then ten soldiers jumped off the back of the steel monster and started firing at him.

Smokey grabbed a Tommy gun and fired back. He was at point-blank range. He stood up in full view and fired away.

A second tank came at him. Smokey fired until he ran out of bullets, then found another magazine in the mud and kept firing. The self-propelled gunship came at him. He kept firing until it stopped moving. Then a second gunship came and Smokey stopped that one too, with his Tommy gun that was glowing red with heat.

He kept firing until he had put out of action one tank and two self-propelled guns, killed four enemy soldiers and sent the rest running.

"We love you Smokey," they sang in the Legion.

Only sixteen Victoria Crosses were awarded during the Second World War in Canada. Twelve went to officers. The only time he remembers hearing his real name, Ernest Alvia Smith, was when he was awarded the VC. Smokey was the only private in the Canadian Army to win the nation's highest honour. It is given for being fearless beyond all measure and selfless beyond all expectations.

"I was just protecting my wounded friend," he said. "And I was scared to death."

They applauded in the Legion. They stood for him. They sang.

"I don't know why they are making such a fuss," said Smokey.

And then they wheeled him out. He was off to France for D-Day ceremonies.

"We love you, Smokey," they said as he left. "God bless you, Smokey," they said.

He thanked them. Then he said, as he always said when he left a gathering like this, "I was just doing what anyone would do. I was trying to help someone stay alive."

We are the Dead. Short days ago
We lived, felt dawn, saw sunset glow,
Loved, and were loved, and now we lie
In Flanders fields.

Lieutenant Colonel John McCrae said he was trying to get into a few words the meaning of endless death which followed the screams which followed the bullets which followed the thoughts that we are invincible, which followed the prayers that we would be so.

It was ugly and it was pain. John McCrae said it was Hades. He would not use the word Hell, but it was, for him, for Smokey, for every soldier who has been there, Hell.

The Cenotaph in Victory Square was built for those who died in the first war. But when it was built it wasn't called the First World War. It was called the Great War, because that was the hell on earth that they thought would end all wars. It was built for those with mostly European faces and names.

Then came the Second World War and the Cenotaph wasn't the last monument, and it wasn't the last war, and it wasn't only Europeans who died.

"Our home and native land," she was singing with a beautiful voice.

She was singing in front of the monument in Stanley Park that is filled with Japanese names. She was singing to a crowd of mostly Japanese-Canadians on a cold November 11 in a home and native land that once did not believe it should be their home because of the colour of their skin and the spelling of their names.

Roy Kawamoto heard me asking about the years of internment.

"You really want to know?" he asked.

It still hurt. You can tell when someone asks in that way.

"It was the fifth of November, 1942. The RCMP swooped down on our house and put us in jail. We were there for seventy-two days."

Everything was remembered in detail. After the jail came the years of internment, which was jail in a camp far away.

While he was talking to me he was standing in front of the monument that has row after row after row of Japanese names of men who died for Canada in World War I. The monument was in the park with those names engraved in bronze on the day that Roy was taken away by the police because his name was Japanese.

He had his twelfth birthday in jail.

Later, he joined the Canadian Army.

Miyoko Grignon said she did not think the pain would ever go away. You could say to her, why don't you just forget about it and get on with life?

She has gotten on with her life and has raised a beautiful family and is an outstanding citizen of Canada.

But forget it?

Her father fought for Canada in World War I.

Then Jim Nishiyama, an Air Force veteran who was standing near the monument for the Japanese, made the observation that brought the reality up to date.

"The same thing happened after September 11," he said. "People with turbans were getting beaten up. And Moslems don't even wear turbans," he added with the further mockery of how stupid the human race can sometimes be. "Just like we were born in Canada but were locked up because we weren't considered to be Canadians."

The national anthem was again being sung. "We stand on guard for thee."

The monument, as all the war monuments, has engraved on it that we must never forget.

It would be good if it added not to forget our narrow-minded stupidities as well as our unbelievable bravery and sacrifices. It is the second of those that ends wars, it is usually the first of those that starts them.

John McCrae's poem about poppies is the reason we wear poppies now, almost a century later. And almost a century later, we are still at war. There have been so many wars. We go out to kill each other, always to make the world better, and safer, and sometimes we accomplish that, but sadly, for some reason it always seems to be temporary. The human species is a work in progress.

The cenotaph in Maple Ridge is beautiful, but not large. It is like Maple Ridge itself: a large town or a small city that is rapidly growing. It is like a hundred other towns and cities in this country.

On November 11 the streets are empty. Almost everyone is at the cenotaph.

This is the story of one family, people who I know. But you know folks like this, just about everyone does.

Frank Aicken, ninety-three at the last ceremony, served in the army during World War II. Standing next to him Gunther Blasig, born in Germany during the war. His father was in the German army during World War II.

Next to him his wife, Ruth Olde, born during the Korean War. Ruth and Gunter's children were all born during the Vietnam War.

Standing next to Ruth, Linnaea, the oldest granddaughter, born during the First Gulf War. Three other grandchildren at other ceremonies in nearby towns, all born during the Iraq and Afghanistan war.

At least in war the human family is all related.

Take up our quarrel with the foe:
To you from failing hands we throw
The torch; be yours to hold it high.
If ye break faith with us who die
We shall not sleep, though poppies grow
In Flanders fields.

Those are among the last words Lieutenant Colonel John McCrae wrote. The poppies are still growing there. He was aching for us to remember who died and why they died, to learn, to stand up for, and ironically, even to fight for, the hardest things of all; for understanding, for forgiveness, for courage, and like John Lennon said in another poem, to give peace a chance.

To fight for peace? It is a mystery of the human condition, but wouldn't it be beautiful to return the poppy to its rightful place as just a flower, and nothing more.

THE POWER OF A GODFATHER

The leaf was floating in the air. It really can't do that, can it?

I mean gravity has to make it fall, or the wind has to blow it away.

But it did not rise, it did not fall. It moved in the breeze, like it was dancing.

Below it a white-haired man was concentrating and holding his hands out, willing the leaf not to flutter to the earth.

A young woman was taking his picture.

"He can do anything," she said. "He's my godfather."

"What's going on?" we asked. Obviously something was happening, a leaf was floating, a man was below it and his goddaughter was telling us that he was keeping it up with his powers.

We got a picture of that, and in a world of amazing pictures that was truly a mind-blower.

"Come here, Crystal, and I'll teach you," he said.

The young woman stepped forward, almost under the leaf, and he took her hands and held them up and showed her how to wave them gently.

"You can do it," he said.

Then he let go of her hands and stepped back and the leaf stayed up.

"It's working," she said. "It's working. I didn't believe it but it's working."

I could hardly believe it. But there it was, a leaf defying gravity, floating in the air below some trees, being held up by a pair of hands that were not touching it.

"It's my birthday," said Crystal. She was nineteen, and her godfather had taken her out for a day of adventures photographed with the new camera he gave her.

"Can you tell us about your goddaughter?" we asked.

"She's wonderful," he said. He was beaming.

"Can you tell us about your godfather?" we asked.

"He can do anything. Look at this."

Then she asked him if she could tell us about that other thing. He nodded.

She did not forget about the leaf. She was still holding it up with the power of her hands, just as her godfather, who can do anything, taught her.

"We thought he was going to die last year. He had open heart surgery," she said.

"Piece of cake," he said.

And then they said they had to go. They had more stops to make on this wondrous birthday. We said goodbye and they waved and walked away.

They must have left their power in the leaf because even when they were gone it continued to float halfway between the ground and the tree where it had spent its life with birds and squirrels and spiders, especially spiders with their clear, silk threads.

After that story ran on the news one guy who has worked with satellite images and strange pictures all of his life asked me how they did it.

I asked if he could see anything holding it up.

"No," he said.

"Well then, it must be the power of the godfather. There is no other explanation."

A BROADWAY PLAY IN GASOLINE ALLEY

What makes a good piece of theatre?

Shakespeare held his dripping quill over a sheet of paper and asked himself that profound question.

It must have all the emotions: tragedy, comedy, evil and triumph, he said, with a few surprises thrown in for good measure. And it's good to have a clown, and maybe an animal.

"There's a body shop with a chicken in it," one of the editors told me.

That's enough for me. I am not Shakespeare. I am just a caption writer to pictures that some fine cameramen take and some brilliant editors put together. A chicken is just fine.

"Have you seen a chicken around here?" I asked a guy in a tire shop on Esplanade in North Vancouver.

He pointed with a lug wrench and a laugh. "Down there. We hoped you would come here someday. That chicken deserves recognition."

We walk, and walk. There are many body and tire and fix-it shops on the east side of Esplanade. The west side has been transformed into swank condos and boutiques. The east side has the flavour.

"Is there a chicken around here?" we ask a woman who looked old before her time and who seemed a bit crotchety.

"It's down there and you can keep it if you get it."

Whoops, I think. The sun is not shining everywhere in Mudville.

I ask someone else about the woman. "She owns one of the shops and is not friendly."

And then a few doors later, I can't believe it. A chicken is pecking at crumbs on the concrete floor next to a mechanic sitting in a fold-up chair eating his lunch. I can't believe it because hearing about a chicken in a body shop and seeing a chicken in a body shop are two entirely separate things.

"What? Who? Why? Etc."

The usual questions.

Camey Kayhan, the friendly, Iranian body-and-fender guy starts telling us the story. He works alone so it seemed anyone who wanted to talk was welcomed.

Someone gave him some eggs from a farm, and said if he kept them warm they might hatch. He kept them warm under a light in his shop while he beat out dents and straightened the results of misjudged turns.

"And one hatched," he said. "It hatched right here. I put my hands around it and it hatched."

This was an excited guy. He smiled. He laughed. He bragged.

He brought it home. And it grew into a rooster. And it did what roosters do, until his wife told him to take it away because early every morning it was doing what roosters love to do.

The only place he had besides his home was his shop, so the rooster returned to the world of fenders and bodies and his one friend.

"We had fun," said Camey. "Here's his picture."

I looked at the chicken. "You mean this is not him?"

"No, this is a chicken," he said. He looked at me in a quizzical way.

"Where did the chicken come from?"

"A cab driver felt sorry for the rooster living alone here so he dropped off this chicken."

"Where'd he get the chicken from?"

Camey shrugged. "Didn't matter, the rooster had a friend."

"So where is the rooster?"

Camey looked sad.

"Someone killed him."

"What! Who? Why? Etc."

The man with fibreglass under his fingernails did not want to talk.

He wiped away a tear. Then he choked out the words, "she hit him with a shopping bag."

"A woman? Who?"

He shook his head.

Down here a shopping bag could easily be filled with lug nuts.

"Why would anyone want to kill him?"

"Too noisy," he said. "But everyone else liked it."

"Do you know who did it?"

He nodded.

"Who?"

He shook his head again.

I think the case could be solved by an amateur detective.

And then to change the subject, I went back to the job of reporting and asked the most probing, basic and revealing question of all, the one thing I tell journalism students, in fact anyone who wants to find out anything about someone else, to ask: tell me about yourself.

It usually works.

"I was a doctor in Iran."

"What?"

"I had seven years of university, and was a licensed doctor when I came here."

This is the jaw-dropping, head-shaking time. I know this happens over and over. A doctor there, wherever there is, immigrates to Canada with a diploma and a stethoscope, but is not accepted here and winds up fixing cars.

You would think the folks in charge here would say, "You just need a little of this and that and you can be a doctor here because we are in great need of doctors here."

But no. The folks in charge here say, "Sorry." Actually, they don't even say that.

"Still feel bitter?"

He gave one of those looks which is done mostly with twisted lips that means I am trying to say no, but yes, of course, what do you think?

And then he said he had to get back to work because there was no one else to do it and this is how he has made a living for the last twenty years.

So far, in one tiny body shop, kindness, birth, death, murder, and bureaucratic stupidity. It needs one thing more, I can feel it but I don't know what it is. It should end on something happy.

"I'll show you something," said Camey. He put down his pneumatic wrench and took us to the back of the shop and a cardboard box. Inside, an egg.

"Every morning," he said. "Breakfast."

SHORT STORIES ARE BEST

I got a letter. In the newsroom I get quite a few letters, mostly saying some-one bakes wonderful cakes and deserves recognition.

Then I got this letter. It was not like the other letters. It had a story. Many of the letters have stories, many of them are about suffering at the hands of whatever the Workers' Compensation Board is now called.

Marjorie Stevens of Nanaimo was different. She wrote: I have a little story you might enjoy.

She said she had seen the back cover of my last book, *The Blue Flames That Keep Us Warm*. The blue flames come from a story that started a long time ago, when I was in the third grade.

My mother had just left my father, who was a difficult, drunken man. My mother told me the first game I learned to play was "fall down drunk like Daddy."

When he came home from the bar he would beat on the bedroom door. My mother would push a dresser in front of it and say to me, "Don't worry. He will fall asleep soon."

She did not think I understood the words "pass out."

Before dawn one morning she woke me. She had a suitcase in her hand. She said, "Shussssh, we're leaving."

I got up in my pajamas, put on a coat, and followed my mother out-side. We took a subway all the way across the city. New York City is very big. We went from one end to the other to move into my mother's sister's apartment.

The sun was up when we got off. We walked down the street filled with row houses. The first thing I saw was my cousin sweeping outside. I had never seen anyone sweeping outside before.

He said he was told by his mother to sweep because today was special. I had never been special before.

The best part of moving in with him was that we took over his bedroom and he, whose name is Dick, was exiled to the hallway outside his apartment. His mother thought that this was terrible. Dick thought it was the best thing that ever happened to him.

He took me to school, P.S. 54. Schools in New York have such romantic names. I was there only a short time when the teacher said we were going on a field trip. If you read the Blue Flames you already know this story, my apology. But there is a point to this.

We left the classroom and went to the basement, then down the metal stairs to the sub-basement. The janitor opened the door of the furnace, showed us the oval of fire that heated the building and said, "Those are the blue flames that keep us warm."

That was it. Nothing more. We went back to our classroom and I forgot the entire episode until half a century later when I was outside our home in Vancouver and our granddaughter, Ruby, was helping me sweep the walkway in front of our house. She, who was four years old, held onto the bottom of the broom, and we were outside. I should have known something was going to happen.

My wife complained that the house was cold. I went to the basement and found the furnace was out.

I called Ruby downstairs and she watched while I lit the furnace. Then I said, "Those are the blue flames that keep us warm."

She looked at me and said, "Now can we have some ice cream."

But I know, or hope, that sometime long in the future Ruby will light a furnace, or something like it with her grandchild, and say, "Those are the blue flames that keep us warm, my grandfather told me that."

It will connect two people who will never see each other.

And now the short story: because of the blue flames, Ruby's picture was on the back of the book.

Marjorie wrote:

"After viewing the back cover of your book, I thought of a little story that you might enjoy.

"I am a seventy-six-year-old with no grandchildren. I have three sons who have for numerous reasons decided to remain single so I really don't think I will ever have any grandchildren.

"Recently I was sitting on a stool in a large shopping mall in the north of Nanaimo. I was waiting for one of my sons to bring me a cup of tea. In the midst of all the people passing by, lining up for food, etc., I suddenly viewed a small girl around two and a half bravely marching along though the crowd holding her father's hand. As she neared me our eyes locked and I gave her a little wave. To my surprise she put her little hand to her mouth and threw me a kiss which I, of course, returned. No one in that mall would ever know how much a sweet little girl had warmed an old woman's heart. This short moment in time is firmly stored in my heart and every time I think of it, it brings a smile to my face.

"Yours truly,

"Marjorie Stevens."

I have only to add: Thank you, Marjorie, and thank you, little girl.

MIKE'S WINDOW WASHING

We just finished coffee in a shop on East Hastings and I said to the cameraman, "What the heck are we going to do today?"

He shrugged.

A rough guy who did not comb his hair that morning, or possibly any morning, was walking along the street, saw me and wanted to talk. He was nice, but I have to go, I have to look for a story to put on television. He wants to talk about the medical system in the province and the housing situation, which he says is bad because people he knows are having a hard time finding a place to live.

I am polite. I listen, but really, I have to go. The cameraman is waiting. Six o'clock is only eight hours away. And I have heard these complaints before. They are real problems, but what am I going to do?

He gives me his business card. Everyone has business cards, even those who wander the streets. I do not have my glasses on so I do not read it because I cannot read it. I thank him and put it in my pocket.

He says his name is Mike and he is in the window-washing business. Mike's Window Washing, he says. I thank him. He says he would give me a good rate. I thank him. He says he could fit me into his schedule because he doesn't have any other work currently. I thank him.

Honest. I got to go.

We shake hands and I get in the cameraman's van and we start going around in circles. That is a good way to go. I have written about this before. We drive or I walk in circles, around and around a block. Someone may come out and be the most wonderful person in the world with the most wonderful story. Or not.

So you go around again. And again. Somewhere out there is something wonderful, fascinating, terrific. The only problem is we don't know what it is or where it is. But the truth is, if you spend your life looking for something good you will find it. It is just that sometimes it takes a lot of circles.

We are into hour four of circles. If we were not such nice people we would hate each other. We have driven to Kamloops without leaving the east side of Vancouver.

"It looks bad," said the cameraman.

And then in a fluke of insight, "What about that guy you were talking to this morning?"

"Just some window washer," I said.

"Well, what's wrong with a window washer?"

"I have done stories on window washers before."

"Look at the time."

"You have a point."

I put my fingers in my shirt pocket and pull out both the card and this time my glasses.

"It's a doctor's card," I say. Doctor somebody or other. "That's not it."

Then I flip the card over, basically by accident.

"Mike's Window Washing," it says in awkward, handwritten letters on the other side.

"Oh, my lord, he has his cards on the back of other people's cards. And this one is a doctor."

I start calling. The line is busy. I call again. Please answer. Busy. Again. Busy.

Time, time, don't you know, Mike the window washer, that six o'clock is now only four hours away? Where are you?

It rings.

"Hello, Mike's Window Washing."

I tell him this is me, and we would like to talk to him, and where are you, and don't leave and don't say you are not available for any reason on earth and please be close by.

111

Surrey. Darn.

"We will be there in forty-five minutes, and by the way, do you make all your cards from other people's cards?"

"Yes."

Good enough.

We rush. He is there. He lives in a tiny, rent-subsidized apartment found for him by a couple of workers with Surrey Mental Health.

"If it wasn't for them I would be on the street with those other useless people doing drugs."

Well, at least we have a clean window washer.

His office is a TV dinner table made of wiggly aluminum legs, with a pile of newspapers on it. Mike is writing on the back of business cards: "Mike's Window Washing, or janitorial work, bonded." And his phone number . . .

"Do these people know you have their cards?"

"Yes, of course."

I don't believe that.

He repeats that he gets permission to use them. But as far as I can tell he is not breaking any laws.

There are many doctors and others whose names and businesses are on the front of the cards. On the other side he is writing "Mike's Window Washing." He spends half his day writing the cards, and then half the day giving them out. Between that he occasionally gets a job.

He has pictures of the Canucks ripped from newspapers on his walls, along with the Virgin Mary, and the Queen.

We have enough. He writes the cards, he has his bucket and pole. He is trying.

We make six o'clock.

The next day a call comes from someone wanting to get in contact with Mike. He is from some company or other and on the answering machine I don't hear clearly the company because the name is so odd. I call back and leave Mike's number on their answering machine.

They call back and leave a message on my machine that they would like to give him some business cards, but they don't want any publicity.

I leave a message on their machine saying that's nice. And if you don't want any notice that is fine because secretly I don't want to give any recognition to anyone who does something for someone else because you saw them on television.

They leave a message thanking me. Which I think is nice.

And I forget about it.

A week later the fellow from the company calls me and says he is having trouble getting in touch with Mike. Mike, I tell him, lives a fluid life. He moves from here to there and sometimes might be hard to get in touch with. I have no idea what I am talking about but what else can I say about someone who lives by the seat of his pants and who I have met twice and I respect but have no idea what problems he has or how to help him, if indeed he needs help, or how to inspire him, which is what I really would love to do.

"I was just like him, sort of," says the man on the phone. "I was broke and didn't know where I was going."

Suddenly, a gift from wherever.

The man on the phone who wants to give business cards to Mike says that fifteen years ago he was broke, unemployed and had nothing.

Where do these people come from, I wonder? And how lucky am I to be listening now instead of playing back an answering machine.

He lost his job when Woodward's folded. He and a woman friend took their unemployment vouchers, asked each other what they would do, and ripped up the vouchers.

They borrowed money to print business cards, creating their own marketing and design company.

Now they have eighteen employees and their last job was redesigning the image of Vancouver International Airport.

And they wanted to help Mike. I said they had to be on television, they must be on television, because they were an inspiration.

I got on the phone and called Mike. No answer did not deter me. I called and called and eventually got him. He was between jobs.

We arranged for him to go to the company. It was called Hangar 18.

"What the heck is Hangar 18?" I asked.

There was a pause. Nigel Yonge, the man with the business cards and the company, explained slowly that Hangar 18 was where the US Air Force had put the contents of the spacecraft that landed in Roswell, New Mexico, in 1947. It was one of the spookiest chapters in the history of the earth.

Did a spaceship really land? Was the Air Force hiding it? Now there's a story I would like to do.

But in an adventurous way, mostly I think to show imagination, Nigel, the fired Woodward's employee, named his company Hangar 18. He has guts. And a heart.

Mike showed up and they had a meeting in his boardroom. Mike sat on one side of a long, executive table. He had never been to a board meeting before.

Nigel and his partners handed him his new business cards. They said the same thing as Mike had written on each of his: Mike's Window Washing. Bonded. Etc. But these cards were beautiful and designed to attract attention.

Then they told Mike their story. He had a great deal of disbelief and was wishing to believe it was true.

"You can do the same," they told him.

He said he thought he could, if he worked hard enough. "And someday maybe I'll have people working for me, washing windows," he said.

Mike left, and started giving out his cards. He did not give out too many. They were too beautiful.

He is still washing windows. And some day, maybe, he will have people working for him. But even if he does not, he will still be washing windows, and a good window washer is hard to find.

HOW HIGH FLIES A BALLOON?

We got a call from Kelly Petrocilli. It was not a big problem, but she felt bad and she knew she had to do something.

"I found a balloon in the lumberyard at Port Kells," she said.

"So?" I said.

"It had a Father's Day card attached to it."

Okay, now I care.

We went to the yard, put on the high-vis vests and safety gear and went out where the forklifts rule. Never argue with a forklift.

About the balloon, she said she found it over there, behind that pile of lumber that was wrapped and packaged for shipment to Japan.

"Father's Day was a week ago," said Kelly. "I don't know how far it came or how I could have missed it."

She took it out from under her jacket. She was protecting it. It was a flattened balloon with a home made card that said, "Happy Father's Day to the Big Cheese. I love you, Anthony."

Below the writing was a drawing of a slice of cheese. You knew it was cheese because it had holes in it like Swiss cheese, which is the only way most of us can make a drawing look like cheese.

"Maybe he was giving it to his father and it slipped out of his hand," said Kelly. She had a sad, but hopeful look.

I told her that we would broadcast the message and if Anthony saw it or anyone who knew him we would relay the information to her and help her and Anthony get together.

And then Kelly went back to work. And I had a feeling. It is the same feeling you might have right now.

Anthony's father might be in a different world and Anthony may have sent the balloon up to him. I did not mention that to Kelly because she was so hopeful.

But I did say it in the story.

"Why'd you say that," someone asked me later that night. "Suppose he just slipped and the balloon flew away. Now you've said his father is dead."

Something came over me. I thought maybe it was true, and if it was not so, we would show Anthony getting the balloon back and giving it to his father and forget about what I said.

The next day we got a call from Anthony's aunt in Prince George. It was true, Anthony's father had died.

We called the number she gave us and the next day Kelly left the balloon and the card for us at the lumberyard. She could not deliver it. She had to attend a funeral of someone who was young and was killed by a forklift. Life works that way.

We went to Anthony's house in Burnaby.

The cameraman was Gary Hanney. As he got out his camera his eyes filled with tears. Before he retired Gary was famous for being the toughest news cameraman in Vancouver. He slept with a police radio under his pillow. He woke in the middle of the night to be at fatal car accidents, and fires and shootings. He was like a cop with a camera.

And now he started crying. His father had died a few days earlier.

We rang the bell and delivered the balloon and card to Anthony. He was nine years old.

His mother said her husband had died three years ago on Monday, the day Kelly found the balloon.

She said this was the first Father's Day they had released the card and balloon from over the grave, which was in Valley View Cemetery in Surrey.

We asked Anthony why he called his father the Big Cheese.

"Because he was the boss. The big cheese," he said.

We told Anthony as far as we knew, his father had gotten the card and wanted Anthony to know that and so he sent it back. Anthony thanked us and said he believed that.

We left. The end of the story.

Until the next day when we went back to tell Kelly what happened.

She was quiet for a moment, then said her father was in Valley View cemetery.

We told her in what part of the cemetery Anthony's mother said her husband was buried.

Kelly's father was in the same area.

"We visit the cemetery on his birthday," she said.

"That's sweet," I said.

"And my kids let balloons go from over his grave. We hoped he would get them."

A forklift went by carrying a load of lumber. It's a busy yard.

She said she had to get back to work. She left, but then stopped and turned around.

"Now I think he did," she said.

How high did Anthony's balloon go? High enough to touch a father, and then back to earth to touch the son.

Kelly believes it. Anthony's mother says it is true. And Anthony sleeps with the balloon with the card next to him in his room. He knows who sent it.

BIG BILL
AND HOW TO COVER A PRESIDENT

I have never done any political reporting. You have to be smart to do that. You have to be smart enough to understand that when politicians say they promise, they do not promise. When they say they will, they won't. And when they say they are on your side, they aren't.

Regular people are much different. If you have a friend who breaks a promise the friendship has a good chance of ending, and the friend will get a punch in the nose.

Promises are important to real people. The same with someone who says they will do something or they will back you up. If they don't, they're out.

That is why I don't understand how politicians survive, when they think outside of the way regular people think.

On the other hand, Bill Clinton was coming to Vancouver and going to speak to the Board of Trade and before I die I had a chance to add one presidential story under my belt.

"You don't have accreditation," said the large, official person at the front door, who probably was packing a nuclear arsenal under his trim suit.

"No, sir," I said. "Where can I stand to see the ex-president?"

"On the sidewalk."

"Will he pass by there?"

"I am not at liberty to answer questions."

So I stood on the sidewalk and saw a cop I know. When he was younger he took kung fu classes with my wife. My wife has a black belt. This guy fought her. I know this guy must be tough.

"A lot of security around here?" I asked in a secretive tone.

"A lot," he said with a pleasant smile.

Many people are milling around the front doors. More are approaching. They are all wearing black, but not just black as in black clothes going to a funeral. These I can tell are expensive black clothes.

"Is that a new dress?" I ask a woman in a black dress that looks like it was designed for a special occasion because it had things that went around here and there in a way in which a guy who only has one suit cannot explain.

"Of course," she said.

"Can I ask how much it cost?"

"No, but it cost a lot."

"Did you get it for today?"

She looked at me like I was utterly without any hold on reality. I get that look a lot.

"Of course," she said.

We started taking pictures of more people arriving. It was now twenty to one. He was due to speak at one. The black suits were picking up the pace.

In any group of four, four held BlackBerries to their ears. "Buy, sell. Alright then sell, then buy."

Also: "Lay them all off. Then tell them you feel their pain. There'll be a bonus for you."

Employees of a bookstore were unloading boxes of Bill's books.

Ten to one and there was extreme rushing outside. Almost two thousand people had tickets to listen to the former president.

"How much were the tickets?" I asked someone flying by.

"Don't know. I got mine free."

I asked the next one. Same answer. And the next. Same. The people with two-thousand-dollar suits were getting two-hundred-dollar tickets free.

I asked the next and the next. Maybe one did pay, but not anyone who I asked.

The rich do get richer because the rich like to surround themselves with others who are rich and influential and powerful, even if they have to pay for them to be there. It is one of those facts of life.

There is another fact.

I saw Bill Wilson, a Native chief of the Squamish Band, who said he also got a complimentary ticket.

He was the only one not in a suit. He wore his vest with traditional Native designs on it.

"I wonder what this free ticket will cost me," he said.

He is a wise man.

One o'clock. The last panic-faced stragglers are running up the street, and their new shoes—which Bill will never see—are getting scuffed on the sidewalk.

The doors close. We are outside. Ten after one, no Bill. Twenty after one, no Bill. One-thirty and we go around the back of the theatre and there is Bill, leaving the hotel next door. He had met Bon Jovi who was staying at the hotel next door and the two of them got into a conversation. A long conversation.

One thirty and we can see the man with white hair halfway down the lane surrounded by Canadian and American security guards with dark glasses. Then Bill sees some construction workers on the other side of the lane. He turns away from the back of the theatre and goes to talk to them.

The amount of times the coded message, "the Eagle has turned" was transmitted and received by secret service and RCMP to men with high-powered rifles on the tops of buildings and others with binoculars in vacated hotel rooms and ambulance drivers standing nearby and other police who were guarding the perimeter two blocks away and to others who we have no idea of, is uncountable.

And he is only an ex-president.

But the construction workers got a personal visit and handshakes, also without paying. Another fact of life: some are luckier than others.

A few minutes later he crossed the lane and went into the theatre. He gave an abbreviated version of his twenty minute speech and was paid $250,000.

Two things I learned that day: covering politics is a breeze; you just accept that politicians are not just people too. And I also learned anyone who thinks politics is a waste of time should give their head a shake.

MORE ON TIES

For reasons beyond anything reasonable I dropped in on the British Columbia Association of Municipalities. Oh, heavens.

A sea of suits was ebbing like the tide, into one meeting, then out to another meeting. The men wore suits, the women wore suits. The only difference was under the suits, but I could not see that.

They all had BlackBerries, ordinary cell phones would leave such a stigma. They all looked important, and they were all in a hurry, and preoccupied with things far away.

And I was about to leave, because in a world of suits I have never found anything interesting enough to give a family in a small town something to remember.

And then came this vision sent from the far end of the hallway, a vision I knew was sent from heaven. Surrounded by black wool-covered shoulder pads and tight-fitting collars was a pair of suspenders. And then more, a baseball cap.

A baseball cap? Indoors? In a high-class meeting? My heavens. You never know. A woman at the mental hospital in Riverview told me that once (check out book one, *Chasing the Story God*, it's a good book) and it has saved me forever. You never know what is going to happen. There is no need to ever despair because: you never know. You never know what incredible, wonderful thing is going to happen in the next moment or around the next corner.

He kept walking toward us and I saw a smiling, bearded face with an open collar and a plaid, flannel shirt under his suspenders. You never know.

"Stop, please, stop. Tell us about yourself."

His name, Miles Fuller. His job, he was representing tree lot owners, which means he was speaking for the world's smallest logging operations, usually one man with an axe and a chainsaw and a F-350 that can haul trees out of the lot.

It is a tough way to make a living. Miles also had a trapline in the north, and took tourists on wilderness tours. But mostly, he was a logger of his own trees.

"A tie? Never had one in my life," he said. His face beamed. He put his thumbs under his suspenders, which had John Deere written on them. "Didn't even have a tie when I got married."

"Did your wife mind?"

"Mind?" he raised his voice. "She wouldn't have married me. She would've thought I wasn't me."

I asked what he thought of all the suits and ties and cellphones passing by.

"They sure look busy, but I'm in those meetings listening and that's all they are, busy," he said.

He said his logging business and his trapping and guiding businesses were all doing well.

"I look at it this way," he said, gripping his shirt collar and pulling it closed probably for the first time ever, "a buttoned-up shirt means lots of talk and no action."

Then he let go of his collar and it fell open. "An unbuttoned shirt means you get the work done *then* you talk about it."

Then he went back into the meeting room. The suits moved aside to let him pass. I suspect they did not want to get touched by his plaid flannel.

Pity, they might have been moved.

TRIBUTE TO A GARDENER

The plaque said "Pete's Place." It was written in paint on a broken piece of wood and was nailed above his gardening shack in the huge community garden in South Burnaby.

That does not matter.

You had to search to find the shack, because it was in a garden only twenty feet by sixty feet. What matters is there were so many dahlias spreading out their large summer faces that everything else disappeared.

The only other thing you could see were the birdhouses, ten of them, all up on poles, again in a garden only big enough for one or two birdhouses. But the birds did not mind the company; all of the houses had families living in them, courtesy of Pete.

I met him because I was standing in the shade at the entrance to the garden looking for someone who looked interesting. All gardeners are interesting. All have a love that goes beyond ordinary mortals. That is another of those facts of life. If you doubt this, talk to a gardener. Some are nuts, but they all have passion.

Then I saw this guy struggle out of his car. He used two canes to walk down the garden path. Anyone who wants to do something that badly I would feel honoured to talk to.

He had a strong Scottish accent and a big smile. He told me he liked everyone in this public garden without exception. That means he liked several hundred people. He also liked dahlias and he liked birds.

"How much time do you spend in your garden?"

"Well, my wife would tell you I spend all my time here," he laughed.

There were flowers surrounding him and the sound of music above his head. The music came from the birds that lived in his garden. That is not a bad place to spend your time.

His shack was about five feet by four feet, just big enough to stand inside and store your tools. He sat in a chair that was half inside and half outside and he looked around. "This is heaven," he said.

"If you don't mind me asking, why do you use the canes?"

"Cancer," he said. "It's in my bones."

Later I walked around the other garden plots and asked if the gardeners knew Pete. They all did. I walked very far, to the other side from where you cannot see Pete's Place.

They still knew Pete.

"He has the best dahlias," they said. "He has so many birds," they said. "He is always happy," they said.

Nine months later, just at the beginning of dahlia season, I got a call from a friend of mine, Ann Dueck. She has her own beautiful garden at home but she visits the garden of the rented plots often, basically to look at Pete's dahlias.

"Pete died," she said. She was crying. A man she had met only briefly a few times had brought enough beauty to her life to bring tears to her when his life ended.

I went back to the garden. I wanted to do some kind of tribute for him, but I had no idea what to do. His dahlias were blooming. His shack was there with the sign above it. We took pictures of the flowers and the sign and his old garden gloves that were bent and creased in the shape of his hands.

This was a few weeks after Leona Helmsley, the billionaire hotel owner, had died and Luciano Pavarotti had died. Big funerals filled the airwaves. At Pavarotti's funeral there were magnificent baritones. Pete Greenaway, age seventy-four, gardener, deserved something too.

I was lost. Then it came not to me, but to my ears. At first we didn't see them, but it was there. Then one landed, and other one. Yes, I know they were just coming back to eat the insects in the garden and to drink from the dish of water that he had put out. But they were there, and they were singing.

We did not have to add anything or say anything or do anything. Pete's memorial was filled with song.

100 IS NOT A SPEED LIMIT

When Ivy Lloyd was one hundred she got a tattoo on her right shoulder. It was a bird.

It went opposite the rose she got on her left shoulder when she was ninety-three. And it went under the butterfly she got when she was ninety-seven.

"They call me the tattoo lady in the old folks home," she said.

"Where will you get one next year?" I asked.

Ivy was tired of me gawking at her. After all, what's the big deal about getting a tattoo, even if you are one hundred?

"On my butt," she said.

"Okay, Ivy, you're my girl."

Charlie Parrott went to the Army and Air Force Club for his one hundredth birthday. The timing was perfect, he said.

"Every third Tuesday of the month they sell beer for half price."

He bought a round for everyone.

Charlie, you are my kind of guy.

But then there was Syd Spinks. What did he do? Go bowling. Bowling?

Come on, Syd, I thought, be original. Be creative. Get a tattoo. Buy a beer. Anyone can go bowling.

He went to the Grandview Lanes on Commerical Drive, a place that has been an old-fashioned bowling alley since 1947. It has been in the same family and they still have five-pin bowling, a truly Canadian invention. Five-pin is not played anywhere else in the world.

Upstairs are the psychedelic black lights and glow-in-the-dark balls. But that is not for bowlers. That is for people like me who bowl twice a year and could not hit the front pin in ten tries.

But Syd has been coming here for twenty years. He used to bowl with his wife. On their fiftieth anniversary Syd and his bride bowled. She died ten years later.

His son, who is seventy-eight, told me his father still climbs up a ladder to clean out the gutters.

Brave old guy.

His daughter told me that he still lives alone and cooks all his meals himself.

Neat old guy.

His grandson Wayne, who is forty-seven, told me that his grandfather is now basically blind. He only had sight in one eye since he was a boy and that has now gone. He has only slight peripheral vision.

"If you stand way off to the side, he can almost see you," he said.

"So, how do you bowl?" I asked Syd.

"I know the pins are down there, so I just throw it."

Then he laughed, and rolled the ball. Right down the middle.

"Do you think he'll shoot his age?" someone asked.

"You mean get a hundred?"

He always does, said someone else.

Syd and I talked. He lost his right eye when he was fifteen and working on a chicken farm and had to spray lime in the barns. It got into his eyes, one of them more than the other. From then on, he lived the same as you would see if you closed one eye. It is hard to judge distances with only one eye.

"What work did you do?"

"Truck driver," he said.

"With one eye?"

"I didn't tell anyone."

And after he retired he drove a cab. Same thing. If you don't tell, no one knows.

Somehow he got through the eye tests. The possibility is that he cheated.

"And now you still go up a ladder to clean the gutters?"

"I know where they are," he said. "When I get to the top of the ladder the gutters are right there."

Then he threw the ball again, but it went in the gutter.

"He's just a little excited because there's so many ladies here," said his son.

The next roll: strike. It came up on the in-house television monitor over where Syd was standing. "STRIKE." It was flashing on the screen.

Syd could not see that.

His score when we left was eighty-nine. But he had to blow out candles on a cake, and eat a large slice and get kissed by numerous ladies who came to the party, and had his hand shook by many men who called Syd a friend. That all gets in the way of bowling.

"Tell me one thing about him?" I asked some of his friends.

From his family I learned about his living by himself and his blindness.

None of his friends even mentioned his trouble seeing. None said that he was a hundred years old. None said that he lived by himself.

All of them said the same thing: "He's always happy."

An hour later I got a phone call. After we left and the excitement died down he scored 110. Happy Birthday, Syd.

THE CHALK DRAWINGS

Every day for the seven years that I went to the Superstore in North Vancouver I would meet Cliff who sold hot dogs outside the front doors.

"I'm doing fine, I'm doing great," he would say, and he meant it.

He had music coming from some speakers and he had his hot dogs and he had friends. And often he would talk about his sweetheart . . . one of the cashiers. She has a son with Down's syndrome.

"But he is always so happy," said Cliff. "He makes me feel good."

Then the store changed its policy and one day Cliff was no longer out front. I saw him later but he said that I should not be upset. He had another place in a park to sell his hot dogs.

And he told me that his sweetheart's son now had leukemia. "But he doesn't know it, so he is still happy."

Of course the boy, about twelve years old I guessed from what he said, suffered and was undergoing chemotherapy and Cliff said some nights at home he was very, very sick.

"But you could not wipe that smile off his face."

Half a year later I was at Children's Hospital during a fundraising drive. Global TV was pouring everything into helping the hospital get new stuff and a new building to help kids. I want to help kids, so do a story.

What story? They have had twenty-four hours of talk and asking and

129

beseeching and profiles of sick kids and kids who have been helped by the hospital and doctors and nurses and new methods of treatment. This was at the end of the telethon. What was left?

I was sitting out front waiting for the cameraman when I saw some little kids behind the hospital in the waiting area drawing with chalk on the ground. That was nice, but no one was there to take their pictures.

Then I saw a balloon that had broken free of some decorations and was floating past the hospital. If only we had a picture of that, maybe I could use it to symbolize freedom or hope or something. But there was no one to take the picture.

In some act of sheer dumbness I chased the balloon from the back of the hospital to the front while it floated up and then came down and then went up again. I was wearing a suit. I was wearing a tie because of the telethon. I was chasing a balloon.

What am I going to do if I catch it, I wondered? But I kept chasing it as it floated out onto Oak Street. In one last lunge before it went into traffic I grabbed it and brought it back to one of the television trucks filled with electronics stuff and things like meters and gauges that I know nothing of. I tucked it between two pieces of very expensive electronic gear.

The cameraman arrived and I told him about the balloon.

"That's dumb," he said. "We are not going to pretend it floated away just in front of me."

"Of course not," I said. "Goodbye, balloon."

"Then what's your plan?"

I did not have any.

We walked around to the back of the hospital and I showed him where the kids were drawing with chalk.

"But there's no one drawing now," he said.

"Maybe they will. Do you want a hamburger? Do you want a coffee?"

Probably not, no and no.

Then some teenybopper girls pick up pieces of chalk and start drawing.

"Whatcha doing?" I asked them.

"Just fooling around."

"Why you here?"

"A friend has cancer," one said.

"He's getting better," said another.

"He's got a nice smile," said the third.

"Can you show us?"

She made a circle, then she put a happy face inside it. Then one of the other girls put curly hair over his head.

"It's growing back now."

The other girl put laugh lines on his cheeks.

"He is always happy," she said.

"What's his name?" I asked.

"Jonathan," they said. "And he's really good at soccer."

They said one day their teacher told the class that Jonathan had cancer. Leukemia.

They had trouble pronouncing the word, but they understood what it meant.

Jonathan was gone for a long time, through Christmas and through the spring, but then he came back to class and they all hugged him.

Jonathan was "cool," Jonathan was "neat," Jonathan was a "survivor." They said those words like they more than meant them. They understood them.

"We came today because of Jonathan."

We finished filming, but something was missing.

"I hate to ask, because I shouldn't, but could you draw a balloon near Jonathan?"

They did, and the story of the boy in chalk was very nice.

Three weeks later I was checking out of Superstore. My granddaughter was with me. I always feel good when she is there. But the line was long, very long. Half the cash registers were closed. I was annoyed. Others were annoyed.

I wanted to complain, but I thought I did not want to be a whiner and things like this sometimes happen.

I got up to the clerk. Her name was Lisa.

"Thank you for putting Jonathan on television," she said.

"Jonathan? Oh, Jonathan."

All I was recalling was a chalk face.

"He was thrilled when he saw it. He said to me, 'Mommy, I'm a star.'"

She said he could not stop talking about it. He smiled and laughed and looked and pointed and looked again. They made a recording of it.

"I'm glad you liked it," I said.

How do I say, "I'm glad you liked it" when the kid saved my day?

But all of that is beside the point. I walked outside with my granddaughter holding my hand and the sun was out and the day was beautiful and the bags in my other hand were pulling my shoulder out of its socket but I would not change it because I would not give up my granddaughter's hand, and I suddenly realized the importance of everything.

It was not that it was a spooky coincidence that the happy guy with the hot dogs was the sweetheart of that check-out clerk, or that the girls at the hospital drew a picture of her son, or that I was standing in that particular supermarket line that day.

What I realized was that the girls talked about Jonathan's cancer and his laugher and his soccer playing. But none of them mentioned his Down's syndrome.

The balloon was truly heading for freedom.

A LONG TIME, A VERY LONG TIME

Sometimes they just click.

There were the young guys and women in spandex running around Minoru Park in Richmond. Many of them were going at a goodly pace.

They wanted to be healthy and beautiful.

And there was Raymond and May. One step, another step, slowly, another step. Raymond held her hand. The runners passed them like a young wind whipping around an old obstacle.

Some of the men runners looked at the women runners and then passed them. Then the women runners passed the men runners. Aerobic courtship.

Raymond and May just kept walking, one step, then another, slowly. He held her hand.

"How long have you been holding her hand?" I asked.

Sometimes you can ask questions like that and get away with it.

"A long time," said May.

"How did you meet?"

"In Singapore," she said. "On a blind date, and we just clicked."

Children, work, money, problems, disasters, tragedies, happiness, thrills, grandchildren, and then the brain tumour.

It was diagnosed about five years earlier in May. Terrifying. An operation and most of it went right, but not all of it. Now she walks slowly. And Raymond holds her hand.

"Did you hold her hand before the operation?"

"Of course he did," said May.

"I always hold her hand," said Raymond. "Just like she said, 'we just clicked.'"

The runners sped by. Raymond and May kept walking, slowly.

Forty-five years, holding hands.

The runners had a long way to go to catch up.

I was at the Pacific National Exhibition. No one calls it that. I was at the PNE and I was off to the side, away from the rides and Whales Tails looking at a logging show.

She had pigtails coming out from under the baseball cap. They were grey.

"Whatcha doing?"

"Sawing some logs, whatcha think I'm doing?"

She was pushing a small log through a portable sawing machine. Honestly, I could have figured that out myself, but then I would not have asked, "Aren't you a bit old to be sawing logs?"

"As long as my man is sawing I'm sawing," she said.

"How long is that?"

She smiled. Her wrinkled face beaming. She was in love.

"Forty-eight years," she said.

"Where's your guy?" I asked.

She pointed to a lean, hard, smiling guy stacking lumber.

Charlie and Gerri went straight to each other as though they were magnets. Then they hugged. They did not hug because they were trying to impress me. They did not know me. They hugged because they wanted to hug. They had not seen each other for five minutes.

"We met right after the war," Gerri said. "I was living in Buffalo and he was in the Canadian Army and he was on leave and came to Buffalo for a night and we saw each other and that was it."

"They call us the Velcro couple," said Charlie. He was still holding her.

They married soon afterwards, and she moved to Powell River. He ran a small logging outfit. Later they developed a portable logging device and were travelling around trying to sell it. But most of all, they were travelling around holding each other.

Children, problems, money, disasters, tragedies, thrills and laugher, and they held each other.

Fairgoers passed by, looking at this old couple with a logging machine and kept going. Most of them were more interested in rides and the donuts.

Gerri and Charlie watched them go. What they needed was what they already had.

"He brings me a cup of tea every morning in bed," said Gerri.

"And if I want her to get up, I bring her two," said Charlie.

"The secret to being happy?"

"We have a honeymoon every year," said Charlie. "And this will be our forty-ninth."

He raised his eyebrows like a devilish kid.

She grabbed him by his ancient, weathered, wrinkled arm, and hugged him. He wrapped both those arms around her.

Like Velcro.

What can you grow in a garden plot only three steps long and barely one and half steps wide?

We will give away the answer: loyalty, love, laugher and tears, plus dinner and memories.

Eleanor was on her knees pulling weeds. Nick was standing behind her watching.

"Do you ever help?"

It is imprudent of me to ask such a question because Nick was large and powerful. Lucky for me Nick was also friendly.

"She won't let me," he laughed. "After all, what would a farmer from the prairies know about gardening?" he asked.

"He always reorganizes things," said Eleanor, who was on her knees pulling up weeds. "He wants his flowers in rows. I like them clumped."

"How long have you two been married?"

"Forever," he said.

"He's lucky," she said.

They laughed, together.

They had been asked that before, and they gave those answers before. And they laughed before.

"You want to hear something funny?" asked Eleanor. And then she went on before I could say anything.

"Someone from the church buried a potato tuber in here," she pointed to the ground which had leaves poking up.

"I asked Nick what that strange thing was growing in my flowers. He told me it was a potato. I said that's impossible."

They both laughed.

"That was six years ago," she said. And then she reached deep into the soil and dug up a potato.

She asked Nick to get her a pail. At last he had a job. He left and she said, "He's very smart about plants."

He came back and she dug up a half-dozen potatoes trying not to disturb her flowers.

"Dinner for a week," she said.

"Tell him about the rhodo," he said.

There was a rhododendron at the end of the plot. The plot was just a narrow strip in front of their home. She had been tending it since they were married, which was forever.

"When my mother died she left me enough to buy a rhodo," said Eleanor. "I always told my mother that's all I wanted."

That was ten years ago.

"She died in the spring, and it blooms in the spring," she said.

Then she added, "Nick planted it."

That was all she said. He put his arm around her and hugged her.

"How long *have* you been married?" I asked again because I was doing stories on endless love affairs.

"Forty-seven years," said Nick.

"You're lucky," said Eleanor.

SONGS FOR A LITTLE OLD LADY

We had been looking, and looking, and looking.

"There is something out there. I know. I believe.

"Remember Reilly at Trout Lake? Believe. Just believe," I am telling myself. We will find something.

"I wish you would," said Dave McKay. "I have meat marinating."

Dave is a North America-wide famous barbeque chef who wins cook-offs in Texas and dreams of opening a barbeque restaurant in Vancouver someday. Meanwhile, he takes pictures for a living.

We had been looking for hours. Four hours! Four hours with me sitting beside him and we have gone in circles and we talk and then go silent and then say, "There's something!" Then we say, "No, that's nothing."

Four hours. We could have driven to Hope and come back. At least we would have been somewhere. Instead we have been on Main Street six times, and Stanley Park three times, and East Hastings four times.

"Wait," I said. "Look. He smiled."

"Who?"

"The guy with the stop sign."

"What guy?"

"The guy with the stop sign who is smiling."

"Does he like you?"

You say things after four hours.

This was on Beatty Street, near Robson. There was construction; lots of trucks and steel plates on the street and barriers and crowds. Dave said he would go around the block again and look for a parking place.

I jumped out at the end of the street and saw the rotund, smiling guy with the stop sign escorting a little old lady around the building site and safely away from the traffic.

"Oh, heavens," I thought. I don't know who or why but this is beautiful. Anyone taking care of someone else is a gift to life and to my employment.

I am running up the street, praying that Dave finds a spot. But I don't see Dave.

"Dave. Please come around the corner."

The man with the sign escorting the woman who is holding onto his arm is getting near the end of the street. I am getting closer to them. He is singing to her.

What? A man is singing to a woman on the street?!!

The end of the world could come in five minutes and I would not ask for more. Except for one thing: where's Dave?

My phone is ringing.

"Hello," I say in one syllable.

"I think I've found something for you." It is Dave's voice.

"But why aren't you here?"

"Because I've found some people juggling on Robson and they look good."

"But I've got a guy singing to a woman."

"So? I've got juggling."

"Singing."

"Juggling."

"I know this is good. He's a construction worker for god's sake, singing."

"I'm coming," said Dave, who did not want to give up his jugglers.

I ran up to the singing man and the smiling woman.

"Wait, stop, please," etc.

"Do you often sing?"

The little old lady spoke. "He sounds very nice. I was just looking for the IGA and I was lost and he said he would take me there."

"Lord! Thank you."

Where's Dave?

"I'm Steve Reno, Mike Reno's brother," said the singer.

I have no idea why he is telling me this. I asked if he sings often and he is giving me names.

"Could you wait a minute until the cameraman gets here and by the way, would you mind if we took your pictures?"

"I just want to go shopping," said the lady.

"Please."

"Just for a minute," she said.

And the construction worker with a name I was forgetting said he would sing a bit more.

Dave was turning the corner and I ran back to his van.

"He's singing," I said, like that was the most important thing in the world, "to her," which really made it important.

Dave got out his camera and asked if I knew who he was.

"He said his name was something Reno, I think."

"Reno?! Mike Reno? From Loverboy?"

"I have no idea," I said.

Dave knows everything there is to know about music. In addition to cooking he sings and has his own band, which he would like to perform in his restaurant when he gets one.

I stopped listening to music in the late 1950s when my life got busy. I know early Elvis when he was innocent. Nothing after that.

"I have no idea about Loverboy or Mike whoever, but I think he said 'Reno.'"

We walked in a way faster than walking and could hear him still singing. He sang a song he made up on the spot. The woman's name was Margaret and he sang:

"I'll be waiting for you Margaret, when the cows come home. You know we need to have a little fun, in a loving home."

"I think I'm going to cry," said Margaret.

Steve went on:

"Save a little love for me baby, when Daddy comes home."

Margaret was wiping away tears.

"Cause I'll be mighty tired, and I'm feeling low, low, low."

He finished walking her to the doorway of the supermarket.

"I didn't get his name," Margaret said to me.

I went back to the singer.

"Who are you?"

"Mike Reno's brother. Steve," he said.

"That's Loverboy, a band, very, very famous," Dave whispered to me.

I went back to Margaret.

"Have you ever heard of Loverboy?"

She looked at me as though I was making a pass at her.

"His name is Steve," I said.

She told me to thank him, and added, "He has a lovely voice."

After endless travelling with his brother and his band while they were on tour, Steve said he settled down to a normal job. He was the safety superintendent at this site.

When we put the story on television we re-ran the first scene, a burly guy in a hard hat escorting a woman past danger. He was singing to her. It was too beautiful not to see again.

We said, "It was one of those perfect, inexplicable, unexplained moments with wonderful folks that happen everywhere every day."

"I think you're exaggerating just a bit," said Dave.

I shrugged. So?

BUILDINGS HAVE LIVES TOO

When they stood on the sidewalk and looked up and up and up they could not believe how high "up" could be.

"Do we really have the tallest building in the Empire?"

Everyone asked because everyone in Vancouver wanted to hear the answer, which was always, "Yes!"

Emphatically, "Yes." Exuberantly, "Yes." Unbelievably, "Yes!"

Most who lived in Vancouver knew that most who lived in London had no idea where Vancouver was, but that was beside the point. The point was we had the tallest building in the British Empire.

It sounded good to say it again.

It was thirteen stories up, but not so. Thirteen is unlucky so the top floor is the fourteenth. In the end that did not help, but in 1910 in Vancouver everything was going up: investments, land prices, the wealth of the wealthy and the finishing touches on the tallest building in the Empire, which just happened to be in Vancouver.

There were just a few minor kinks. First, the name of the tallest building in the you-know-where at the corner of Hastings and Cambie.

It was started by the Imperial Trust Company which commissioned the work. Imperial Trust was making a good deal of money during the real estate boom of the early twentieth century. They could build the tallest building and call it the Imperial Building.

Then someone at Imperial made some bad deals and they were bought out by the Dominion Trust Company. Imperial ceased to exist.

It was now the Dominion Trust Building that was rising higher than ... you know.

But they needed more money. Has there ever been a building going up that did not need more money? A fellow named William Arnold, the vice president of Dominion Trust, was in charge of the building as well as most of the investments of the company.

He was wheeling and dealing with loans for real estate and buying real estate and doing those things that high rollers get paid a great deal for doing. He would be a hedge fund manager now, or a real estate tycoon living close to the edge but sure that everything was going to keep going up.

Then he met Count Alvo von Alvensleben, a handsome, young German aristocrat who arrived in Vancouver in 1904 basically broke. Within five years the count was rolling in money.

It was not that his investments were so good, but through family connections he had become the conduit through which German money was flowing into British Columbia. His main source of cash was the Kaiser, who was trying to make money in British Columbia real estate, and to use up some of the large wealth he had accumulated through various means, some of them legal.

In short, in modern newspaper terms, Count von Alvensleben was laundering money for the Kaiser. The count did very well. He built a large, rambling house for himself in Kerrisdale. It is now the Crofton House School. And he built the famous Wigwam Inn at the head of Indian Arm on Burrard Inlet.

William Arnold and the count became good friends. Arnold could offer the count a good, secure, investment. The count could offer Arnold cash, in large quantities. Nothing could go wrong.

Within two years the Dominion Building was finished, the tallest skyscraper in the empire, and now many in Britain were starting to hear about it.

"Who paid for it?" they said along the Thames.

"Germans? Germans built the tallest building in the British Empire?"

Imagine hearing that with a British accent trying to hide the insult with incredulousness.

"Aren't they our enemy?"

In this case, size did not matter. The British, including the Queen, were not impressed.

At the same time real estate began falling in value. You have seen this happen in your lifetime, several times. You know it happens. However, the vice-president of Dominion Trust did not believe it would happen to him. Loans on property were not being repaid. Risky investments were being shredded. The vice-president's head was hurting.

And he could not turn to Count von Alvensleben. World War I had started and suddenly the count was nowhere to be found. He was out of the country. But many in Vancouver believed he had cannons installed in his home and was plotting to blow up the government buildings in Victoria. It was not a good time to ask him for a loan.

The count's property and bank accounts were seized by the Canadian government and he never returned.

And just to add insult to misery, less than two years after the Dominion Building was finished it was no longer the tallest building in the you-know-where. Just three blocks away a newspaperman built another skyscraper, later to be called the Sun Tower. It was higher than the Dominion and now *it* was the tallest building in the . . . Okay, that's enough.

And vice-president William Arnold went up to the fourteenth floor, which was really the thirteenth, and blew his brains out. The police said it was an accidental discharge of his gun.

If you ask just about anyone working in the Dominion Building today if there is anything spooky about it they will tell you there is a ghost wandering the hallways.

Check it out, if you believe in such things. You can walk up the circular stairway in the building yourself. Admire the opulence. No one will stop you.

Ghost or no ghost, you will feel the story.

THE SUN TOWER

You love newspapers. I love newspapers. They are so much simpler than television. A reporter sees an event, listens to those complaining, screaming, cheering, groaning, encouraging, then asks some basic questions and writes a simple story about what he or she thinks has gone on. Sometimes the story is close to accurate.

Period.

It does get in your blood. You don't actually have to work. You watch, ask, and write. You could be good, or bad, accurate, or not, but it is still fun and exciting.

Louis Denison Taylor had that feeling. He worked in a small town newspaper in Revelstoke, BC, in 1896 and he had a dream. He wanted to be a big city newspaperman.

He applied to an ad to be the editor-in-chief of a new paper called *The Vancouver Daily Province*.

"Well, how about starting in the circulation department?" they said.

He wound up running the department. He was diligent. He saved his money. Then he heard one of the oldest papers in the city was up for sale. The owner had died and his widow was not able to run it alone since she was the managing editor, editorial writer and occasional reporter.

"Wow," or something like that, said L.D., which is what everyone called him. "Imagine, owning a newspaper."

It was not a very big paper, it had only twelve pages for news and advertisements, but it was a newspaper in a big city.

He rounded up some friends and the short of it was with some borrowing and some begging he now owned *The World*, one of the original newspapers of Vancouver. It began in 1888, only two years after Vancouver was born.

He pushed for good reporting. He pushed for exciting reporting, and with those combinations you get more readers, which means more circulation, which means more money for the owner.

And there is nothing like being in the media to let your own importance go to your head.

"L.D. for mayor."

That is what folks were saying.

L.D. ran and L.D. won.

Mayor and media star, what a combination. And now the money really started rolling in. But it had nothing to do with his politics or his reporting. It was time for another real estate boom in Vancouver.

This one was in 1909 and 1910, the same boom that was fueling the Dominion Trust Company in the previous story.

In the early days of Vancouver, real estate booms came in quick waves with sudden troughs between them. The fact that most expected the waves to go on forever and the troughs to be a thing of the past is one of those human quirks.

With a real estate boom comes advertising, and the best place, in truth the only place, to advertise in 1910 was in newspapers.

L.D. said his paper had more display ads, which means advertisements with pictures in them (the real money makers), than any other newspaper in North America. It does not matter if that was true or not, L.D. believed it and said it. Not bad for a small-town guy.

"We need a bigger building to publish our paper," he said.

"How big?"

"Big."

"How big?"

"This big." He stretched his arm up as high as it would go. He wanted the biggest building for the biggest paper in North America.

And so the tower started going up, and up and, well you know. Seventeen stories up, taller than the Dominion Building only a five-minute walk away. Taller—here we go again—than any building in the British Empire.

"It should look dignified and old, like the buildings in London," said L.D.

So the domed roof was painted green to make it look like aged copper.

Not only were real estate and the economy and, most important of all, advertising in his newspaper booming, but people were taking notice of his building.

It was not just because it was the tallest, the biggest phallic-like tower in the wherever. It also had something seven stories up that you could not take your eyes off.

Possibly L.D. was a forefather of Hugh Hefner, who made billions out of one thing: naked women.

L.D., more than a century earlier, had the same thought. When he was approving the plans of the new office for his *World* newspaper he may have said something along the lines of:

"Why don't we have some naked women on the building?"

He may have phrased it a different way, but the outcome was the same.

Nine unclothed, naked, breast-revealing women, there is no other way of putting it, line the seventh floor of his enlarging tower. We will leave the symbolism for others:

"Hey, wait a minute. He has naked women wrapped around an enlarged tower. He must be perverse."

We only know that the local upper-crust women said: "WHAT? He CAN'T DO THAT!"

But he did. Nine women naked from the waist up, breasts pushing out into the air, pretty women, sensuous women, sweet women. Okay, that's enough.

We know the bluenoses were appalled. We suspect the men were not. Many men came to stare at this atrocious affront to the dignity of decent people. They looked and looked and were appalled. Then they looked again.

The World Tower was a success. Like Playboy, no one said they ever went to see the ladies, they just passed by to check out the building. But the way home from work often took a new route.

The World newspaper was pumping out wonderful numbers of copies and everyone was happy, except those who did not like naked women right where you could see them.

The dream of L.D. was fulfilled. Everyone who read *The World* in Vancouver could look up and see the World Building where the news of the world was printed.

And then came the trough between the waves.

It had to come. You knew it was coming.

But L.D. did not. He thought he was above the waves. Silly man.

Come 1914, only two years after the tallest building was finished, and the collapse came.

Real estate fell. Stocks fell. Investments fell. And worst of all, advertisements dried up.

Eventually, L.D. lost his newspaper. He lost the building. He went back to the only job that took no other credentials—he was re-elected mayor of Vancouver again.

The history of the World Tower after that was like a roller coaster, rapid down, quick up, then down, then up.

After *The World* left, the Human Fly settled on the outside of the building. Just like today some folks figure out oddball ways to make themselves famous.

In 1918, four years after the fall of the newspaper, a fellow named Harry Gardiner made some headlines from the building.

He called himself the Human Fly and starting at the base, with his suit and tie and street shoes, climbed the building that was still called the World Tower.

A crowd of tens of thousands gathered and despite the police trying to stop him, Harry climbed and climbed. I have no idea how he did it. I have stood outside the building and said, "impossible." No one could find enough grips and handholds to get off the ground. But he did. And he went up to the roof, which was painted green.

There is a lot of media attention when you get to the top of the World.

The crowds cheered. The Human Fly was arrested and released, and never heard from again on the west coast. Somehow he made a living out of doing what he did.

For several years the tallest building with the grandest view stood empty. Then in 1924 it was sold to Americans, the Bekins Moving and Storage

Company of Seattle. Whoops, good thing it was no longer the tallest building in the British Empire.

The Bekins people put a large sign on top saying: BEKINS, which could be seen from all over Vancouver. This would be the down part of the roller coaster.

For thirteen years the World Tower was known as the Bekins Tower.

And then someone yelled, "Fire." That was 1937 and it was across the street from the Bekins Tower. The blaze was in the *Vancouver Sun* building and gutted the place. This would be the up part of the roller coaster because the *Sun* now desperately needed a place to write and print its newspapers and there it was, right across the street.

The *Sun* bought the Bekins Tower, which was the World Tower, and renamed it the Sun Tower.

Roller coasters and history can leave you dizzy.

In 1964 the *Sun* moved out, but the name stayed. Whew. The ride was over, the name is famous and the building is now one of the smallest in the city.

And with each passerby whom I talked to about the building, none of them had ever noticed the naked ladies.

FIRST THE BIG, NOW THE SMALL OF IT

66**T**he World Tower is so beautiful. But what a shame if we can't see it," said an alderman of the city of Vancouver. It was 1912 and the tower had just gotten its instant green dome.

They were in Chinatown on Pender Street where the Sun Yat-Sen Garden is now. They were looking west over an empty lot at the corner of Carrall and Pender and smiling at the towering structure, which was the tallest building in the British Empire, they reminded each other.

"If we widened Pender Street no one could put a building on that corner."

They pointed to the corner on the southwest side of the street.

"If no one puts up a building there we can always see the tower," reasoned one alderman.

"But Chang Toy owns the lot," said the other alderman. "And he will be very angry if we take it away."

We know they said that because Chang Toy owned the lot and was well known in Vancouver for his temper.

Now we can only imagine what happened next.

"But he's Chinese, and what's he going to do, stamp his feet?"

"We expropriate the land, give him some cash for it, and that's that."

They would leave him with just a tiny strip of his property.

"Look, it's not even two steps wide." Ha ha.

In short, it was not a good time to be Chinese in Vancouver. There was a head tax that had been increased time after time. By 1910 it was $500 a person, equivalent to more than $10,000 now. Chinese were not allowed to buy land or even live in several cities of the lower mainland. Chinatown was where they should stay, or go back to China.

And even Chinatown was not safe. Just a few years earlier, 1907, whites again went through Pender and Keefer Streets smashing windows and beating anyone who was Chinese.

It was not beyond reasonable to figure that if they left Chang with just four and a half feet of land for himself that they would be cheating him out of that space.

But the truth was, don't mess with Chang Toy.

He was raised by his mother. His father died when he was three. He was seventeen when he came to British Columbia as part of a shipment of human hands that would work for close to nothing in the canneries. From there he worked in a sawmill in New Westminster until a white foreman pushed him too far with racial insults.

Chang was good with kung fu. The white foreman was knocked out cold. The other Chinese workers saw Chang as their hero.

From there he moved to a laundry, then a grocery store in Chinatown and then to an import and export business. He was as good with his mind as with his hands. He did well and wound up owning the Sam Kee Company, which had been in business for several decades and was involved in contract labour and real estate.

There Chang blossomed. He bought land, then hotels. By the time the aldermen were trying to pull a fast one over him, Chang was one of the most successful and wealthy Chinese businessmen in the city.

"That is all the space you are leaving me?" Chang said through an interpreter. He was too busy to learn English.

They tried to hide their smiles.

"If that is what you left me, that is what I will use," he said.

Then he bet the aldermen that there would be a building on that four-and-a-half-foot-wide space.

"This is the favourite spot for tourists," said Rod Chow, who now owns the building.

He was spreading out his arms on the Carrall Street side of the building.

The fingers on his right hand touched one side of the building, and the fingers on his left hand touched the other side.

"That's the whole thing. And Chang won his bet."

There is no known record of how much the bet was. But Chang did better than the money. What counted was he beat them, just like in the sawmill.

Rod is the son of Jack Chow who bought the building in the 1980s and restored it. The second floor has slightly more room, six feet wide with bay windows. The basement had baths with glass bricks in the sidewalk above it to allow light. It is the only glass-bricked sidewalk in the city.

When Rod sells insurance, or marriage licences, he does it though an open window onto the sidewalk like selling burgers or coffee. And he has a thriving business. Anyone who works in the brilliant, unbeatable world that Chang created would do nothing else.

The building is in the *Guinness Book of World Records* for being the thinnest occupied business space on earth.

But you can no longer see all of the World Tower, which is now the Sun Tower, from the sidewalk because a movie theatre was later built a few blocks away. Life works that way.

But what does not change is the lesson you can get from a building too narrow for two people to pass each other without a questionably tight squeeze, which is not recommended with all ground-floor windows.

The lesson: when you get painted into an impossibly tight corner, bet on yourself.

FISHERMAN OF IRON, CAMERAMAN NOT

66 "Why did we do that?" asked cameraman Karl Cassleman. "I'm getting calls from everyone saying I'm a wimp."

I have told you about Karl in earlier stories. He is one of the strongest, if not the strongest, of all the cameramen and cameramen are all fairly strong. They spend their working lives with the equivalent of a large sack of potatoes made of steel on their shoulder.

In their other hand they have a tripod, which weighs as much as the camera. Around their waist or in knapsacks they carry more potatoes in the shape of batteries and extra tapes and tools and things, lots of things because you don't want not to have a "thing" when some reporter who carries nothing but his or her good looks suddenly wants to do a stand-up and needs a radio microphone pinned to his jacket so he doesn't have to hold a microphone in his hand.

"Sure I have the transmitter and the mic to pin on you and the receiver to attach to my camera, all in my pockets," says the cameraman. "I'm glad I carried them for you. You look so good without holding an ugly old microphone."

You get the picture. If you want to go into television news and wish to take pictures, start lifting weights as well as going to school. This applies also to camerawomen who are called cameramen and don't argue with them. They are stronger than you.

"Why did we do that story?" I replied. "Because you told me to get out of your truck and talk to that guy, and it was raining and cold and I was going to get wet. That's why."

It is also impossible to get mad at Karl. He bubbles with enthusiasm from minute to minute.

The man I was sent to talk to was an old fisherman we saw hauling around some ropes in one of the storage lockups at the Fisherman's Wharf across from Granville Island.

"Hello."

"Hello." All the usual stuff. It turned out that he was retiring from the business after sixty years and was cleaning out his huge locker. His name, George Arnet. Age, seventy-two.

He had gone fishing with his father when he was twelve, and never did anything else. He walked around the locker sorting things and slowly dropping them here and moving other stuff. He said he was going slowly because of the arthritis in his back. Ouch.

He was coiling some rope and tossing it into a large box. While talking to him I casually picked up one end of the rope.

"My good god," I said. "What the heck is in this?"

"Lead."

"But you are moving it like it is cotton."

George looked at me like I was odd.

I saw an anchor. I tried to pick it up. To my great self-admiration I got it off the ground.

"How much does this weigh?"

"About fifty pounds," he said. He tossed dozens of them into the ocean while halibut fishing, and then pulled them back in, by hand.

"Pick it up," I said.

He did, over his head. With one hand.

If you are a guy, there are truly only a few things that impress you: beautiful women who you know would never look your way, beer, and muscles. Okay, some guys now like wine, too.

All guys try to flex their bicep when a woman touches their arm.

I could hear Karl saying, "My gosh," or stronger words, in admiration of George.

We went on talking about fishing and life and he went on moving stuff around. Karl was taking pictures of him. Then George picked up a rope, a regular rope without lead, attached at both ends to a long cylinder of steel. It was about the same length as I am tall.

George tugged on it, dragged it, then to move it over some other things in his way, he hoisted it off the ground and dropped it on the other side of the junk.

He used one hand.

"What's that?" I asked.

"Oil cooler," he said, like who would not know it was an oil cooler?

"See if you can pick it up," said Karl.

I want to be strong. I wanted to pick it up. When I was a kid I wanted to be a garbage man more than anything else in the world because they were strong.

I grabbed the rope, with two hands. I pulled. I, in simplicity, basically ripped my arms out of their sockets and my face nearly exploded. It did not leave the ground.

Karl laughed. He was taking my picture.

"Okay, wise guy," or words stronger than that, "let's see you do it," I said to him.

I took his camera, and turned it on. As I've said before if you keep it on wide angle and don't move too much, anyone can take a picture. It's like those disposable cardboard cameras, they all have a wide-angle lens that keeps everything in focus, but don't expect art.

Karl took the rope in one hand. He lifted. The cooler did not lift with him. He took the rope in two hands. He pulled with more than all his might. This was important. This was the manly thing. He is about twenty-five years younger than George. Karl, as I said earlier, is one of the strongest of the strong of his generation. His face was bursting.

His integrity was at stake. His reputation, his honour, and more important, he knows the camera is on.

He grunted, he groaned, he cursed. He moved his hands to the front of the rope and there, sort of, one end of the cooler rose almost off the floor.

"Darn." Or words stronger.

George just smiled.

What was this all about? Every boy's dream, and nightmare.

George was our hero.

And the next day the calls started coming to Karl.

"You wimp. You poof. You useless waste of human skin."

He has friends who are cruel.

Which brings us back to the question, why did we do that story?

Fate. And a look at a man who knows what it is like to have to move an oil cooler in a boat by himself.

He came from an amazing generation.

THE UNDERSIDE OF SCRABBLE

"**Y**ou what?! You cheat at Scrabble?"

"I don't cheat. I bluff."

He was ten years old. He could put down a word and get fifty points. I get that after half a game.

His name is Matthew and he had a soft, chubby face and a tight, athletic mind. We met him because we were standing on the sidewalk at Eighth Avenue and Granville Street on Sunday morning and we saw a woman not putting money into a parking meter.

"Ma'am, it's none of our business but you forgot to put money in the meter."

"But it's Sunday," said the woman. "Do you have to pay on Sundays in Canada?"

She was from Seattle. She was getting lunch for her son who was in a Scrabble tournament in the Masonic Building across the street.

"Can we watch?" we asked.

She had gotten Matthew's favourite lunch: fried chicken, potato chips and cupcakes—six of them—with strawberry icing. Playing Scrabble takes a lot of brain calories.

We have been at other Scrabble tournaments. There are players who specialize in two-letter words who are amazing. They can get out of any predicament. And I met a woman, an African-Canadian in the correct way of describing her. She was from North Vancouver and seldom got less than eighty points on any word.

I watched her with my eyebrows glued to the ceiling. She rejected words that had thirty points, and rejected those with forty. Sixty, maybe. And this was all from one set of seven letters. There, that one over there on the board that no one saw, she slipped the letters in with others already out there, counting them this way, that way and back and forth, plus double word score: eighty points. Next.

But today we were watching Matthew playing Joel, a Chinese-Canadian so long as we are into unimportant race. Actually, it is important. And I mention it for a reason. If you want to dispel prejudice go to a Scrabble tourney. Whites, blacks, bikers, immigrants who learned the language in their adult years, the old, the young, competing letter by letter and knocking the illiterate socks off most of us. A game of Scrabble at an official tournament will humble you.

But we were watching Matthew, the youngest player in the room. He put down A-D-A.

Joel, twenty years older, and a Canadian border crossing guard, shook his head.

"You don't think so?" Matthew stared at him.

Joel bit his lip. Paused. Then said, "No."

They went off to the official Scrabble computer dictionary.

It is tough to challenge a word at a tournament because simply it can be embarrassing if the word you think is not a real word turns out to be an acceptable word and you have to say, "Oh. Whoops. You are smarter than me."

Matthew's mother was holding his chicken. "It's getting cold," she said.

Joel and Matthew came back to the game.

"It's not a word," said Joel. He was trying not to smile.

I asked Matthew, "Do you get away with that a lot?"

He nodded. "Usually they don't question me."

He is at the level where doubting someone is often futile.

"Isn't that cheating?" I asked.

"Bluffing," he said.

"Like poker?"

"I don't play poker," he said.

Off to the side was W.P. Kinsella who wrote the novels that became the movie *Field of Dreams*. He plays at all the Scrabble tournaments. If he wins he can get $100, sometimes.

For his novels he got millions. But he once told me that writing is hard, playing Scrabble is fun.

Matthew lost to Joel, who was ranked a level higher.

Matthew's mother stood in the back of the room with his lunch. He bit into the chicken then went straight to the cupcakes.

"I feel better now," he said. "I'll do better next time."

And he did. And not only was his mother proud, but she did not get a T-I-C-K-E-T, which in Seattle can be challenged on a Sunday, but not in Vancouver.

This is a personal note, just as all these stories are.

My mother loved Scrabble. When she was dying of cancer and was no longer able to speak or communicate in any way we brought her old Scrabble game to the hospital and spread it out on her bed and played.

She lay at one end of the bed, barely breathing, and doing nothing else.

We were at the foot of the bed trying to put together letters.

She died a few hours after our last game. I think she was watching, and I think she knew we had a few words that would have counted as bluffing.

THE SOUND OF RAIN

Blip, *blip*, then *blop, blip, blip*.

Raindrops fell off a picnic shelter roof and hit the plastic top of an empty paper coffee container that was standing upright next to a stone on the grass and they made music. It is funny that the music is easier to describe than the instrument.

Blip, blip and then the rhythm changed. *Blip, blip, blip, rat-a-tat, tat*. It was raining harder.

Holy mackerel, we have a story. But then laughter. The music was interrupted by someone having fun. How can this happen in the rain?

We were at Trout Lake, again. It is a good park. There is a picnic shelter, just one, with a roof and four picnic tables under it, and honestly, what more could you ask for if you are fifteen and you have your buddy there and you have an hour off from school and nowhere else to go?

They were playing plastic pop bottle football under the roof, passing, dodging, using the tables as players, trying to fake out each other and then passing to each other. Teams change by the instant.

And laughter. And then bottle cap soccer. And then jumping from the ground to the top of the table. You can't do that when you get mature because your legs say, "Are you kidding?"

Then jumping from table to table. What happens if you slip? You don't ask that because they don't. They are fifteen.

And then holding the bottle that was the football out under the edge of the roof and letting the water fill the bottle. And then pouring it over your own head.

"What?" Okay, now we have to intrude and ask, "What? Why?"

"Because he dared me to," said James Clark.

"And you did it?!"

"Why not?" asked Tan Hui. "We got soaked anyway."

Their hair was dripping from the rain, from sweat, and from the leftover water from the bottle that did not go on James's head, which now went on Tan's.

Plus the steam was rising up from both of them because the air was cold and they were wet and their hearts were pumping out heat. The picture of happiness.

Then they went back to bottle cap soccer.

Basically, every adult in the world can remember the same story. And later from their mothers or teachers or someone old who doesn't understand:

"How the heck did you get so wet? It looks like you were pouring water over your head."

MEN IN PARKING LOTS

This was so easy to do. Cameraman Mike Timbrell suggested it because he does the same thing. All his friends do it. Guys he has never met do it. And guys on the other side of the world do it.

"Go into a parking lot outside a mall," he said, "and what do you see?"

"Cars," I answered, trying to have the right answer.

"Of course, cars." He was already impatient because I did not see the obvious which was right there, and there, and there, he pointed out.

"What's in the cars?"

"Guys?"

"Brilliant," he said. "And why are they there?"

"Because they drove to the mall?"

"Do they really pay you?" Mike asked.

I thought I was going to have to try to explain that when he added, "So if they are at the mall why aren't they shopping?"

"Because they're guys and guys don't like shopping."

He looked at me like someone who has been fumbling with two plus two and finally came up with the right answer.

"Oh, I get it. We can ask guys why they are sitting in their cars."

"Brilliant," he said.

So we asked guys sitting in their cars why they were sitting in their cars.

"Because I don't like shopping," said the first one.

"Because I hate shopping," said the second one.

"Are you weird or something?" asked the third. "Do you like shopping?"

We put together a string of comments from men who did not like shopping and preferred sitting inside their cars, with exhaust fumes passing by, reading newspapers, listening to the radio or just sitting, and waiting. Many still had their seat belts on.

The next day reaction poured in. It did not trickle, it poured. And it was summed up the same way over and over.

From men: at last someone said what I feel.

From women: now I understand. I thought he just didn't want to be with me.

Mike Timbrell, thank you. Your insight has saved some marriages.

OUTSIDE 7-ELEVEN

About eight or ten or twelve kids were there, sitting, drinking Slurpies, a few were smoking. The number was hard to pin down because they were fluid, coming and going.

It was the classic lunchtime outside a 7-Eleven which is across the street from a high school. This one was at Broadway and Nanaimo and the school is Vancouver Technical, but it could be any school and any store that may hate having the kids hang around but could not stay in business without them.

Just on a lark we decided to ask teenagers what was on their minds. I realized as I approached them that it might be a stretch to think anything was on their minds, which is a seldom-used organ during the time of hormonal imbalance.

"Hello, can we ask what you're talking about," we asked four girls who were sitting on the ground leaning up against the store.

"Boys," one said. "Except her," she elbowed the girl sitting next to her. "She already has a boyfriend."

"So, you can't talk about boys if you have a boyfriend?" we asked.

"She doesn't know what it's like not to have one," another girl said.

"How old are you?" we asked.

"Fourteen," three of them said.

Fourteen is an age of great romantic suffering, we know.

We asked the boys who were standing what they were talking about.

"Girls," they said.

Then one of them spit on the ground.

"You shouldn't do that," I said.

We went back to the subject.

"Girls, we talk about girls," another boy said.

They were standing right next to the girls.

"Do you talk to the girls about girls?" I asked the boys.

They looked a bit taken back. Nothing much will faze a teenage boy, but there was a hint of, 'Are you kidding? Talk to girls about girls?'

"No," said one of the boys. "How could we talk to them about girls? They don't understand like we do."

These boys and girls are standing in one group but they are not talking to each other, at least not about the things that they say they are talking about.

The boy who spit started to spit again, but looked at me and tried to stop, which is impossible to do and it went on his chin. This made everyone laugh and he wiped it off with the back of his hand.

One of the girls said that was disgusting. Then they laughed again.

We were relaxed now.

"What are you really thinking about?" I asked the girls.

"My father. I wish I could see him," said one.

"I'm sorry. Where is he?"

"In a logging camp in the north. I saw him last summer. He doesn't live at home anymore."

Sorry, again.

"I would like that more than anything," she said.

Then one of the boys said they had to get back to school or they would be late.

As they walked away the boy who spit looked back, and did not spit.

They crossed Broadway, in the middle of the block, against the light, and all I could think is that teenagers have a lot of adult deep inside, they just don't let it bother them as much.

ONE LAST TEETER ON THE TOTTER

They found the board. It did not matter where. In the old way of measuring, it was about twelve feet long, almost too much for two nine-year-old girls to carry.

They got it over to a big rock and we saw them just as they were lifting it so that the rock would be in the middle of the board. They were laughing.

The board had been out in the weather for a long time. It could not be used for building. That time was long gone. In truth, the only use left was cutting it and burning it. That or landfill.

But first, one more moment of life. One girl put her leg over one end and the other at the far end. It was harder for the second girl because the first had sat down on the ground.

And they laughed some more.

"Are your parents around?"

One pointed to a house nearby. We got permission to take their pictures. Once again, this is the way the world should work.

They went up and down and I asked, "Shouldn't you be in school?"

No, it was a professional day.

"Is the board fun?"

They both laughed more. "Yesssss."

They went up and down and held on and pushed with their legs.

"What's more fun, having a day off from school or doing this?"

"This," they both said.

And then one of them said, "He's stepped on my gum."

"Who?"

They pointed.

"The guy with the camera?"

They nodded and laughed.

The cameraman tilted his camera down and shot his own shoe.

"There's nothing there," he said.

"On the side," said one of the girls.

And there, on the side of his shoe, was a glob of sticky, used bubble gum. The girls laughed louder.

And then we left with pictures of laughter and a board that was given one more day of life and a shoe that needed cleaning.

This happened during the same summer that the government started removing all teeter-totters from playgrounds because they were deemed to be dangerous for children.

Maybe they should just give kids rocks and boards instead, and let them laugh at the adults who can't safely watch where they walk.

GAMES PEOPLE PLAY

He cast and the line went out and out, too far to see. He was good at casting. And then he started reeling it in.

That's all there is to fishing, plus hoping you will get something at the end of the day. Those who say just the enjoyment of a day on the water is enough, that you don't need fish, are fibbing. But you have to say something when you come home empty-handed.

Bill Relkoff started reeling, and walking. The end of the line stayed right where it landed and he walked to the sinker as he reeled in the line.

"Isn't that backwards, Bill?"

And then he counted: "Thirty-eight, thirty-nine, forty."

"Forty what?"

"Forty steps," he said, "which I times by three, one hundred and twenty feet. Not bad."

Each step he took was three feet long, sort of a metre in unromantic measure.

He was fishing on an empty field in Queen's Park in New Westminster. No hook, no bait, just a six-ounce sinker and a long line, and determination.

"I'm hoping to land a forty-five footer," he said.

He checked around to make sure the field was empty and cast again. Again, it went too far to see, but my eyes are not so good any more. I was sixty when I met him.

"That's a good one," he said. "I'm eighty-four and this got me out of my seat at home."

He used to fish. He got older and stopped. Then one day he thought, "It's not the fish, but the fishing. Sure I can't eat it, but I can burn off what I ate."

He was a funny guy. And his new self-invented sport was not passive. He cast, he walked, and he counted.

"Thirty-nine, forty, forty-one. Almost." He was as excited as seeing the big one that got away and knew it was still out there.

He reminded me of the people at the horseshoe pitch in Central Park in Burnaby. Every day a group of them throw horseshoes, which is what you do when that is your sport.

Then came winter and I saw them trying to clear away the snow, but more came down and when your horseshoe lands under a pile of white flakes you can't tell who is the closest. So they invented a new game.

"It's sewer pipe," said one of them.

They cut a pair of plastic drain pipes each about a foot long and stood them upright in boxes.

They put the boxes with the pipes about twenty steps apart indoors in their clubhouse and while it was snowing outside they stayed warm and tossed washers into the pipes. Very simple. For someone who likes horseshoes it would get you through the winter.

I told my wife about that and while we were on a picnic with friends she invented a game. Very simple again. She drew a circle in the dirt and then gathered some stones.

We stood behind a line and tried to throw the stones in the circle. There were near misses and bull's eyes and stones that rolled away and cheating.

"I did not step over the line."

"Yes you did."

That made the game authentic.

In a picnic that was wonderful with good friends and wine and salmon and bread and fruit, the stone game was one of the best parts.

Then I started researching the history of games and it turns out that rolling or tossing stones had its beginning in the earliest cultures. This is not hard to imagine. Gather some people, especially kids, who are temporarily not at war and they find a use for stones other than throwing them at each other.

It was basic marbles, which in the history of games is the grandparent of bocce, lawn bowls, ten-pin bowling, polo, golf, soccer, football and hockey. They are all the same game with different-sized balls, and all came from marbles.

And it is the same as tying a sinker on a fishing line and casting it.

"Forty-two, forty-three, darn," said Bill. "Enough for today."

He said he was getting tired. He had already walked around the field three times, exercising his arms, his back, his legs, his heart, his lungs and his imagination. He said he would be back the next day to go after the big one.

"I'll get that forty-five footer yet."

He left with his rod bouncing in his hand. Whoever said you don't need fish after a day of fishing was brilliant.

TO WALK THE LINE

It has been a long time since I walked a picket line. You may have done the same. It is one of the low points in life and you are doing it because you think you should and actually you have no choice and after a week or two you lose all perspective on whether you should or should not be there. You just walk.

The last time for me was with some well-known reporters and editors and photographers and all the behind-the-scenes people who work harder than the people who are on television, except no one was on television.

Picket lines go up just outside the company's property, which in Greater Vancouver means the area from the sidewalk to the curb. That means you have a strip of concrete, which is the sidewalk, and a strip of grass between the sidewalk and the curb to walk on.

You walk in long circular paths, half on grey, half on green.

While you walk you don't think of contract language, you think of rent. You spend your days walking outside while others indoors are fighting over your future.

You read a lot, but your mind is always on other things and you don't remember what you just read. You don't jump up on a picket line and shout, "Hey, this is a great book." You just put it down and start another one.

And as you walk the grass starts to fade away. It can take just so many shoes before the blades break and then get crushed and then die. The green stretches become brown.

Hot dogs are eaten over the grass. There are always hot dogs on picket lines. And a fire burns in a barrel set up on the grass. There is always a burning barrel on a picket line, even in the summer.

And lawn chairs get put on the grass because after a while sitting replaces some of the walking. You sit, others walk.

And you wait, because that is your purpose, and while you wait the sun does not reach the grass that is in your shadow.

There are good times, the ball games, the endless game of Hearts, the meeting of people from other departments. Then you have someone new to walk with.

No matter how much we all wish for the good times, bad times happen. So you walk, and the grass dies.

And then suddenly it is over. It may take weeks or months, but suddenly it is over. The negotiators negotiated and the signatures were signed and the lawn chairs get packed up and the fire in the barrel is allowed to go out.

The next day everyone is back at work and the grass says:

"For creatures with brains much bigger than vast fields of us you sure have a dumb way of settling conflicts."

MY HERO

I started to write this comparing Canadian heroes with American heroes because just by the numbers game there are more down there than up here. They are all equal, they are all good, but America's got the numbers.

The only reason I compare them is because there is just one hero in my life, one, no matter where I grew up, that inspired me, elevated me, inflamed me with the feeling that I could do something to make the world better.

And he is Canadian. He is Terry Fox.

I was lucky. I met him. I remember when the news director at BCTV twigged to the reality that, "He's running a marathon every day! My god, no one can do that."

That was Cameron Bell, the very tough old news director who had seen uncountable thousands of stories but now was moved almost to tears and in awe by one of them.

"Twenty-six miles a day!" said Cameron. "That's a marathon, every day, on one leg."

Yes, that is what Terry was saying, "A Marathon of Hope." But it did not register.

The difference in hearing the slogan of Terry's run, "A Marathon of Hope," and realizing what it meant was profound.

Others who run marathons do two or three a year. Professionals train with two or three a month. Terry was doing one a day, on one leg.

I went to the hospital to do a story about Terry after he had to quit his run. His cancer had returned. He had gone almost halfway across the country, twenty-six miles every day. He could only feel the ground beneath one foot, his left. His right was a piece of metal and plastic.

But each step was pain. Each step brought a wince to his face. I saw it. Each step was felt from his stub on his thigh to his brain and stung his tongue and his jaw and his cheeks. It was not a fun run.

When he had to quit he said he was not giving up. "I will keep fighting, I promise."

And there he was in the hospital after they found the cancer had spread to his lungs. He knew he was waiting to die. I knew it. His family knew it. We did not talk about it.

We did not talk much about his run. We did not talk about his heroism. We did not talk about the pain or the money he was trying to raise for cancer research.

It was Christmas Eve, 1980.

"If you could give everyone a Christmas present, what would it be?"

"Faith," he said.

"You mean in yourself?"

"No, in God. Then yourself."

Religion is a hard thing to talk about. Especially on non-denominational television, which does not want to seem like it is preaching or to offend anyone's belief.

"I want them to believe in a God, and to be like that God; good, you know what I mean?"

I was looking at a guy in a hospital bed whose cancer was spreading through his body and who was becoming the most famous person in the country and he wanted people to believe in God.

"Not the Sunday morning television God," he said. "I don't know what they are talking about. But the God who wants us to do better."

Terry was not walking across a stage with a microphone in a two-thousand-dollar jacket and a sweating face telling people that "GGGOOOOOODDDD had saved them. And GGGGGOOOOOODDDD had died for them. And seeennnnddddd MOOONNNEEEYYY."

Terry was in a hospital bed and telling me that God had given him something to live and die for, and he wished others had that feeling. It was a feeling more than a belief of someone with a beard sitting on a throne with angels around him. Believe in something bigger, and then you believe in you.

Very basic. Very simple. Very Terry.

"All I wish is for others to have a feeling of hope," said Terry.

"In what?" I asked again.

"In everything," he said. "It makes living better."

"If by some miracle you got better what would you do?" I asked.

"Finish the run," he said, "just like I promised." He tried to smile.

He wished the world a good night and a good day, and a Merry Christmas. Then without the energy to say he was tired he closed his eyes and fell asleep.

We took down the lights and folded up the tripod so quietly we heard nothing but Terry's breathing.

He was the bravest, strongest, most honest, plainest speaking, most inspiring person most people who knew him said they have ever known. Me too.

There should be a statue to him over Ottawa that is higher than the Parliament Buildings so the people who run the country could look up to him.

There are millions of Canadians who have saved their Terry Fox dollar coins after they were minted in 2005 on the twenty-fifth anniversary of his run. He is still the only Canadian who has ever been on a Canadian coin.

We are lucky to have a national hero who was not a member of royalty or in the military or in the tough world of business or the talented world of the arts.

We have a hero we can follow.

HISTORY OF BC

I was shocked. I mean it blew my socks off. Big, beautiful San Juan Island, just a rowboat ride away from Victoria, should have a Canadian flag on it. But one stupid and bullying man who happened to be given some authority lost it.

And I was thrilled that in the streets of old Victoria, when they were just stretches of mud, that a wacko guy who wanted to keep that city and island British would get into fist fights with anyone who disagreed with him. He became the second premier of the colony.

Talk about colour and romance and insanity. The birth of British Columbia is a four-star blockbuster movie waiting to be made.

It was the boss at Global BC, Clive Jackson, who asked me if I would do some stories on the history of BC because it would be one hundred and fifty years old in 2008.

I didn't know that, I'm thinking, but of course I'm not admitting it.

Sure, I say, knowing that what the boss wants the boss gets even if the boss doesn't know what a dull bunch of stories that will be.

I go to the library and start reading.

What?! What's this? I can't get my eyes off the page.

Someone finds gold up near Hope one hundred and fifty years ago. Not just a little gold, but pounds of it. There is gold all over the place, nuggets the size of your fist.

Imagine trying to keep that secret.

Within a few months thirty thousand Americans are coming up from San Francisco wanting to get those nuggets. All of the gold seekers have guns. And of course they do because it is not only in their Bill of Rights, but it makes sense that if you find some gold you don't want anyone else taking it from your knapsack.

They get to Victoria by boat and then learn the Fraser River is way over there.

Over where?

Over there, across that inland ocean called the Georgia Strait.

So they build rafts and rent Native canoes and paddle across with their gold pans and guns and whisky. They row where big ferries now go, then paddle straight up the river and start panning.

There are only about one hundred British subjects in the entire mainland.

The governor of the colony of Vancouver Island writes to Queen Victoria.

"Do something quick, or you won't have any land to do anything with."

That is the Cole's Notes version of British Columbia.

In official history books the stories are longer and have more dates and treaties and government officials and pronouncements.

But here are some of the stories as you might hear them over the back fence, which is where stories bring people together. There are tales of gold, guns, fist fights and dumb bosses.

Happy one hundred and fiftieth, British Columbia. You rock.

THE BIRTH

“**M**y God, we’re going to die.”

Simon Fraser looked down, and down was a far ways off. This was an exciting job he had, but it would not be so good if he was killed.

Simon Fraser was following the Columbia River and when he got to the end and it lead out into the Pacific on the coast of America he could go home to Ontario.

He had been brought to Ontario by his widowed mother when he was an eight-year-old child. She had joined the migration from England to Upper Canada to start a new life.

Simon got a job as a clerk in the North West Company, which was looking for ways to get furs from west of the Rocky Mountains to the Pacific coast.

After ten years with the company he was given the job of setting up trading forts in the west and finding a river that could be used for exporting the furs. The river had to be calm enough to get canoes through, but the one he was standing far above now looked like a stick so far down and a canoe would not have a chance of surviving.

He established Fort McLeod, which became the first European settlement west of the Rockies, and Fort George, which became Prince George. And then in 1808, he took an incredible journey down this unnamed river and at the end met a hostile reception from the Musqueam Indians.

It was not the Columbia that he had been looking for, and whatever it was it could not be used for safe navigation. He called the area he went through New Caledonia, meaning New Scotland, after stories his mother had told him about what Scotland looked like.

Caledonia was the name the Romans gave to Scotland when they arrived there. It means land of trees.

The river was later named after Simon Fraser. But he did not know that when he left after exploring the river, the wrong river. He was a failure, and went back to Ontario and spent the rest of his life farming and grinding wheat and died in poverty.

For fifty years New Caledonia changed basically not at all. By 1858 less than three hundred non-Natives lived there. It was bigger than France, Germany and Holland, or bigger than California, Oregon and Washington combined and the entire population of non-Natives would fit in a high school gym. Most of them worked in Fort Langley, which was the Hudson's Bay trading post.

Then in 1858, boom. Everything changed, basically overnight. In that river that Simon Fraser had been disappointed with because it wasn't the Columbia, gold was found.

A piece of shiny metal, just north of Fort Langley. On a sandbar by a wandering prospector. And not just one piece. Pounds of it. Nuggets the size of fists.

The prospector must have felt like a real estate agent in Yaletown when the first condo went up.

But news of finding gold cannot be kept a secret for long. As soon as the gold was brought out the hordes came in.

They swarmed up, mainly from the gold fields of California, which had gone dry. They walked up over the border but mostly, the quickest way, was by ship from San Francisco and Seattle. The ships went to Victoria. Vancouver Island was then a colony, and Victoria was the capital with all of three hundred people living there.

On April 28, 1858, an American steamer arrived with 2,800 men. They would not wait for boats. They bought them from Indians and made them from logs and paddled across the route that BC Ferries now takes and straight up the Fraser River.

By the summer thirty thousand had arrived. They swarmed up the river and some fought with the Natives and some fought with each other and they were pulling gold out with unbelievable ease.

Victoria grew overnight, literally. In six weeks 225 buildings were put up, mostly by American businessmen trying to cash in on the Americans who were arriving. Outfitters and pack trains were created overnight.

And it was not just those looking for gold in the ground who flooded in. American ranchers started bringing in cows and whisky to feed the prospectors.

Looking at all this and wondering what would happen was James Douglas, a giant of a man with mixed blood of a Creole mother and Scottish father, who was governor of Vancouver Island. It appeared to him that the Americans would simply take over. They brought their flag and basically 99 percent of the population of New Caledonia was American.

The mainland was British property, but the British had not done anything with it except make a few tiny forts for fur trading. That was not enough to hold onto the land. The rules were simple, much as they are now. The strong man takes it, whether it is gold or land.

The Americans had taken Texas and California from the Mexicans. There was little to think they would not take New Caledonia also. Many of the tents and log cabins up and down the Fraser River had American flags flying over them. James Douglas wrote to Queen Victoria telling her that the Americans would take all the gold, probably the land, and the only thing they would leave behind would be empty whisky bottles.

It took a while for the letter to arrive. The ship had to go down to the bottom of South America and then back up the other side and then across the Atlantic. But when it did, Queen Victoria made a quick decision. She proclaimed the land filled with Americans a colony of Britain, which at least gave Britain a legal right to argue in court.

She was about to sign into law that New Caledonia was hers when someone looking at maps of the world ran into the throne room, at least that makes a good story, and told her, "Stop, Your Majesty. A New Caledonia already exists."

It was an island in the South Pacific.

"What do we know about the land?" asked the Queen.

"Well, it has the Columbia River running through it," someone said.

"Then we shall call it the colony of Columbia."

"But the Columbia River also runs through America," the aide said.

The Queen thought for a moment, then in a flash of queenly brilliance, said, "Then we shall call it *British* Columbia.

The proclamation was put on a return ship and just before the end of the year, on November 19, 1858, in the mud and the rain that would not let up, James Douglas, the governor of the new colony, signed the paper in Fort Langley, making it official. The Hudson's Bay flag came down and the British flag went up.

British Columbia was born. The non-Native population was 99 percent American. Those darn immigrants, they always change things.

JAMES DOUGLAS

James Douglas never joked, not about anything. He was afraid of being mocked. He developed a stern face. He never smiled. He was afraid he would not be taken seriously.

We have so few pictures of him. But just keep looking at this man who was the father of British Columbia and learn about the troubles a man can have, and overcome.

When James Douglas moved to Victoria it was Victorian. It was white, and all other races were beneath those who were white.

James Douglas was not white. His Scottish father was the administrator of a sugar cane plantation in Barbados. He married a local woman. Even though he was light skinned, James Douglas was not considered white in Victoria.

While he was working his way up through the ranks of the Hudson's Bay Company in a remote part of the place that is now our province, he married a woman who was also mixed. Amelia was the daughter of a Native woman and a white fur trapper.

He rose through the ranks of the Hudson's Bay Company simply by being diligent and hard-working. Also being big and strong helped.

Even when James Douglas was the governor of the colony of Vancouver Island he and his wife were invited to basically no social gatherings in the tiny capital city.

When he convinced Queen Victoria to declare the mainland a colony and stopped it from being taken over by America, most of the citizens of the new colony thought he was unfit for the job.

The recorded public words of a barely literate white woman in Victoria were:

"James Douglas," she said, "has been all his life among the Indians and has got one of them for a wife. So how can it be expected that he knows anything about governing one of the colonies of England."

Most folks agreed with her.

Few women spoke to his wife.

Together, James and Amelia had thirteen children. Four survived. One of them, a girl named Martha, was sent to a boarding school in England. There she told stories that her mother had told her about her childhood with the Natives.

The headmistress of the school told Martha that she would be allowed to tell the stories, but she could not mention that they came from her mother.

But it was only through the efforts of James Douglas that British Columbia is now under a Canadian flag in a culture made up of every race that the British flag ever flew over, which is basically every race on earth. He would be able to joke about it now.

THE GOLD IS STILL THERE

"The old guys skimmed the cream off the top, but there is still plenty of gold for all of us."

Those tempting words were spoken by a miner I met in Dawson City in the late '70s. He was neatly dressed and showed me a nugget that he kept in his pocket. It was the size of a Zippo cigarette lighter. In this non-smoking age, that means it was big. He said it was worth about $10,000.

I was astonished that he carried it with him. Wasn't he worried about being robbed?

He looked around at the vast emptiness. The Yukon is almost the size of British Columbia but has fewer people than Port Moody.

"If they took it, where would they go?" he said.

There was also a former CBC television cameraman from Montreal who saw a documentary on gold mining in the Yukon. He quit his job the next day and moved there. When we met him he was wearing a beaten-up cowboy hat with gold nuggets pinned on it. He was a happy man.

I mentioned them in an earlier book. What I did not talk about were the amateur gold panners who line rivers and streams whenever the price of gold starts going through the clouds, as it is once again.

When I saw them out there they reminded me of the words of the miner with the Zippo lighter nugget. "There's plenty left for the rest of us."

They were just south of Hope, near where the first miners stopped in

1858. They were wearing gumboots and had long-handled shovels and were digging up small scoops of gravel and dumping them into gold pans.

They could have been spending the weekend fishing, except there were no rods and no bait, just the same dream that has been in every gold miner's eye since shortly after time began.

Round and round they swirled the pan with the water and the gravel as the want-to-be-rich city folk felt the thrill that something yellow might be in there.

The object is to move the flakes of gold to the bottom of the pan because gold is heavier than the pebbles and sand. You use water to get it all to move then pour off the top layer of debris. It is the same technique that was used one hundred and fifty years ago in this same spot, and it worked then so why is it not working now?

The city miners would drive back home at night and watch the news that would tell them the price of gold had gone up yet again.

"Marge, we got to get out there tomorrow. We can make a fortune."

But the next day it rained and they stayed home.

"We don't want to get wet making a fortune."

But the following weekend the sun was out and they were back on the shores of the Fraser digging and swirling and dumping out their pans and starting again.

"There's no gold here," said Marge. "Those old miners took it all."

I met one of those old miners living in a shack hidden in the woods. He paid no rent, had no mortgage. He also had no electricity or running water. But he did have gold.

People are weird. All of us. We want things we cannot have, we want more of everything, we want bigger things, we are jealous of those who have more than we have, and criticize them for being what we want to be. And when and if we do get more, we often don't know what to do with it.

That was like the old miner I met in the woods south of Hope. In his shack with a broken front door and with his only companion an old dog, he had jars filled with gold sitting on his window sill.

The jars once held jam, but now were each worth thousands of dollars. They were lined up like beer bottles of some college kids. Except instead of being empty of brew they were filled with shiny yellow metal.

"I have looked for this all my life. It is what I do," he said.

He was from Quebec with a heavy accent. He wore a multicoloured toque. And when he shook my hand I saw he was missing two and a half fingers. He had his thumb and index finger and half his middle finger.

I looked at them and he answered without being asked.

"Lost them in the search for gold," he said.

I asked why he didn't cash this in and live in luxury.

"This is my life," he said. "This is all I want. I search for gold and live well."

I told him about the people digging down on the banks not far from his shack and how they were finding nothing.

"They are impatient," he said.

He came with us to the gold fields, the cameraman, myself and the old miner.

He watched them dig, swirl and dump.

"There's gold in those pans," he said.

He pointed to a woman who could have been a clerk or a college professor or a cop or a nurse who was working the edge of the river.

This happened before the camera, one of those things you pray for. The woman had been hunting all day for gold and was frustrated and quitting.

The old miner asked for the pan that she was holding. She had been swirling, she had been dumping and her head was slowly shaking back and forth in the universal language that said: "This is useless, this is dumb and I am quitting."

The old miner looked at the gravel and sand and said, "There probably is gold in here. Be patient."

The woman smirked.

The old guy with the multicoloured toque and missing fingers started swirling her pan, carefully pouring off a teaspoon of debris. Then he bent down, scooped up more water and did the same. Again, and again, until there was nothing left but a skimming of black sand on the bottom of the pan.

Near us we watched others swirling, dumping, digging, and swirling. They were in a hurry to become rich.

But the old miner was already rich. He had time.

I thought that this final layer of sand would be gone through on the next swirling, but no. He put water over that one layer of sand and swirled so slowly, so carefully you would think he was watching each grain slide away.

And then one more time; a little more water, just enough so the sand would move when he swirled, and then he handed the pan back to the woman.

"There's your gold," he said.

He was pointing to a speck half the size of a grain of sand.

"You're almost rich." He laughed, she laughed and we left.

At least the old miner and the cameraman and I left. When we looked back a crowd had gathered around the woman. It was like seeing someone win $10 at the lottery counter and others say, "Congratulations, wow, and what numbers did you play?"

It is easier to go to work, but once that little golden bug bites it can change a life, or a country.

How mesmerizing can that bug be?

I was with cameraman Ken Chu, who had been in Canada only a few years from Hong Kong. He made fun of his own driving. It was not racist, it was not prejudice. It was a joke between friends based on a stereotype.

"No one in Canada knows how to drive like me," he would say.

On this particular golden day we were in the basement of a high school teacher who could afford to live in the British Properties in West Vancouver, possibly the most expensive housing area in the country.

We had to promise not to publish his address or a picture of his house. But he wanted to show us his hobby, gold collecting.

He said he had read about the early miners and how they easily discovered that here in a stream or there or even over there no gold would be found. But in between those spots, ten steps from where he was standing was a deposit of flakes or nuggets or maybe a finger of gold that would keep him searching for another month, or longer, or maybe a vein that would run from here to lifelong wealth.

You never know. But this teacher had an idea. He would add just a little modernization and comfort to his quest and see what happened.

He bought a wet-dry vacuum cleaner, a scuba diving face mask and a snorkel, and from a mining supply store, a rocker, which is a small machine that does the swirling for you. To run the rocker and vacuum he got a small portable generator. Then he put a foam mattress in his Volkswagen van.

On his summer vacations from school he combed the creeks of the province, following the gold trails of the Fraser River and the Cariboo. He would walk out into the creeks, put his face down into the water with the mask on to see what he was doing, then suck up the gravel with his vacuum.

In the afternoons he would have wine and read a book while his gravel was being rocked away.

Maybe he was just lucky. Maybe he was good at figuring where gold might be. But whatever the reason, when he took us into his basement there were rows of shelves with scores of baby food jars sitting neatly on them. I have seen jars like that from other collectors. They have been filled with pens, or buttons or dead insects.

In this basement, the collection was of gold. Each jar weighed about four ounces. Gold was then selling for $800 an ounce.

The baby food jars came from his kids. He did not want to waste them.

He said he wanted to share his hobby. The opportunity is still there if you work hard enough. And then he said almost the same words as that miner in Dawson City. "The guys long ago took most of it. But there's still plenty left."

When we left, Ken kept repeating, as though it was a mantra and I was not there: "Did you see all that gold? Did you see all that gold?"

He put his van into reverse to leave the man's driveway.

"Did you see all that gold?"

He was still saying it when he drove backwards across the street and smashed into a telephone pole, bending his back bumper.

He looked at me like this had suddenly snapped him out of his trance. We both started laughing.

"Say nothing," he said to me.

We got out and looked at the bent bumper.

"Gold is very expensive," he said.

THE DUMB PIG WAR

Imagine you are looking at a map, between the bottom of Vancouver Island and the mainland of the US.

Wait. This is too unbelievable to imagine. Take a look at a map.

The map says San Juan Island is part of America. But it is way over to the west, very close to Canada. If you drew a line straight down between the islands it would seem like it naturally would belong to Canada.

This is how the line got zigged and how one dumb, arrogant bureaucrat lost the island for Canada.

When Britain and America compromised on the 49th parallel in 1818 they said the boundary of those islands would go through the middle of the strait and then continue down through the middle channel.

This was forty years before this problem popped up and everyone on both sides assumed the middle channel meant the middle, which gave San Juan Island to Britain. The Hudson's Bay Company had a trading post on the island for half a century. There were a hundred British subjects living there. It was only a rowboat ride away from Victoria.

But in a move of administrative stupidity the British got rid of an autocratic, miserable plant manager named Major DeCoursie, a title he gave himself, by exiling him to the Hudson's Bay post at San Juan. You ever have a boss you swear was a son of the devil? That was him.

At that time there were only nineteen Americans living on the island, including women and children. They were all farmers.

One day one of the Americans got tired of a pig rooting through his vegetable garden. This was a boar pig, almost wild. He shot the pig. Whoops. The pig belonged to the Hudson's Bay Company.

Instead of taking the $10 that the pig was worth, Major DeCoursie demanded $100, basically a quarter of a year's pay. He was going to show those Americans what happens when you break the British rules. Then he put the pig killer in jail, in the stockade at the trading post.

Simply speaking, that was a stupid thing to do.

The Americans got mad and sent word to their friends on the mainland. About sixty US soldiers invaded the island demanding the farmer be freed.

James Douglas, the governor of the colony of Vancouver Island, said this will never do. You can't have Americans invading a British island. The Americans will take over. He sent in a British war ship.

The Americans sent fifty more soldiers.

Douglas sent in six more war ships.

The Americans sent fifty more soldiers and ten cannons.

Douglas sent four more ships, eleven in all, and 1,500 Royal marines.

There is nothing like escalation to make a problem get larger. The Americans dug in, and the British dug in, facing each other, daring one another to shoot first.

Douglas rowed out to the island. "Don't give in," he said.

The commander of all the US armies travelled by train from Washington DC to the west coast, and then by boat to San Juan. This was an important matter.

"We will not lose to the British," he said.

But he did not want a war because, basically, the United States was moving closer to civil war and a war with Britain would not be good at this time.

The general proposed a compromise. They would pull out most of the troops and move back the others so they would not be in each other's faces. Each side left about one hundred soldiers on the island.

It would be good to be a forgotten soldier, so long as you are stationed on an island with a beautiful climate and no shooting. For the next twelve years the soldiers from the two countries faced each other with guns ready but with friendliness growing. They got to know each other quite well and shared a lot of stories and whisky across no man's land on the idyllically peaceful island.

After the Americans got though killing each other with their civil war, officials of the US and Britain would get back to the problem of the pig. But by now the pig was forgotten and the issue had become one of ownership. After all both sides had an army there. So who gets to stay?

Both countries gave the dispute to the only neutral country in Europe at that time: Germany.

The German chancellor pondered this; however, during the past decade while nothing was done about the island, about three million Germans had left Germany and immigrated to America. Basically only a trickle had gone to Canada.

As I mentioned in an earlier story, in the 1870s there were more German than English newspapers in New York.

The chancellor probably thought about this for a long minute and said he would simply side with his people. He drew a line down a map that went zip, zap, zap and zip.

"That looks like the middle, more or less," he said.

In short, San Juan became an outpost for Macy's instead of the Hudson's Bay.

If only that British guy in management had charged $10 for the pig you could take a ferry to San Juan today and you would not need a passport.

But as it turned out, the Americans so admired the British fortitude for hanging in for so long that the Union Jack is now raised every day over a park where the English soldiers had their camp. It is the only place in the entire United States to officially fly a flag of a foreign country.

MATTHEW BEGBIE

You know him as the hanging judge. And he did hang them. Thirty men swung with a rope around their necks when Judge Begbie said, "guilty and you are sentenced to death, by hanging."

But when he believed someone was innocent even though his accusers said otherwise, Begbie spent weeks and tons of brainpower going over the testimony looking for little fibs that would free the accused man.

He was a strange bird, educated at Cambridge and became a lawyer and was involved with high society, but when the crown needed someone to be the first judge of this new colony in a distant land, and they selected him, he said yes. The fancy social life was over.

He came to this land of forests and streams and rivers and fell in love with it even though he was a cultivated man who spoke French and Italian. There was little need for either here.

Unlike Britain where he would take a carriage to court, in British Columbia he was the only judge between New Westminster and Kamloops, and he took his feet to work.

Until he got a horse, he walked up the Fraser carrying his tent and his judge's robes. He listened to cases involving gold claims and murder. His courthouse was the forest and his bench a stump. When he sentenced someone to death he wore the traditional black hat that he carried in his knapsack.

And then he went fishing for dinner. The next day he walked to another camp to administer justice.

More than any other single person he turned a wide, lawless land of gold and guns into a place where arguments were settled in a dignified manner.

He did not marry. His first and only love was the law and deciding which side would win in a dispute.

But he did miss the culture of Europe. In a rare personal letter to a friend in Europe he wrote, "When you write back to me, please include gossip. I can't send you any from this place. The unisexual character of the population"—it was basically all men—"almost precludes any stories of interest."

He was a tough man who hungered for a little touch of a hot, romantic story to balance out the tales of murder and greed that he dealt with in his rustic life.

But if he were around today I think he would look at the criminal justice system and say, "This is no way to treat a criminal."

"You, for the crime of murder," he would say, "will pay with more than a half-dozen years in a cell with cablevision."

SAPPERTON AND ITS HEROES

I knew he was buried somewhere in the New Westminster Cemetery, and figured he would have at least a small headstone. It would be old and worn, so I carefully read one after another. A few of the dates were in the 1860s, some in the 1870s, and many were weather-worn beyond being readable.

A burly guy named John with tattoos covering his hands and arms asked if he could help.

"I'm looking for the grave of John Linn, one of the original Sappers," I said.

He said he could probably help me find it, but then added, "What's a Sapper?"

What's a Sapper? So sad. And such an opportunity. We live and work in places that have names and histories but sometimes we can spend our lives there and know nothing about it.

It is really not our fault. You are born at Royal Columbian Hospital right at the edge of Sapperton. You tell your friends as you grow up that you live in Sapperton so they know what part of New Westminster you are in. But unless someone says to you, "Hey, do you know how this place got its name?" it seldom occurs to us. And honestly, when was the last time in general conversation anyone said, "By the way, the price of gasoline is up and how did this place get its name?"

193

"Sappers were among the greatest, strongest, bravest guys on earth," I said to John.

That got his attention. And then he got mine.

"I'm the gravedigger here, and I'll help you find him," he said.

In his office he pulled out an ancient book, so big he needed two hands to lift it.

"This goes back to 1860," he said.

"We need 1878," I said.

He turned the big pages carefully. Each was covered with lists of neatly handwritten names and dates and locations of graves. All of the writing had been done with the sliced ends of large feathers which were dipped in ink.

"Here," he said. He was excited. He read out loud the location of the final resting place of John Linn, also known as Jock, and copied the location of the grave on the palm of his hand with a ballpoint pen.

I followed him outside. He was in a hurry.

"What's a Sapper?" he asked again.

So the story began:

In 1858 when British Columbia was a new baby wrapped in a Hudson's Bay blanket it needed protection as all babies do. James Douglas, who was the father of the new colony, asked Queen Victoria for someone to babysit the new child. Preferably a strong babysitter.

He did not ask for an army, but just enough men in uniforms to say to outsiders, "Don't try anything foolish and no one will get hurt."

The Queen sent only 160 men, but they were the best. A regiment of Sappers. Never in the history not just of BC but all of Canada had so few done so much with so little.

Sappers: the odd name came from the French, who long ago devised a method of warfare by digging zigzag trenches through which they would drag their cannons closer and closer to the enemy. The object was to keep your soldiers alive while killing the other solders, which is basically the object of all wars.

The zig and zag gouges in the earth were called *sappe* by the French. And the poor guys who had to keep digging them while the enemy was trying to kill them were called *sapeurs*.

All armies steal winning ideas from each other and when the British got hold of this they said those poor sods with shovels and guns are actually combat engineers. It is good to have a title between work and getting killed.

But the British, with unusual admiration for the French, kept the name and designation of this new breed of soldiers with just a slight English change in the spelling. As they lined up with wheelbarrows and cannons they were called Sappers.

Under the command of Colonel Richard Moody, the 160 Sappers left England in 1858, sailed around the bottom of South America and got off on the muddy banks of the new capital called New Westminster.

"Your duties are simple," we could hear the colonel telling his men. "You must patrol an area the size of France and Germany, plus the Netherlands. And keep the peace among thirty thousand men, all of whom have guns, and many have whisky, and they are all looking for gold and so they will be in a strongly protective mood.

"And in your spare time you will build roads so that the Hudson's Bay Company can sell supplies to the miners.

"And you will have to survey incredibly rugged woodlands so that we can build new towns.

"And you will be poorly paid, and you cannot look for gold yourselves.

"Could we have a rousing cheer now?"

The colonel said just one other thing. Anyone below the rank of sergeant would not be allowed to own any civilian clothing. They would have to wear that itchy red shirt whenever they were awake.

The reason was in case any of them tried to desert they would be spotted more easily.

I could see John the gravedigger starting to feel itchy.

But amazingly, not one of the Sappers did leave his post or desert his duty. They kept the peace and built the roads and laid out the towns and made their first permanent camp at the edge of where the cemetery is now, right near where the BC Pen was later built.

That is why this area is now called Sapperton.

After five years all the hard work was done and the regiment was disbanded. Everyone was offered a ride back home to England. Most of the officers, including Colonel Moody, got on board and did not look back.

All the lower-ranking men stayed, including Jock Linn. They had nothing to go back to. They were each given a small parcel of land in return for their services, and Jock Linn took his on the north shore of Burrard Inlet next to a small creek and raised a family.

Years after he died the village of North Vancouver was looking for names for its creeks and valleys. Someone remembered the old Sapper who used to live there and said his would be a fine name.

Except no one bothered to check the spelling. Hence: Lynn Valley and Lynn Creek, with a "Y," instead of an "I."

John the gravedigger had found the spot in the cemetery.

"That's where it should be," he said pointing to some grass between two graves.

He got down on his knees and started pulling away the turf with a small garden shovel. It hit something hard. He peeled back a patch of grass and under it was a flat stone, so small it could be totally covered with two hands.

John ran his fingers over it and found some grooves. He cleaned them out with his index finger. It said simply, LINN.

To call you a pioneer doesn't come close, John Linn. We salute you.

GASSY JACK

The whole time you are reading this pretend you are also listening to honky-tonk music on an old piano. They did not have honky-tonk music during this era, but it sounds good.

You are in Vancouver, in Gastown, looking at that awful statue of Gassy Jack standing on a barrel. The image is romantic. And the father of this city standing on a tipping barrel is the truth. The bad part is in the statue you can't tell if his face is a man or a glob of clay.

In the only picture we have of him, he was a good-looking guy with fat cheeks, broad shoulders and a beer belly, which makes him the perfect grandfather and many folks' idea of a founding father for any city.

Forget the politicians, forget the railroad and the lumber barons and real estate tycoons, the real father of Vancouver was a saloon keeper.

Mr. Jack Deighton, if you would use the proper form of the name, but no one ever called him Mister. He was Gassy. Gassy Jack.

But once upon a time, as all good stories begin, before there was a Vancouver there was a busy, smoky, noisy place where big trees were cut up. A sawmill, a huge one, called Hastings Mill. Somewhere in a history course you heard of that mill, and then forgot about it along with James Douglas and Colonel Richard Moody.

The Hastings Mill was amazing because you can still go there, walk there and say, "What's he talking about? There's nothing here."

Right on. If you leave the PNE and walk north across McGill Street you see a large, probably empty, park and a swimming pool called New Brighton. But keep looking, squint your eyes. Tighter. Now, can you see the sawmill, the giant sawmill, one of the largest in the world?

Smoke. Steam. Men. Horses. Shouting. Ships. And trees larger than anyone had ever seen being hauled out of the water by muscle.

Walk down to the swimming pool and right next to the men's room, darkened by time, is a bronze plaque. It says simply, "Here Vancouver began."

The plaque says "all was forest towering to the sky." They were poetic plaque writers back in those days.

What it doesn't say is that the owners of the mill had one desire, to make money.

And they took a novel approach for 1867, only nine years after the first gold rush and after the colony of British Columbia was created and in a time when men were men and men had beer and whisky whenever they wanted.

The owners of the mill forbid drinking at the mill and anywhere around logging areas. It is not just the smokers of today who find life hard.

"What? What are we going to do?" asked the men who routinely had a beer on their way to work at six in the morning, and who often would bring more to drink during lunch and whenever they felt thirsty.

"Drink and you will not work here," were the official orders. They were enforced to keep the mill running efficiently. And the mill did run well, and the men grumbled.

Jack Deighton had a saloon in New Westminster. He had started out searching for gold, but could not find any. So for a while he was a pilot on boats at the mouth of the river. But there was no money in that.

So he opened a saloon in New Westminster and called it the Globe. That was where the money was, selling beer and whisky to the gold seekers. It was also a perfect place for the one passion that Jack had: talking. In any saloon you talk a lot, and no one talked more than Jack. Stories, gossip, whatever. And in the cliché of the day, anyone who talked a lot was called gassy, as in "you gas bag." In time, Jack Deighton became Gassy Jack.

But Jack made a business mistake. He went away on vacation to what later became Harrison Hot Springs and left the saloon in the hands of an American friend. Whoops.

Sometimes you don't know how you do such a stupid thing without thinking. While Jack was away the Fourth of July popped up, and his friend, his American friend, invited everyone in town in for a drink, on the house. And everyone came. By the time Jack got back all his beer and whisky was gone and the cash drawer was empty.

Jack had to do something fast, before he got too hungry. But New Westminster by now was full of saloons and competition was tough. He figured he would start over somewhere new, somewhere where he could be in demand. He had heard about Hastings Mill and thought their no-whisky rule could mean a full house for him, if he just stepped outside the rule.

He begged and borrowed enough money to buy one barrel of whisky, loaded it into a rowboat along with his Native wife and mother-in-law and brother-in-law and started rowing. He went down the Fraser, around where Steveston is now, up past Sea Island where the airport is now, around where UBC is now, then into Burrard Inlet, still rowing, and under where the Lion's Gate Bridge is now and he kept rowing until he reached the muddy banks of a shantytown about where Water and Carroll Streets are now.

There was nothing there, but what a perfect place. It was just four blocks outside the "no drinking" boundary of the sawmill.

He stopped the first two men who walked by and offered them whisky in return for building a shack that he would call once again the Globe Saloon. In twenty-four hours they had put together a twelve by twenty-four foot room, with a bar inside to serve drinks. It probably could hold ten or fifteen if they did not mind elbows in their ribs.

On the first day it was packed. The thirsty, whisky-deprived mill workers flooded in. And then they came back for more.

In a day he had enough money to send his brother-in-law back to New West to load up another barrel and the rest of the story was simply wealth and happiness for Jack. His business thrived, he had friends, and he continued to talk like a gas bag.

Within a month there was a row of buildings behind Gassy Jack's saloon. It is sort of like putting in a Sky Train station. Immediately a row of condos grow up alongside it. Within a year there was a townsite with about fifty buildings surrounding the saloon.

Officially it was called the Granville townsite in honour of the British Colonial secretary, but everyone called it Gastown.

By all accounts Gassy Jack lived a happy life, a saloon keeper trying to earn a living and giving birth to one of the world's greatest cities just by taking one daring step outside the law of the land.

Toast, to you, Gassy.

EMILY CARR

If you came to visit and she did not like you, and she did not like most people, she would pull a rope which was attached to a pulley in the ceiling. The other end of the rope was tied to the only other chair in the room. The chair would go up and you would have no place to sit.

In modern terms, she would be called an eccentric nut case. We are outside the Emily Carr School of Art on Granville Island. What do you know about her?

"I know she painted trees. That's about all I know."

Speaking was an art student with paint-spattered hands.

Yes, she painted trees. Over and over and over she painted trees, weird-looking trees, heavy, strange trees that never looked in the forest like they do on her canvases. But you sure knew they were trees the likes of which you had never seen before and you either loved her art or hated it. Most hated it.

"I don't know if I have any thoughts about her. I just have an image. You know, an image of the trees," said a woman artist sitting cross-legged out front of the school.

The Emily Carr school does not teach about Emily Carr. It teaches young artists who are as free and nutty as Emily Carr to be free and nutty, which is what artists should be. In fact, that is the only kind of artist that Emily liked.

She also painted totem poles. She loved painting totem poles. She loved being around aboriginals even though she really did not try to understand them and they certainly did not understand her.

When she went to France to study art and to paint she said one of the best things about being there was that she did not speak French, and almost no one she met spoke English. She got along with smiles and nods. That was communication enough for a woman who liked the person she was inside her own head better than those she met outside it.

A young man coming out of the school was asked the same question: What do you know about her?

He bobbed and weaved while giving his answer.

"Emily Carr was like someone who was like, you know, like way out, like weird," he said.

Emily Carr's thoughts were also a little difficult to follow.

Her life, though, was impossible to avoid. She was different. She was a misfit, right from the time she was a little girl in Victoria at the height of the Victorian age. Little girls were supposed to be sweet and nice and clean and starched and obedient and quiet.

Emily Carr rolled in the dirt, planted her tiny feet and said "No" to adults. She fought authority, and she was rude to those she did not like.

Yes, she sounds like most kids you know today. But in the 1870s in Victoria she was an endless embarrassment to her family. She had a mind of her own, a rarity for a girl in those days.

"I like her, because the little I know about her she rebelled against her family," said a young art student with expensive sneakers and newly bought pants that had holes in them for which she paid extra.

As well as in France, she studied art in England and California. Art became her solitary life. The society she saw around her was stiff and lifeless, she said. She liked her pets more than any people.

She said she first started painting in the woods not so much because she liked trees, but because she did not want to be around people, and people did not go into the woods. When she began painting totem poles they were mostly in abandoned villages. The poles are now gone. If not for her art there would be no memory of them.

But after all her work, and all her studies, she could not sell a single painting. Victorian men and women wanted paintings that were nothing more than ornaments in their Victorian homes. Art was then looked upon as a decoration of approved subjects, which were almost always scenes of an English countryside that really did not exist, except in the paintings, and artists were seen only as presenters of those mythical but nice countrysides.

Emily, in her forty-second year, gave up painting. She put down her brush and said this was useless. And she was hungry.

She became a landlady in Victoria and entered the most depressing period of her life. She hated her tenants more than she hated other people because she had to clean their floors and dishes and cook for them. This was not the way life should be. She wanted to be free of the social restraints, and now she was a servant to those who believed in the restraints.

She wrote that her tenants were a bitter collar around her neck. She needed them to make a living. Beyond that, she could not wait for them to move out. And then more moved in.

But then something happened. How do things like this occur? You could search the books of all histories and religions and still not have an answer. Why do things happen, sometimes?

After fourteen years of not painting, a government curator who was working for the National Gallery was sent to British Columbia to find paintings for an exhibit of west coast native art. He discovered some paintings of totem poles. He thought a Native had made them.

When he found Emily he offered her a return trip railroad ticket to Ottawa. Her paintings would be displayed in the National Gallery.

She was threadbare broke. She took the tickets and went across the country with her art.

And there she was discovered by some members of the Group of Seven, the most powerful group of artists in the country. They liked what she was doing.

Suddenly, she was about to become famous. But recognition did not change the way she saw life. She fought everything she thought was phony, and that was basically everything in the straitjacket of Victorian life where women were expected to be pleasant, serving and anonymous.

"I think I heard that she had it hard being a woman," said a student smoking a cigarette and wearing rings through her ears and lips and nose.

What hurt Emily the most during her later years when her art was being accepted was that critics said it was impossible that a woman could make great art or have creative thoughts. Even her few friends said she painted like a man.

She spent her last years with her monkey and dog and pet rats, and she died still boycotting a world that would not let her live life as she wanted to live it. She would not allow those who were so proper and polite to hammer her into an obedient mold.

To call her an artist with paintings in museums is only the first line of the story. She was a rebel against small-minded, self-righteous, self-pious, socially constrained Victorians. Her brush was her sword.

And even if they don't know much about Emily, many of the students at the Emily Carr school are just like her.

BILLY MINER

There is a Billy Miner Pub in Maple Ridge, which is odd because Billy Miner drank sparingly. He did not want to give up to a bottle the little bit of freedom that he squeezed out of life.

There is a Billy Miner chocolate dessert in The Keg restaurant, strange again because a large part of his diet was bread and water.

And there is a picture of him at the entrance to the Keg restaurants. He is a lean, aging leather-faced cowboy wearing a cowboy hat with a large brim.

He seldom wore cowboy clothes. He either bought the finest suits available, or he wore striped prison shirts and pants with a number on the back.

Billy Miner was a train robber, a hold-up man, a gunslinger, a no-good criminal vermin who spent most of his life in prison, escaping prison or hiding out from the law.

On the other hand you don't name desserts after men like that. He was also a hero to ranchers and farmers in British Columbia, a distinguished gentleman who was good to children and old folks, and although he carried a gun he never killed anyone.

How do you come to be a criminal? Well, having a brutal, drunken father is not always the cause, but it helps. I cannot analyze how it happened. Criminal psychologists try to do that and have not figured it out yet.

The facts are that as a teenager Billy Miner started robbing stagecoaches.

And he was caught. While he was a teenager he was locked up in San Quentin prison in California.

Beatings from guards were commonplace. They used thick rubber hoses. And they would tie a prisoner's hands behind him. Then they would attach a rope to his wrists and sling the rope over an overhead bar and pull the hands and arms up and the pain would be unbearable.

The prisoner would scream and go on his toes. Screaming was just part of the fun for the guards. Begging did no good. The practice in San Quentin then was to leave the prisoner like that until he passed out from the pain.

Sexual brutality was rampant. The older, stronger prisoners had their way, repeatedly, with the younger inmates. Billy Miner was one of the youngest. And there was no one to complain to.

He was in and out of prison. There were no education or counselling services. By the time he was in his young fifties he had spent more than thirty years in damp, noisy cells. He had been beaten and locked in solitary confinement, which meant no light, no toilet, only bread and water, and a concrete floor to sleep on, which the guards threw water on to make it more uncomfortable.

The only reason I give you so much detail is despite his suffering somehow he came out of that as a gentle man, well-spoken and kind. No one can understand the strength of the human spirit.

His only overriding problem was he did not know any other way to make a living. But robbing stagecoaches was finished now because while he was in prison stagecoaches were replaced by trains.

So he robbed trains. And with the money the first thing he did was buy the best clothing he could find. He looked distinguished. And then he moved to Princeton, BC, to avoid American law enforcement. As a personality you could not top Bill Miner: polite, gentle, well-read, kind to children and old folks, generous and neat and tidy.

He changed his name to George Edwards and for seven years lived as a most respected gentleman, who occasionally had to go away for business.

One of those business trips was to Mission where he boarded the Canadian Pacific's Imperial Limited, westbound to Vancouver. At Silverdale he and an accomplice ordered the engineer to stop the train.

Then he had them uncouple the baggage car from the rest of the train.

They left the passenger cars behind and ordered the engineer to drive to Whonock.

There they emptied the safe of the modern equivalent of six million dollars in gold and securities. It was this country's first train robbery.

There was outrage in the CPR's head office. The railroad had no insurance and was libel for the loss, and even worse, it hurt its reputation. Folks would stop shipping gold and bonds on the train if it could be so easily held up.

"Catch him at all costs," said the railroad police.

Three years later he was caught, but by then George Edwards had become one of the most popular men in the province.

No one came right out and said they thought he was Billy Miner but they were proud that he might be. When the police came snooping around they said they never heard of such a man.

"Nope, not around here. No one like that."

Bill Miner was their hero, because they said the CPR stole from the ranchers and farmers and Billy Miner only stole from the CPR. He did not give much money to the poor, but it was still close enough for them to call him their Robin Hood.

Because of his previous crimes he was sentenced to life in prison.

The trial was held in Kamloops and when the train left with Bill Miner onboard a band came out to play, not because he was a criminal in shackles surrounded by guards, but because he was their hero.

When the train neared New Westminster the authorities learned there were so many people waiting at the station to greet him that they wanted to take him off early and then sneak him into the prison. The train slowed at Sapperton about three miles before the scheduled stop, but there were hundreds of people lining the tracks waiting to wave at Bill.

More crowds were waiting at the New West Station. This was not the way to instill humility in a train robber.

He was transferred to a wagon and when it pulled up to the entrance of the stone-walled prison there were hundreds of local residents waiting for him.

"Hi, Bill. How you doing, Bill? When you get out come and visit us."

His reputation was so good and his appearance so suave and gentle that the daughter of the deputy warden took a special interest in him and wanted to save his soul.

He was sixty-two years old, an elder statesman of prisons and holdups and charm and politeness. He had many visits with prison officials possibly because of the influence of the deputy warden's daughter, or possibly because of an outside influence. We will never know.

Soon after he went behind the grey walls he was transferred from the prison shoe shop to the brickmaking yard. And there he and three accomplices dug a hole under a fence, slipped through it, then used a ladder to climb the wall to freedom.

When their escape was discovered there was a half-hour delay in chasing them while guards locked all the other prisoners in their cells.

The three who went with Miner were quickly recaptured. Miner never was.

"I would like to ask the Prime Minster, how did such a thing happen without inside help?"

There was thunder in the Parliament in Ottawa. The questions went on. The answers never came. But the CPR stopped whining about its missing securities.

More than likely there was a deal. The CPR got back its stolen papers, Bill kept the gold and moved to Georgia where, naturally, he robbed another train.

He was caught, imprisoned and escaped again. It seems like robbing trains, getting caught and escaping were his best qualities. If he had put that energy and talent into running a business or a city or country we would have had a better world.

He died behind bars. Usually when a prisoner perished without family his remains were given to a medical school to practise on.

Bill Miner had already become so popular in the community in Georgia that the citizens paid for his funeral. It was the first, and last time, that happened.

In New Westminster, just outside the old BC Pen, which is now a comfortable housing subdivision, there is a street named Miner.

It is the first, and last time, that has happened.

PAULINE JOHNSON

It is amazing that it ended like this, her face and her name carved in stone. You are looking at a profile of a Native woman, but she is not really Native. No, her image is somewhat different. But she wears a Native headband with a feather in the back, and her necklace is made of bear claws. The top of her dress across her shoulder seems to be made of buckskin with fringe.

The white Victorian women of the late 1800s and early 1900s did not dress like this. They would not associate with anyone who dressed like this. They would not talk to them, only about them.

The name carved below her image: E. Pauline Johnson. 1861–1913.

She did not use her first name, Emily. She was simply Pauline Johnson, and at the time the memorial was placed she was the most well-known woman in the English-speaking world.

You sure would not have believed it in the beginning. Her grandparents on both sides said words to the effect:

"Poor Pauline, we hope she doesn't suffer. She's the child of a mixed marriage, her health is not good and she is, after all, just a girl. The best we can hope for is that she gets married at a young age."

Even though her father was a chief, since she was born on a reserve she automatically became a ward of the British government. But she was too sickly to attend residential schools like her older sisters. So her English mother taught her at home, and she taught her well, and she taught her poetry.

Pauline also listened to the stories from her aboriginal relations. And then she turned the stories into poems and a magazine in New York bought a few of them.

Simply put. "Wow! Mother! Father!! Look!!!"

At a time when not much, at least not creatively, was expected of white women and even less of Native women and even less of women mixed Native and white, Pauline started pouring out poems about everything.

She even wrote one about a body of water that she paddled her canoe around in the young park named after Lord Stanley. It was a beautiful lagoon, but in extreme low tide it almost disappeared. She played with words and images and wrote a poem she called "The Lost Lagoon." She had a way with words and images.

That was before the road was built through the park which cut the lagoon in half, sealing up part of it and turning it into a lake. But we still use the name Pauline gave it, even though it is no longer lost, nor a lagoon. She would have laughed at that.

She did a lot of laughing. We have no copies of the ad lib remarks that she made during speeches, but all of the reports of them were the same. "Pauline Johnson is very humourous. She is a jokester. She made the audience howl."

She was, in effect, our first standup comic.

She took her poems and stories on the road, going on speaking tours. She travelled by wagon in remote villages of Ontario and British Columbia, telling and retelling the stories and comedy of her Native ancestors and her white mother.

From Canada she branched out to the US and then England. This was the girl they hoped would marry young and disappear.

In her one-woman show she wore buckskin and bear claws and feathers and then halfway through her talk she would switch to high society dresses. Canada was a place like nowhere else in the world. People of nature who wore a silk dress.

Pauline Johnson lived in a small apartment in the West End of Vancouver. But when she was not in there she was in Stanley Park where she spent literally all of her time. She wrote about Siwash Rock and the flowers and trees. She explored the park and wrote about it and loved it.

When she was dying of breast cancer at fifty-two she had one wish, to be buried in the park. But there were rules against that.

However, this was Pauline. Her grave with her ashes is a few steps away from the Sequoia Grill, which used to be called the Tea House restaurant. It is strange that there are no sequoias in Stanley Park. Pauline would have said some funny things about that.

She is officially the only person buried in the park. She requested that she have no headstone. That was Pauline. You got to love a person who has such humility.

But there is also human nature to deal with. In 1922 the Woman's Canadian Club decided just before the tenth anniversary of her death that she needed a memorial, so they erected one over her buried ashes.

Her grave became a shrine. At the beginning of the 1900s when people heard of Canada they pictured Pauline.

Pauline would have said something funny about that too.

A small candy company named themselves after her. Pauline would have laughed.

And then she disappeared. We don't read much poetry any more. I asked ten younger Canadians who I work with about Pauline Johnson and none of them had ever heard of her.

But while she lived she overcame prejudice without ever complaining and made a living by writing about the good parts of her life and her country.

After the story ran on the air I got a letter from Mavis Toll of Vernon. She said they had to memorize Pauline Johnson in school. This was in the late 1930s and '40s. She sent me a copy of one of the most famous poems of Pauline's: "The Song My Paddle Sings."

The last stanza is:

And up on the hills against the sky,
A fir tree, rocking its lullaby,
Swings, swings,
Its emerald wings,
Swelling the song that my paddle sings.

Thank you, Mavis.

Thank you, Pauline.

And if your grandparents had only lived long enough they would have bragged, "We knew she could do it. We never worried at all. We were rooting for her all the time."

JOE FORTES

"Seraphim, what the heck kind of name is Seraphim?"

Seraphim turned around slowly.

"Come on, tell us, where the heck did you get a name like that?"

Seraphim faced the drunk and said, "My sainted mother gave it to me."

Did it happen just like that? Well, probably, because Vancouver was just a tiny, miserable, cold village in 1884. In fact, it was not even Vancouver. The village was still called Granville, and there were more saloons than grocery stores and Seraphim was a bartender.

He was also just approaching his twentieth birthday and was tall and powerful. He was also the only black man you would probably see all day, or all week or month.

There were a lot of strong, tough guys in town. Most of them cut down trees or hauled lumber with no chainsaws or forklifts to help them. But Seraphim was stronger. And fearless.

Joe Fortes now is a trendy eating place. So who was Joe? We asked nicely dressed, good-looking patrons going in for a wine and steak.

"Was he a cook?" asked a smiling-faced guy with his arm around a pretty young woman.

"It's a restaurant. I'm just guessing," he said, somewhat apologetically after he realized that his BlackBerry was still in his pocket and the answer was not in his head.

"He was a lifeguard," I told him.

"Oh," he said, with a tone that made it clear that that was the most disappointing answer we could give.

"Not a cook, huh?"

Cooks are now IN. Lifeguards are not.

But in the late 1800s and early 1900s one lifeguard was the most well-known, well-loved, well-respected, most trusted, most admired man in the city.

But first his name had to be changed.

At the same time as Seraphim was tending bar, most of the songs people knew and sang were slow and had simple lyrics. Stephen Foster, who was drinking himself to death, wrote the songs that everyone sang.

"Oh! Susanna" was the anthem of the California gold rush.

"Jeanie with the Light Brown Hair," and "Camptown Races" are still recorded in popular music.

And "Old Black Joe."

In 1950 in a public school in New York City we sang "Old Black Joe" with the principal playing the piano in front of the auditorium. They did not tell us that Stephen Foster drank himself to death at thirty-six in a flophouse in the Bowery. He had feeling and poetry, just no common sense.

Gone are the days when my heart was young and gay.
Gone are my friends from the cotton fields away,
Gone from the earth to a better world I know.
I hear their gentle voices calling, "Old Black Joe."

The song is now banned. We do not have Old Black Joes any longer. We do not remember or speak of the cotton fields. When that song was written Old Black Joe was a slave.

But when Seraphim was standing behind the bar everyone knew that song.

"You're Old Black Joe," said the drunk looking at the young black man whose name was not Joe.

But Joe Fortes was born.

He was seventeen when he left Barbados, the child of a black woman and a Spanish man. He left the island on a sailing ship on which he would do any work they gave him, and he ended in Liverpool where he earned a living cleaning toilets.

He arrived at the Hastings Mill a few years later on a ship that was supposed to take on a load of lumber, but the ship sank and so he had to stay around the new town, but that would be just for a while, until he could get on another ship.

Then came work in the bar, and living in a flophouse on a muddy street in what was being called Gastown.

We don't know how or when or why it happened, but there was a day that he wandered away from the boasting and arguing men in the bar and walked until he could walk no further.

He stopped at a large bay. It was probably summer and he stripped off at least his shirt and went into the water.

In Barbados he swam like a fish. In Liverpool he won several swimming races. In English Bay he found a home.

The newspaper articles about him say he pitched a tent right next to the water and began swimming every day. This was an age when most men could barely float and no woman would go further than getting her knees wet.

In a short time he built a shack, which was near where the Sylvia Hotel now stands, and supported himself with labouring jobs.

As more and more people began to spend the summer at the bay he made himself the guardian of the beach. In the record books he saved twenty-nine lives. Unofficially, he saved hundreds.

At the turn of the century the city gave him the title of the job he had been doing for free for ten years and gave him a small salary, enough so that he could stop searching for odd jobs and now spend all his time at the beach.

Just before World War I the city wanted to clear away the shacks that were lining the beach. Joe was not the only one who liked waterfront views. The city crews moved in, got the folks and their belongings out, then set fire to the shacks.

Until they came to Joe's shack. There they found more than a hundred local citizens surrounding Joe's home.

"You are not going to burn this one," they said. "Joe is our friend."

It was a standoff, at least for a while. But Joe had friends in City Hall even though he did not know any of them personally. Again, what exactly happened is not known, but it is easy to guess that the mayor and aldermen were hearing from their wives and children how this old black man had saved, "Who? You mean he saved him and her and him and her?"

And the list went on. And the city fathers had a very wise moment of insight. If they wanted to go home to a family that would not hate them for the rest of their lives they would do something about Joe's home.

The next day several wagons were roped together and the city crews hoisted the small cottage on the wagons and a team of horses pulled it several blocks away to Beach Avenue.

They gently placed it in its new home and gave him an official address, 1708 Beach, less than a block from the bandstand. Joe was now living in the cultural, musical and happy centre of the world he stood guard over.

He spent the rest of his life there, saving lives and teaching children to swim. Basically every child who was raised in Vancouver in the 1890s and early 1900s and who went to the beach learned to swim from Old Joe.

He never married, that would not happen in white Victorian society. But in the evenings and during the winter he had a never-ending stream of visitors. He was everyone's grandfather and friend.

He died of pneumonia in January 1922 in Vancouver General Hospital. As his funeral cortege, pulled by two horses, rode along East Hastings hundreds of men, women and children lined the route. As it turned up Granville more came out to say goodbye. As it approached Davie Street thousands were standing silently.

When the horses finally stopped at the beach where he lived and made his home and friends, tens of thousands were waiting for him.

In 1927 a drinking fountain with his image on it was installed near the bandstand, near where his home was. It is still there.

In 1986 this man who arrived with nothing was named Citizen of the Century.

To the young couple who went into Joe Fortes Chop House: it is entirely possible that Joe Fortes saved one of your great-great-grandparents from drowning. Just think if he had not.

THE LIVING ROLLER COASTER

It seems impossible, but the story of life has so much pain and joy packed into half a week.

Monday I am on East Hastings talking to poor people who hear voices inside their heads. The voices are real and they shout, and when you listen to someone who is holding his head to stop the screaming inside you ache inside.

When they grab their heads to push away the voices that are tormenting them and you are standing there watching and hearing nothing you feel so weak.

I talked to Robbie, who looks sixty and is forty, and when he tries to get a job they tell him there are no jobs available and he walks out of the store and looks at a sign in the window that says "Help Wanted."

And we talked to Jazz, who is young and is wearing much makeup, and she tells us "they have to open the window, just open the window." We have no idea what she is talking about, but she keeps repeating "they have to open the window."

They need help. But they are on East Hastings and most everyone drives home on Broadway or Oak or over the Lion's Gate and so they are invisible. They show up on television once in a while or they are seen when you make a mistake and drive down East Hastings and you say, "This is unbelievably pathetically terrible. Something has to be done."

And years go by and nothing is done.

The day after that story I got phone calls from parents of kids who were in Riverview and then got released and then killed themselves.

And then life goes on.

The next day we are looking for happiness because I do not want another soul-crushing story. However, I have to go to the bathroom and so Mike Timbrell, the chief cameraman, tells me he will go to a nearby Starbucks.

But when we get there it is closed.

Closed??!! You can't be closed! I have to use your toilet.

But they mouth the words through the window that the power is out. An idea strikes like a gift from the heavens.

No power?? Well then, let's do a story about no power.

Mike gets his camera and we talk to the people in an insurance company and a Telus store and a Subway sandwich shop about working without electricity. Everyone is up for the challenge and funny and friendly and a short time later we are done. Miraculous, amazing. I don't know how that happens. From nothing to a something that makes you smile in a few minutes.

But I still have to go to the bathroom. The manager of the Subway shop points to the back of the store and gives me a flashlight. Joy and relief, even if it's in the dark.

And the next day, we meet the old fisherman who has the strength of a man who has worked with his back and arms all his life. He picks up things in his storage lockup that neither cameraman Karl Casselman nor I can budge off the floor, and Karl is very strong.

Presto, another story. Another moment of joy and admiration of someone who may be seventy-two years old, but does not give in to the years.

Pain and happiness, tears and laugher between Monday and Wednesday. Homeless, schizophrenic drug addicts to a dark toilet to a humble, hardworking retiring fisherman.

It is called life, hang on for the ride.

THE BIG COJONES

"We can't say that," I said to Karl Avesfelt.

"Well, there's no other way to say it," he said. "They got big cojones."

Karl is the editor choosing the pictures that are going into the story about the linemen for Hydro who are two hundred feet up a steel tower next to Highway 1 in Burnaby. Just looking at them on the tape on the TV in his edit room is making my cojones shrink to safety.

"They got cojones," says Karl. "Big ones."

"I am not saying that on the air," I say.

I record the next line of the story.

"They define the word brave. They give meaning to cool courage," I say into the microphone.

Karl takes the mic from me and says into it, "And they have big cojones."

I got to admit, even to him, that it sounds better than what I said, but I am not allowing cojones in a story that is going out at dinner hour, so he erases it.

"And you don't," he says to me.

We start yelling at each other in the friendly, loud exchange of ideas that fills Karl's room every day when he thinks he can write better than the writer, which is usually true.

"Will you guys stop arguing about cojones," shouts Ron Tupper, who is in his edit room a few feet away across a dark hallway. "I'm up to my butt in problems here and all you're worrying about is cojones." He used the English equivalent for cojones.

The fact that cameraman Karl Casselman's voice is in the story saying "holy, s . . ." while he is describing what he is seeing through his telephoto lens is irrelevant. He is taking a close-up picture of a guy basically strolling along a thin steel girder twenty stories up over the highway.

"Holy, s . . ." I'm thinking too. The word may be vulgar, but it fits, and besides he muttered it, so it was not clear enough for me to lose my job.

"But no cojones," I say again.

"These are men, real men in one of the last jobs that men do," says Karl, "and they have cojones."

At that moment Doriana Temelo walks down the hallway. She used to be an anchor in the '80s and now is a producer on Global National. She is tall and bright and beautiful.

"Stop," says Karl to her, "Can we use cojones to describe these guys?"

She looks at the picture of men up near the clouds and says, "I was up there once doing a story about them."

So much for the real men theory. And so much for Karl proving his cojone theory with Doriana.

He goes down the hallway looking for support. Editing is not a passive art.

He finds Marco DenOoden, who is in charge of grabbing satellite images out of the air and putting them on TV. Marco reads a lot, he always has a book in front of him. He even reads through his lunch break, so you know he is a smart guy.

"Can we use cojones?" Karl asks Marco.

Marco has a kind of puzzled look. "I guess so," he says.

"Why you siding with him?" I ask.

"Cojones are okay," he says. "It means courage."

Karl is gloating.

"Okay, you're right, but we're not using it," I say.

Then Marco comes in the room in a rush.

"I didn't know it meant THAT," he said. He had just looked it up on the Internet.

"Ha," I say to Karl.

The story was wonderful. Karl as usual contributed half the lines and chose the best of the best pictures. The order that pictures go in can make or break a story. He makes them.

But there were no cojones in it. Just really brave guys who have something many of us don't.

THE SHOES IN THE WASHROOM

Everyone loves inside, behind-the-scenes scoops. This is the juiciest of them all.

There is something going on in a men's toilet at Global News that should be shared with the world because you will then know we are just ordinary mortals, like other forgetful people.

Someone left their shoes behind. They are sitting on top of the heater near the sink and have been there for three weeks.

How does anyone walk away without their shoes? Didn't they notice their socks were less than comfortable when they left the building? When they got up in the morning didn't they see a space on the floor where their shoes should be?

One of the most popular stories I ever did for television was about a shoe in the middle of the street. Everyone has seen them and it is a mystery on how they get there.

Perhaps someone drank too much and forgot to tie their laces and the shoe fell off while they staggered home. Or perhaps they were having a lover's intimate moment in the back of a taxi cab with one foot sticking out the window and no one wanted to stop whatever it was they were doing just to grab a falling shoe.

Those are reasonable ways to lose a piece of leather tied around your foot.

But not in the bathroom of the major television news station in British Columbia. No way. We are sober journalists, no staggering allowed. And no office affairs, at least none that I know of. We are too busy trying to uncover the affairs of politicians to have time for any of our own. And if anyone did do such a thing in the newsroom you could be sure that shoes would be the last things to be removed. We keep our priorities right.

And why two shoes? How does anyone lose two shoes? They could have been put there because they were wet from snow or rain, and another pair worn home. But no guy on this planet goes out in the morning with extra shoes. Women do that, but they are smart. Guys are lucky if they remember to change their socks.

I checked below the cuffs of all the anchors. But anchors dress way too well to go to work without shoes.

And I checked all the hardworking reporters, but they of course walk over hot coals and broken glass to gather the news, so they don't dare lose their shoes.

I would have checked the executives on the top floor but their carpets are so thick you cannot see their feet, and besides, they have their own washroom.

They are still there today, size 11—I checked—black leather dress shoes. The custodian is too kind to remove them.

If you see any Global employee walking around town with worn-out socks yelling "Ouch," tell him to go to the bathroom in the northwest corner of the newsroom.

He will owe you big time.

P.S.

Two months later the shoes were moved to just outside the door of the washroom. A month later they were pushed to the other side of the entrance to the newsroom next to a large potted plant. They are still there.

MOUNTAINTOP RESTAURANT

One of the most amazing stories I have ever been at was at the top of the Lion's Mountain, the twin peaks that literally loom over Vancouver. I have written about it before, but then this year something happened.

Often climbers and skiers get lost in the mountains around the peaks and they are rescued by a volunteer group of fantastic individuals who at a moment's notice, usually in the middle of the night when they are sleeping, usually when it is raining and cold, or snowing and cold and dark and windy and dangerous, go out and save them.

They don't ask who, they don't ask why and they don't ask for pay. They are honest to god heroes who are the usual assortment of office workers, mechanics, a few doctors and even a lawyer or two over the years. They love to climb mountains. They are good at it and when someone gets lost in the mountains they get out of bed, put on their boots and raingear and go out into the dark and find them.

And then came the day sometime in the late '70s when they had a celebration dinner. They could have gone to a fancy restaurant. They could have gone to a park for a picnic. But not these guys. They are mountain people.

They looked up at the Lions and said, "That's our restaurant."

Straight up the side they went. On their backs they carried two long tables and chairs, a grill and charcoal, a boom box and steaks and potatoes and corn on the cob and wine, and then they added fancy candelabras and red tablecloths and napkins and dinner plates and forks and knives and butter and bread.

Up and over the top on the peak on the left, the highest one, and they were in their world. And then came out the tuxedos and floor-length gowns and dance shoes and the music played and they set out a formal dinner for twenty up where the air was thin and crisp.

I was a wimp. I flew up in a helicopter along with camerawoman Naomi Stevens. She filmed the entire amazing event. After dinner they had Grand Marnier and then danced in their make-believe ballroom in the sky.

And all the time the music was going and the feet were waltzing Naomi and I were leaning over the edge watching a fellow slowly pulling himself up the side of the mountain. It is tough near the top, nothing but rock and crevices to pinch your fingers around, and when you get up that high you think you have really accomplished something.

Naomi filmed the climber as he struggled. She filmed him as he got closer. She filmed him as his head crept up to the top and she filmed his eyes as he saw a crowded ballroom where there should have been barren rock.

She filmed him as one of the rescuers in his tux approached the man and asked, "Do you have reservations?"

They cooked a steak for him. These are not people who abandon anyone.

I have told and written about this story so many times it is like a piece of comfortable music. It makes me feel good. But then last Christmas I was at a party where a woman in her early thirties introduced herself to me. She said her father was the man in the tux who asked about the reservation. She was so proud. She was a little girl then but after the story was on TV and they all watched it together just after her father came down from the mountain, she said she could not believe what he had done. She spent years after that bragging about him.

When the young woman told me the story twenty-five years later she was still bragging. It's good to grow up with someone who makes you proud.

Naomi and I flew down with the helicopter. At the bottom we looked up. There were barely a few dots at the top of the peak, at that exclusive private dinner club that was open to only the most truly select clientele.

We are all footmen at their table.

THE SAINT OF COOKIES

For almost ten years the firemen in West Point Grey did not buy dessert. They had the cookie angel.

"Here she comes. Here comes Margaret." And the door to the fire hall would be pushed open by a muscular young man and under his nose would pass the aroma of warm cookies.

Margaret would go inside and put the plate on a long table and be immediately surrounded by a dozen firemen. That, I am told, is a woman's idea of heaven.

Margaret Green was old and sick when her husband frantically pushed in 911 on their phone. His wife was not breathing.

Within minutes the sirens were stopping outside his door and the firemen were inside putting life back into his wife's body.

Her doctor told her that five minutes more and she would have been dead.

Instead, because they got there quickly, because they did what they knew how to do, she lived and so she did the only thing she knew how to do to thank them. She baked.

She baked them cookies and cheesecakes and pies. Other fire halls came to steal her cookies. She did not mind. She baked every other day for more than fifteen years.

When I met her she was inside the fire hall giving out cookies when the bell rang. The bell that meant someone else was dying, or that a building was burning, or that a car had crashed and someone was trapped and screaming and in pain. And her boys dropped their cookies and ran to the trucks and left.

"I pray for them," she said.

She stood alone in Fire Hall Number 19.

The trucks vanished and her cookies grew cold. It did not matter. Her heroes would be back.

"I ask the Lord to bring them back safely," she said.

Others might have brought cookies and said thank you after being rescued. They might have done it once, and it would have been appreciated. Most who are rescued always mean to, but never quite get around to, saying thanks.

Margaret brought fresh cookies to the fire hall more than two thousand times. Only an angel could be that warm.

A LESSON IN SHAKESPEARE

So you have a story of someone killing another, perhaps a father, or a brother. And there is someone who sets up the murder. And that is followed by guilt, so bad that it cannot be washed away even if the skin was worn off by scrubbing.

Or perhaps you have two men in love with one woman and they get into disguises to find out who she loves the most but the disguises get switched and who you think she loves is not who she loves.

And there is always a clown, who is fat and jolly and lets you breathe in the middle of the story and you laugh before going back into deep despair. And we are not finished yet. Suppose you hear someone say something and suddenly the deepest problem of your life is right there, exposed and solved.

Not bad for one ink-stained writer who turned out play after play five hundred years ago just to keep himself in beer and kidney pies.

Some say Shakespeare did not write his plays. Who cares? It does not matter if they were written by Sir Francis Bacon or anyone else, the truth is they exist and the finest stories in the western world are all in one book by one writer and every story on "Law and Order" and comedy by Chris Rock somewhere had its roots in a play by Willy Shakespeare.

You should clear your appointment calendar and sit down and read *Hamlet*. Read it slowly so you get the meaning of the words. When the actors onstage say them they come too fast. The audience understood what they were saying when they were first performed but we are accustomed to a slightly simpler version of the same language and generally pay less attention to anything that has words. Look at a beer commercial—no words, just women and beer.

And so when Bard on the Beach has its rehearsals I try to do a story. But what? I have done the setting up of the stage, the costume makers, the battle scenes and the backstage workers.

And then there he was, like in a play by Shakespeare, the lost man. He was Richard Au, a photographer for the *Sing Pao* newspaper, taking pictures of the rehearsal.

I have seen him at fires and crime scenes and press conferences. He is a member of the true working press, a camera in hand and an eye looking for something to make page one. He is Chinese. He is an immigrant who speaks passable English. He is in the tent where Shakespeare is performed. He is lost. There is no blood. There are no guts. There are no corrupt politicians.

I take advantage of the poor and the innocent.

"What do you know about Shakespeare?" I ask Richard.

He looks at me like, what am I doing asking him? He is just a poor, lowly photographer hoping to get a shot and then move on to his next assignment.

"I know he made plays," he said. His assignment editor had told him that.

"Do you know anything else?" I ask.

He shakes his head.

At that moment Christopher Gaze sees him and overhears the question. Christopher Gaze created Bard on the Beach. He started playing Shakespeare in England and turned it into a career. He is a brilliant actor and director. And he knows what Shakespeare would have done with such an opportunity in front of him.

"Would you like to learn some Shakespeare?" he steps forward and asks Richard.

Richard only wants to get his picture and get out but he is polite. He nods his head.

"Say this, 'All the world's a stage.'"

Richard tries, but his English has been learned on the street and "All the world's a stage" is like shifting gears without pushing down on the clutch. It is grinding and misses.

Christopher is wise.

"Good," he says. "Try again."

"All the world's a stage and all the men and women merely players."

Christopher's play is being rehearsed on the stage right behind him but he is ignoring it in favour of teaching an ESL photographer one amazing line of literature.

He reminds me of a time when I was interviewing Jimmy Pattison about some matter of business and I was a young reporter and had not yet started doing stories at the back of the show. After the interview with Jimmy and when the camera was put away he said to me, "Do you understand anything of what I just said?"

I said no, but I'm sure it would make sense to those who need to know.

"Not good enough," he said. "Forget the camera, just sit down."

For the next thirty minutes he explained the economics behind what he had been talking about. He told me the history of similar stories and the theories of what happens when world events influence local activities. He was not saying what he was doing was right or wrong, he was not defending his position. He was a university teacher giving a lecture to a classroom of one.

He had already made his point on camera. He was earning maybe two or three hundred dollars an hour, maybe more. He had half a dozen businesses to run. I was a nobody.

When he finished he asked if I understood. I said yes. He got nothing out of that half-hour. I got an education.

Christopher Gaze was doing the same.

". . . and all the men and women merely players. That means we are all in a play."

Richard tried over and over and finally got it: "All the world's a stage and all the men and women merely players."

He was so delighted he smiled and asked Christopher if he could have a job.

The rest of that speech talks of the seven stages of our lives, from childhood to doddering old age which resembles childhood. It is a capsule of every psychological development textbook written since then.

When I left I saw Richard sitting in one of the hundreds of empty chairs in the audience watching the rehearsal. His camera was in the seat next to him. He was concentrating on the strange words, but actually they were not so strange.

Most of Richard's pictures of crime and fashion and struggle and laughter were taken on the street, which suddenly to him was looking more and more like the stage in front of him. Shakespeare would have written him into his next play.

LAND OF OPPORTUNITY

Canada is what America was in the nineteenth century. I grew up hearing endless stories of the land of opportunity. I did not see any of them in our neighbourhood, but we all heard about them in school when courage and determination and plain hard work were enough to give you the golden egg inside your nest of straw.

Most people in my neighbourhood were stuck with the plain hard work and then they died.

I think too many wars and too much money spent on missiles had something to do with that.

Not so in Canada. Despite high taxes and endless rules and regulations I have seen and reported on examples of poverty to wealth that I have tripped over and found in the oddest places.

In 1994 I was with cameraman Karl Casselman again. I have been with him in alleys around East Hastings and the diamond district of the East Side of New York.

"I think we have to go the other way," I said. We had been hunting for something for several hours.

He started turning.

"You can't make a u-turn here," I shouted in something close to panic. "I didn't mean the other way here." It was the middle of Granville Street.

He had done the same thing in New York.

"In New York I drive like a New Yorker."

I yelled. "New Yorkers don't drive like this."

"I'll give them a lesson," he said.

Then he went up on the sidewalk.

"Nooooo," I said.

"I took a taxi ride last night after you were asleep," he said. "They do this all the time."

But on this day we were looking for a story in Vancouver. I like Karl because he always tells me in the worst places to go out and talk to someone. After his u-turn we were under the Granville Street Bridge next to a seedy-looking gas station.

"Go find something in there," he said.

I think he had to make a phone call. So I got out and talked and talked and talked to the grease-covered mechanics working inside. They were all working on Black Top cabs.

"They do five or six thousand kilometres a month," one grease monkey said. "We fix them and keep them going."

The place was so small that the cabbies would drive in, get whatever fixed and then back out. There was not room to keep driving through.

They had the taxi contract and were happy with that. It was incredibly hard work but a steady income.

Then I met an East Indian guy who owned the place. He had his head under a hood and was fixing a spark plug.

He said he immigrated here ten years earlier and now owned this place as well as two houses and was in love with Canada.

Nice story, and that was the end of it, an immigrant did well.

A decade passed and in 2004 I was driving around with another cameraman, Paul Rowand, looking for a story.

"Why don't you try that place?" he asked.

"Did it, with Casselman," I said.

"Well maybe you can find something different," he said.

We stopped. I went inside. Nothing different. The same Black Top cabs, the same smell of grease and sound of motors and power drills loosening lug nuts. The same soiled blue coveralls over the same-looking guys.

"I know you," said a voice.

He was a friendly-looking East Indian guy in coveralls with grease-covered hands.

"You came in here ten years ago. I just got a job here. It was my first day," he said. "I was in the background of one of the pictures on TV. My name is Dave."

Nice, I thought. And you are still working here. Good. And I was ready to leave.

"Now I own the place," he said.

One more golden story from gasoline alley.

KILLER INSTINCT

Istill have it, the killer instinct. It's not really dangerous, I'm not a threat to anything living or imaginary, but when you get older and you learn you still have it, it makes you feel good.

On Monday, cameraman Tony Clark and I are tooting around in his camera van looking for something, as is done every day. Now Tony is a very bright guy who wasn't born when I was sharpening pencils in a newspaper office. But he is a superb photographer and a kind guy.

"What are you doing?" I ask when I see him using an electronic pencil on some gadget sticking out of his dashboard. "Is that a GPS? Which I don't think we need because I don't know where we are going."

"No, I am trying to find some music that you might like."

Well this is very thoughtful of him because between police and fire radios and the office radio some of the younger cameramen listen to music which is very strange to me and which I do not consider music, because it does not have a nice, soft melody and words I can hear and understand.

He tunes in the equivalent of 600 AM, which is the only station I listen to because Frank Sinatra and the early Elvis were the only people who sang songs that entered my ears without resistance.

He says that should keep me mellow.

Mellow old men do not have killer instinct.

We drive over the Georgia viaduct and he says, "There's a guy down there and it looks like he has flowers."

That is good enough for me. A guy, flowers, and the guy is vertical, what more would you want to check out a possible story?

As we approach, Tony the kind cameraman says, "I saw him on television yesterday. He was in a promo for CTV. They're doing a story on him tonight."

"Tonight?!" I almost shout. "Tonight? It hasn't run yet?"

"No, that's why I said 'tonight,'" Tony says, being very gentle with my slow grasp of reality.

"You mean we can do the story on the same night that they promo it for their special of the night?"

Again Tony the insightful cameraman nods. He is dealing with someone who likes music from distant age.

What I am thinking of is beating or at least going nose-to-nose against the competition.

This is like the old days when I was young and doing police stories and the most important thing in the world for holding onto your job was getting the story before anyone else. That was newspaper competition when you would be at a crime scene and sucking in the facts like a reporting sponge and then running, literally, running, to a pay phone and jamming in a dime and dialing the number with a shaking finger, calling the city desk and praying that you are the first one to tell the city editor what's happening.

News is only news when it is new.

John Daly still does that. I swear he prowls the city at night looking for crime. I don't think he sleeps. And I know he is on the phone to the news editor pumping in hot tips like he was a fresh young reporter and he is almost as old as me.

But I chose the gentler side of reporting long ago and competition was left behind. I am not going head to head with another station with stories of old men fishing in Como Lake.

But wait a minute. CTV is doing a story on the homeless guy selling flowers. And here I am standing in front of the same homeless guy selling flowers. And CTV hasn't run their story yet.

I can taste the instinct. And it takes away the years.

"We are doing the best story this side of the moon on this guy," I say to Tony.

Of course, with Tony taking the pictures it will be fairly easy, since he takes such good pictures.

The homeless guy, TJ, is wonderful and warm, and is wearing socks over his hands because he has no gloves and he is thankful that he has these rejected flowers to sell.

A delivery guy buys a bunch, but doesn't have any money. TJ lets him have the flowers. A cop passes on a motorcycle and says TJ's not hurting anyone and not breaking any laws. The delivery guy comes back and gives TJ $20. This almost makes the flower man cry.

It is an absolutely beautiful story. Check it out on my web page next to the blog.

If you want to learn more about how rejected flowers are making some lives better look up Flowers for Food on the Internet. It is a great idea.

And not only did we get a chance to tell you about it, and to meet TJ, but we also had our story on one minute before CTV's. Now that is what a killer instinct can produce.

P.S.

It also makes for something good. After the story ran someone sent a box to me for TJ. It had warm clothes and gloves. It had no return address, just a note asking us to deliver it.

It also had a one hundred dollar bill.

This time TJ did not almost cry.

GETTING THERE

Tears are in my eyes and wind is in my face and I cannot lift my hands from the handlebar because I am afraid. I am going down a hill only two miles from my home and I cannot make it. I am going too fast and the bike is not steady and I have not ridden for fifteen years and no, I am not prepared to ride to California. I am in Canada and California is more than fifteen hundred miles away—almost twenty-five hundred kilometres, which sounds further.

But my kids are in front of me and I must catch up to them because, well, because we have just left on this trip and if I pull out now it would be too soon to quit. Also I cannot stop because I do not know which brake to squeeze. I am afraid of pulling the front brake too tightly and going over the handlebars, but I do not remember which hand has the back brake.

It was my daughter's idea. Colleen was fourteen and she simply suggested that we visit a friend of ours in San Francisco. That seemed like an averagely good thing to do. Then she said, "Let's go by bike."

Why not, I thought. I was a bit flippant, but in our lives we say many things we do not mean. Her twelve-year-old brother, Sean, heard about it and in a sullen twelve-year-old mood said, "Sure." He had nothing else planned for July.

Little is left of that trip except a photo on a wall that shows the three of us in front of the Golden Gate Bridge. We had ridden thirty-two days to get there and in the picture you cannot see the bridge because of fog. Sean is standing alongside me, his head level with my shoulder. Now he towers over me. Colleen now has a daughter of her own, Ruby, who is riding a tricycle.

I was twenty pounds overweight. I had not trained for this trip. I thought we could easily ride fifteen miles an hour for eight or ten hours a day and thought it would be a good family adventure. The adventure part was right.

The first night we camped in White Rock. I fell asleep before I made dinner. They ate crackers and canned peaches.

And then it rained. I got soaked trying to put the tarp over the tent. I went back to sleep with wet clothes. I was so tired I did not even notice what the kids were doing. We left in the morning without breakfast and cold and hungry and miserable. And then came the first flat.

There is a rule about buying bicycles. Buy good tires. I did not follow that rule. We fixed the flat and then went through Customs and the nice man at the border just shook his head.

We might quit soon, but first breakfast in Blaine. And after bacon and eggs and pancakes the sun came out and we were all feeling good. Can't quit now, I would tell them later.

On the way out of Blaine we had another flat. Take everything off the bike. Turn it upside down. Get out the tools. Pry off the tire. Find the hole. Patch it. Pump it. Put the wheel back on. Try to figure out how to put the chain on. Load up the bike. And ride.

Mileage during that time: zero.

"I think I have a flat," said Colleen.

"But we just fixed Sean's."

That did not matter. It was flat.

By the time we got to the coast there were three more flats. But the Pacific Ocean and the coast road are too beautiful not to keep going. We would quit when we got to Oregon. That is far enough. On the way to Oregon, three more flats.

"We're not getting very far," said Sean.

But Oregon was too beautiful to turn around and go back. The further we went the better the ocean looked. And we were feeling a little stronger. At least I was feeling stronger, the kids were already that way.

Fixing flats and riding and eating were becoming our lives.

When we had a chance to eat in a diner we ordered four breakfasts, each with eggs and potatoes and sausages and pancakes. The fourth we split. Then back on the bikes.

The soreness of our bottoms was vanishing and a strength we could all feel was growing in our arms and legs. Eating, then pushing on the pedals. Sweating, pushing, pulling on the handlebars, then more eating. We stopped for milk and juice and junk food and each time the clerk in the store would look at our dirty, tired, glowing, sunburned faces and see the bikes outside leaning against each other like pack horses and say: "You must be having a great time."

Then we went outside and saw one of the tires was flat.

Before the trip was over we had nineteen flat tires. We were getting very good at fixing them but wondered why was this happening to us? I did not know the rule of tires.

At the northern tip of California we got the last space in a campground and had our tent up and a fire going when another fellow on a bike came into our site. He had a scraggly beard and looked like he had not combed his hair for weeks and had two of the smallest knapsacks hanging over his rear wheel that I had yet seen. He was so polite I did not trust him.

The campground was full and could he stay with us, he asked.

I looked at Colleen and Sean. They were both smiling. Kids are good at judging character. His name was Richie and he stayed and we all shared a campfire and talked about riding until the night was black and the fire was a small glow.

We compared bicycles, which everyone riding does, and he said we really should have better tires.

"Be careful," he said. "Those cheaper ones can get a lot of flats."

The visitor told us he had spent the previous five summers touring the US and Canada and Alaska on a bike that looked like it had come from a garage sale. It was battered and scraped and stripped bare. He guessed he had 100,000 kilometres on it and almost never had a flat.

He lived on a house boat on the Mississippi River and he worked as a short order cook at night and wrote novels during the day. None of them had been published as yet. But riding during the summers gave him ideas to write about and the winters gave him time to write.

Colleen and Sean listened from one story to the next and then on to another.

"I didn't know there were people like that," Colleen said later when she was wrapped up in her sleeping bag. "I think I like this."

After they were asleep I brought our dishes to the bathroom to wash them. I know that was forbidden by a sign on the wall, but I thought I could sneak them in. It was too dark to clean them at the camp site and I did not want to leave them dirty for the animals.

The door opened and a man about sixty with a baseball cap and a flashlight and an orange reflective vest came in. He snorted at my dishes but said nothing. I was trying to use as little space as possible and was wiping up the sink when he came to wash his hands. He chose the sink next to me although there were five others available. He tried to bang my pots with his elbows as he washed his hands but they were just out of his reach. He snorted again and read, muttering to himself, the sign about no dish washing. One more effort to knock my pots off the edge of the sink, but he missed. Then he left.

At the door he said, "Some people can't read, can they?" Then he was gone.

I saw him heading for his trailer, which is a fine way of travelling. I'm sure his dishes were neatly stacked inside. I'm sure he had a fine vacation. I only wish he could have heard the stories about riding across Canada and writing novels in the winter while his dirty dishes were still sitting behind him on the table. He might not have gone to sleep so angry.

The next morning the visitor was gone before any of us awoke.

Our breakfasts were soon becoming enough for five. Our lunches could feed six. For dinners we would stop in the mid-afternoon at a grocery store. We bought snacks to eat immediately and stocked up with chopped meat (two pounds), spaghetti (a box), tomatoes (six), bread (one), a quart of five percent milk, plus cake for dessert and junk food for later in the night.

After thirty-one days on this diet I lost fifteen pounds, proving again that if you move a lot you can save a lot of money on diet books.

But I was still not smart enough to buy extra flashlights. In fact, I was irresponsible and dumb. Every day I was sure we would get to the next campground early and be sleeping by dark. Except at 9 p.m. it was dark and we were still riding.

The sun does not set gradually in the Redwoods, it just hits the earth and disappears. By 9:05 p.m. it was hard to see each other. By 9:15 it was impossible. It was too dark to see the road and I hit a broken bottle and blew out my front tire. In the virtual blackness by the roadside, relying on passing headlights and a dying flashlight battery we changed it using our last spare inner tube.

Someone told us a campground was about ten miles down the road. We kept going. One mile, two. Peddling is slow in the dark. We could not see our own bikes. We called to each other, coasting slowly down hills with our feet out scrapping the ground, praying for cars to pass so we could see for a quarter of a minute. I tried our last flashlight. It was dead.

Soon we were walking the bikes with our front and rear wheels nudging each other so that we would know we were staying together. Then the logging trucks came, returning after a day of gathering the fallen children of the fallen giants. The trucks are big and they travel fast and their logs bulge out of their sides and stick out the rear like long drooping scythes cutting off anything that gets in their way when the drivers make curves.

They could not see us, although that probably would have made little difference. They own the road and they seldom give an inch. Every five or ten minutes we would hear one coming from the rear. They are noisy, old trucks that spend most of their lives on rough roads carved out of the forest. They rattle. Their steering is sometimes erratic. They came up behind us and passed us at fifty miles per hour only an arm's length from our bikes. After the first one passed way too close, we got off the road each time they came. But when we were off the road and the trucks had passed we could see nothing. The blackness was so complete we stumbled into bushes and fell into ditches.

We tried riding because the walk was so slow, but then Colleen said, "sorry, my tire is flat." Poof, right there in the blackness with no flashlights and no idea how far we had to go the tire was not acting as a tire should. We could feel it more than see it and it was a puncture from broken glass. Why would we think beer bottles would not be thrown along the road in the Redwoods? What do we think, they are sacred or something?

It was too dark to think of patching it, and we had no more tubes. So we pumped it up and we went on, then we pumped it again and pumped it again, about every hundred yards.

We guessed we had about seven miles to go. But we were afraid we might miss the entrance of the campground if the lights were turned off, which they were at several other places.

But stopping here was impossible and going on was impossible. We could not see the road. We were feeling our way along except for the brief passing headlights and even they no longer helped. When they came from behind we had to get off the road. The cars and trucks could hardly see us.

We thought of sitting by the side of the road until light, but when we stopped we heard a loud and frightening crash in the blackness behind us. Sheer terror. My skin crawled.

I did not know if it was a madman or a bear. But it was big and by the sound of the crash it was strong. None of us said anything. We got on our bikes and shuffled and pushed as best and as fast as we could, with Colleen riding on a flat tire. We said nothing. This was not the best night we had.

We went for many minutes without talking; no screams, no tears, not even a word about fear. I thought we were going to be attacked and there was nothing I could do. I could not fight back. I could not even see the thing coming. The blackness was complete. Just keep going, kids. Don't stop. To say it was frightening is too petty. To say it was terrifying is getting only close.

Time crawled. We could still not see each other except in passing headlights. And except for those brief moments, I would not have known the kids were still with me. Eventually we whispered, and that was a salvation. I was proud of them. They were having it rough and neither one complained.

Then we almost bumped into two fellows standing by the side of the road next to a van. I do not know who scared who the most. They did not see us coming. We did not see them standing there. We were lost and alone and frightened and tired and hungry and they asked us for help.

Their battery was dead and they needed a push up to get it started. They were going the other direction. Colleen steered and popped the clutch and we pushed and it worked. But they also helped us. They told us the campground was only another mile down the road.

That mile was easy. Then we saw a light in the distance. God knows how beautiful is a light. Colleen pitied blind people.

The light was held by one camper. It was a lantern and he was carrying it into a tent where in another minute it would have been put out. We called to him which must have been frightening. Sounds out of the darkness are not reassuring.

He told us the entrance was a few hundred feet up ahead. A park ranger was not only still on duty but he and his wife greeted us like grandparents. They asked if we were travelling with another biker, a fellow with a straggly beard. He had saved us half his site. The campground was otherwise full.

What fellow? Sure. Where, who? Don't ask, just say thank you.

It was Richie.

"I thought you might be late, so I saved you a space."

He had been there since mid-afternoon, relaxing and reading. He would be gone, he said, when the sun rose. He never rode in the dark. "No sense in that, you can't see all the sights."

You can look him up on the internet. Richie Swanson. He is still living a simple life in a houseboat on the upper Mississippi. He writes for many magazines about bicycling and nature. And he is still writing novels, and won the National Peace Writing Award for an unpublished novel in 2000.

Over the next few days we met Ritchie several more times, mostly because he was now riding much slower with two girls he had met along the way. They were sisters and going to Mexico.

We shared another campsite with the three of them just north of San Francisco and it was apparent that Richie and one of the sisters were starting to hit it off.

In the morning they were all gone before we had the eggs out of the frying pan.

Long after the trip was finished Richie wrote me a letter. He and the sister whose name was Lori had been growing fond of each other. He had planned to meet them again somewhere between San Francisco and Los Angeles but they never showed up. He continued on with his riding and pedalled his way slowly back across country and followed the Mississippi River up to Minnesota and his tiny houseboat.

He went back to work on his novel during the day and cooking in a diner at night. Three months later he got a letter from Lori's sister. Lori had been killed just south of San Francisco. She was hit by a car that kept going even after it ran over her. It happened the day after we all sat around the campfire on that night just north of the city.

By the time we got to the Golden Gate Bridge the fog was rolling in. It was getting dark and cold. We stopped for a picture. I put the camera on the seat of Colleen's bike, which was the only one that still had a kickstand. I set the delayed automatic shutter and ran back between them where they were standing with the other two bikes. In the background was the bridge, now covered with fog.

I put my arms around them and the shutter snapped and I glanced at Colleen and she had a look of shock on her face. Then I looked back at the bike in time to see the wind blowing it over with the camera heading for the ground.

That picture is on our wall. It is one of the happiest moments of my life. It was the last picture that camera took.

We rode to our friend's home and dropped our greasy, mud-caked saddlebags on her floor. We ate peanut butter sandwiches and talked and took showers and slept, and slept, and slept.

We spent a day touring the city and talking about the trip and then we rented a car and drove thirty-six hours straight back home with the bikes strapped to the roof. We stopped only to sleep in the car.

There is only one PS.

The following year, we did the trip again.

With flashlights.

And better tires.

And no flats.

EMAIL? WHAT EMAIL?

Global television has some of the best photographers in the country. These folks stand in the rain and snow or heat or pre-dawn morning to get pictures that explain and illuminate our lives.

Theirs is a world of the outdoors and some of them are almost strangers in the newsroom. And it is in the newsroom where others work on computers with emails.

A company order went out a few weeks ago for everyone to change their password.

"What password?" asked John Chant, a cameraman who started here when cameras used film.

He walked into the newsroom. It was not raining inside, he noticed.

One of the IT guys sat down with him and helped John work his way back through the computer dust to his closet of e-mails.

"What!! I can't believe it," said the computer guy.

"Is something wrong?" asked John.

"This is fantastic. I've got to take a picture of it. I've got to show someone."

It was obviously a big moment for an IT guy. John was not sure if he was being promoted or fired.

"I've never seen this," said the IT guy.

"What?"

"What? What, you ask. Look."

He pointed to the number of backed-up e-mails.

"I haven't been here for a while," said John.

The IT guy was trembling as he read out loud:

"Eleven thousand, one hundred and seventy-four," he said.

"Is that a lot?" asked John.

"I've got to tell someone," said the IT guy. "Amazing."

It had been four years since John checked.

"Did I miss anything?" he asked.

The IT guy erased everything except the last three months and John started reading.

"I don't think I did miss anything," he said.

Then John met cameraman Karl Casselman. The camera vans passed each other under the rain in Kitsilano.

"I had only 3,000 to go through," said Karl. "But I can't remember anything exciting in them."

I was riding around with John while all this was going on. We marvelled at 11,174. We said that was indeed a very large number.

Then John's phone rang. It was cameraman Ken Chu. He wanted to tell John about a story he had just done. Ken has been around an extremely long time and has lived with cameras basically all his life. He is getting ready to retire soon.

John asked if he had any backed-up e-mails.

Ken, unlike John or Karl, has never put his fingers on a computer at work. Never.

"I had a few," he said.

"More than 11,174?" asked John.

Ken said nothing. I know because John said again into the phone, "Well, more than 11,174?"

Then John's face changed. "Goodbye," he said to Ken.

"Well?" I asked.

"He said it was more than 40,000 when they stopped counting."

"Did he miss anything?" I asked.

"He didn't think so."

TWO MINUTES IN THE TELETHON

It is 10:58 in the morning on Sunday. The show has been going since 7 p.m. Saturday. Strain is starting to creep in although the faces still have smiles.

Some of the producers have been up all night. They are staring at automatic stopwatches on their computers.

"Darn, darn, darn. We are way over time."

When you interview someone live, ten extra seconds here and twenty there are so easy to do.

"Why, here's another question I forgot to ask, and you are so kind and generous to donate so much."

But extra seconds add up to minutes, and then more minutes, and then suddenly, DARN, in the most polite of words.

I have just finished taking a cheque from someone donating to the children's charity, and before the ink is dry, Brian Smalley, the floor director is spinning his hand in the air off to my side vision. He means hurry up. Then hurry up more. And I am thinking I haven't finished talking to the generous donor yet.

Hurry. The hand is getting desperate. The super producer sitting in the dark at the main control desk is telling Brian through his headset to get me off because we are getting further behind in time. Brian's hand moves faster. Brian is one of the friendliest guys I know. He would be calm in a tornado. But he is being told to get me off the set.

I am hoping the kind and generous person who has just given the cheque will come to the end of his sentence so I can say thank you, but it is a long sentence.

Finally he finishes and I say thank you, as naturally as I can and Brian the floor director is gentle and complimentary. "Very good interview," he says as he ushers us offstage and brings on the next guests.

What he is doing is keeping blood pressure low and removing the tension from the next interview.

As I leave the set and step into the darkness behind the cameras I hear Bob McGrath asking if he can take a break. He has been standing and talking on camera for hours and he is getting tired.

Bob is the founder of "Sesame Street" and I remember him when we had a black and white TV and my kids were in preschool. He helped teach them about life. Back then he was the older man on the show.

Now my daughter's daughter watches "Sesame Street" and Bob is a bit older, but just as sweet and gentle. He is a tiny bit stooped over and I don't think he weighs more than 120 pounds, but still working and full of energy.

They tell him he can take a break because there is a ten-minute pre-recorded segment and everyone can rest while it runs.

Bob goes through a door.

Unknown to him and to those who told him he could take a breather, another super producer timed out the next seven hours and said, "aggggag-gghggg." It was more than ten minutes over time.

"Drop the recorded segment. Call in the next interview subject. And where's Bob?"

They look around.

"Bob?"

"He took a break."

"Where'd he go?"

The look of horror.

It is now 10:58, the time we started telling you about. The interview must start at 11 a.m. because the following segment is based on the interview.

"Where's Bob?"

More horror. People with worried faces are running everywhere, "Bob? Bob?" But they can't shout because the show is still going live only a few steps away.

They are in the lobby, now frantic, "Bob!" Here they can shout, but no answer.

10:59.

"Check the bathroom!"

"Which bathroom?"

"The men's, you idiot."

"I know that, but upstairs or downstairs or in the lobby."

10:59:30. The producer's eyes look like a cork screw. "All of them!"

"He's coming. He was in the bathroom." No one cares which one.

Twenty seconds to go. Arms are waving him in like he is a runner at the end of a marathon. He is jumping over the cables that are lying on the floor connecting the cameras. Each cable has a cable puller behind the cameraman keeping the black wires from getting tangled. Each cable puller is praying that Bob doesn't trip over his cable. Please God, keep him going.

Ten seconds. I can hear the timing through a small radio near me. The couch with the young interview subject and his family has been waiting under the spotlight for almost two minutes.

Bob jumps up on the tiny platform and sits between two adults. "You are the mother? You are the father?" he asks. He is panting a bit, but he is a professional. He has done this all his life. It doesn't matter that there are only five seconds left. He is ready.

"My God," says someone. "He doesn't have a microphone."

Keri Nelson, one of the two most super of the super producers of the telethon, grabs a mic out of someone else's hand and in two steps is off the floor, on the platform, hands Bob the instrument and back out of camera range as the I hear "Three, two, one."

And then, at 11 a.m. precisely, the camera and lights go up—on another part of the stage for another cheque presentation. As a backup in case Bob didn't make it, a director had moved the cheque presentation into the 11 a.m. interview slot. The countdown was too close, so they went with the cheque.

Thirty seconds later the presentation was over and the camera came up on Bob and his trademark casual, calm and friendly chat with the little boy in the wheelchair, and it all looked like it had been planned just that way.

What was Bob doing?

He was in the bathroom fixing his contact lenses. He had only one of them in when he ran from the bathroom and jumped over the cables.

THE BAREFOOT BRIDE

Roger Hope's favourite story is the barefoot bride. It is not mine. My favourite story with Roger Hope is Roger Hope's story.

Roger Hope is a cameraman at Global television and is the husband of Deborah Hope. She is one of the most recognizable people in the province. She is on the air for several shows every day and is the spokeswoman for several charities. At the end of the stories I do on the air she usually smiles, which makes me like her.

Her husband is one of the massive crew of behind-the-scenes people who shoot the pictures and edit them and others who do the writing for the anchors, not to forget the people who set up the lights and find the old stories in the library and answer phones and do research and the accountant and the schedulers, which is a headache job because in television almost everyone works in oddball shifts around the clock and seven days a week.

In short, there are a lot more people behind the scenes than on the scene. And Roger is one of them.

"Put me in your book, will you?

"What's your favourite story?"

"The wedding couple."

Oh, that was wonderful. A couple from southern California had come up here to get married because they had visited here before and loved Vancouver.

She had a knee-length white lace dress and he a dignified black suit and they got married by a JP and then went to Stanley Park for their pictures.

But this day was in the midst of the coldest, rainiest, most miserable day of the spring of that year. She was soaked. He was soaked. She was barefoot.

"Why don't you have shoes on?" I asked.

"I felt free up here the first time I came," she said.

"But it's raining and it's cold," I said.

"It's like love," she said looking at her soaked new husband. "The first time is what you remember. And that's what it always is."

"Wasn't that beautiful?" asked Roger. "Wet love."

"Nice story," I said to Roger. "But my favourite was a snippet he told me when we first met that day."

I had slid into his van and he was bouncing his head off the steering wheel. Okay, he wasn't actually doing that, but I am telling the story and that's what he was wanting to do.

I said, "How are you?" and he said, "You wouldn't believe it."

The night before he was in a supermarket. His wife had again made the cover of *TV Week Magazine*. "Please, pick me up some copies," she said to him.

He did as he was asked and grabbed a handful of copies and put them down on the counter.

"Beautiful woman," said the cashier.

"She's my wife," said Roger.

"You wish," said the cashier.

"No, I mean it. She's my wife."

"And I'm Geena Davis," said the cashier.

"Honest," said Roger.

"Whatever," said the clerk. "If you say she's your wife then she must be your wife." Then she chuckled. Just a low chuckle, not enough to get her fired. Not enough so that any jury would say that it was beyond a reasonable doubt that she was not laughing, but just clearing her throat.

But she did chuckle. And Roger again said: "Honest."

"That'll be thirty, sixty-eight," said the clerk.

He picked up his groceries and the magazines and walked out. He turned his head enough to see the clerk whispering to another clerk and pointing to him and them both chuckling, but not enough to get fired.

"She's a sweetheart," he said of his wife, "but I don't think she knows that it's not easy to be married to one of the most famous women in the province."

Now, let us vote. Which is your favourite story? The barefoot bride, or the unbelievable husband who shot it?

THE NORTH SHORE NEWS

I was lucky enough to meet Peter Speck when he was a millionaire and we were cruising on his concrete, sixty-foot sailboat, because ten years before that he might have asked me to lend him bus fare.

This is the story just as it happened to him. He had been recently fired from his job as a salesman for a small community newspaper. He had had a car accident, which I believe he said he caused, and his car was totalled. His girlfriend had left him. He had no bank account.

But he was no quitter. There was no whining or applying for unemployment insurance or getting a bottle of whisky.

He scraped together $2 and walked to Edgemont Village in North Vancouver, near where he lived.

He went into a stationery store and bought a receipt book, and a map of North Vancouver. He drew a circle around Edgemont Village and then went to every store in the village and offered them an ad in a newspaper that did not exist. He collected no money. He said he would be back for payment if and when the paper came to life.

He sold more than twenty ads, and then with his receipt book and nothing else he got a loan from a bank to start a newspaper.

It was 1969 and he used the money to print a four-page paper, the *North Shore Shopper*. He wrote every story in it, edited it himself and created the ads. He paid a printer to make several hundred copies.

Then he delivered by himself, on foot to every house inside the circle on his map. On the masthead the newspaper said "reaching every door in Edgemont Village."

He then went back to the stores and collected for his ads.

He used that money to publish a second paper a week later, still writing every story himself, and laying out the ads and delivering the paper by foot. The next morning he was out selling ads for his third week.

Soon he paid the bank back and hired someone to help and he repeated the process.

By the time my kids were delivering the *North Shore News* in the late '70s the paper was being published twice a week and it had over a hundred pages and there were enough heavy full-colour inserts to wear out a twelve-year-old.

The paper was now reaching every door on the North Shore. It won so many awards there's no more room left on the walls of their office. It made so much money that it became temping to others and was bought by the owners of the *Vancouver Sun*.

"I couldn't help selling," said Peter. "I will be rich for the rest of my life."

That is wonderful incentive.

And that left Peter Speck sailing on his sixty-foot sailboat to wherever in the world he wanted to go. How did he get success? He tried.

When I last saw him he was going off somewhere. It did not matter where. He had started with nothing but disaster and fifteen years later he was master of his own ocean. How? He tried.

Now every map he looks at starts with a little circle around Edgemont Village, and ends wherever he wants.

BROOKLYN DODGERS

Y ou know when they say it's all "relative" and you nod because that sort of explains away the problem, and then you go on to another topic and are thankful because you don't have to ask, "What the heck is relative anyway?"

Thanks to a young guy who had no idea what he was teaching me, I now know what relativity is, and it makes me feel good.

He is Darren Twiss, a news editor at Global. You look at this guy and you are immediately impressed. He is tall, good-looking and lives with his wife in a trendy condo on trendy Main Street. He has been around the world and has at least one and probably three university degrees.

He is an excellent editor who can work the new editing computers like they are a yo-yo. Plus he puts pictures together in a way that makes them look like they belong together, which is basically what a video editor does, along with correcting the English of some less than bright reporters. In short, he is an up-and-coming guy.

We are doing a story on three young men who were throwing a ball around and practising their batting at a baseball diamond in the middle of January with snow piled up on the mountains on the horizon.

Baseball in January?! This meets the requirement of being wonderfully wacko so we will try to put it on television.

After it is taped and the interviews done, then Darren, the young editor, and me, the old reporter, are putting this story together. He is shaping the picture, I am scribbling the words. After changing one, then changing another, then rewriting, then reorganizing the sentences and the adjectives, and then dropping the adjectives, the words and pictures will be joined together in a way that seems natural and easy.

He asks me if I played much baseball when I was young.

"Baseball? It was our only sport," I say.

Then I say, as I always do when talking about this topic, which is nearer to my heart than anything except my granddaughter, "I even saw the Brooklyn Dodgers play."

I am waiting to hear a "Wow."

Instead, Darren, the bright young editor, looks at me and says, "Who were the Brooklyn Dodgers?"

I stare, in disbelief. His question I do not answer. I do not answer because it is impossible to believe it is being asked.

"Who were the Brooklyn Dodgers?"

I have never before heard those words. Never.

The Brooklyn Dodgers for a guy growing up in Brooklyn were the reason for living. For the rest of the western world, even those who knew little about baseball, they were the eternal underdogs who one time, and one time only, beat the New York Yankees in the World Series and there was dancing in the streets. They were the first major league team to have a black player, Jackie Robinson.

And then they moved to Los Angeles and became overpaid playboys.

I try to explain some of this to Darren, the editor who is holding the fate of my story in his hands. He has a look of someone on their first day of conversational Greek.

Then Darren apologizes and tells me he was born in 1980, and baseball of the 1950s was not taught in university. I do not believe anyone could have been born in 1980. That makes them too young to be allowed out on their own. I have shoes older than this man who is editing my story.

But then comes the part where he teaches me about relativity.

He was watching the Junior Hockey games from Europe a couple of weeks ago and he said in "relative terms" he knows what I was talking about.

"Some of those players are just sixteen and seventeen," he said in disbelief that anyone could be so young. "And I'm twenty-seven already. That makes me feel so old."

We finished the story on baseball in January. It was an educational day for Darren. He learned that it's not too soon to start planning for his retirement, and he learned about some mythological team called the Brooklyn Dodgers, which has no bearing at all on his life.

And I learned that, relatively speaking, I am glad I saw the Brooklyn Dodgers, because when I remember those old guys I feel so young.

P.S.

The next day Darren came back to the newsroom and said to me, "My wife just shook her head sadly when I told her about what we were talking about."

"What do you mean?" I asked.

Darren looked sheepish. "She couldn't believe I didn't know about the Dodgers. She said everybody did. And she grew up here too."

I felt much better.

BURRARD BRIDGE GARDEN

In a way it is like Butchart Gardens. In the early 1900s after her husband had dug all the limestone out of the ground Jennie Butchart said that hole is darn ugly.

So she started pouring in topsoil that she got from neighbouring farms. The dirt was hauled in wagons pulled by horses.

Butchart Gardens is pretty nice now.

And in a way it is like Queen Elizabeth Park. In the middle of the 1900s it was an empty quarry of jagged rocks. An executive of the Park Board, William Livingstone, said that hole is darn ugly.

So he started filling it with soil and flowers.

Queen Elizabeth Park and its Quarry Garden is now the second most-visited park in the city.

And in a way it is like VanDusen Garden. In the later 1900s, which means in the '70s when hippies were growing their hair on Fourth Avenue, an abandoned golf course was going to be turned into housing. The people of Vancouver said that's a darn shame.

So a kindly and well-off fellow named W.J. VanDusen donated a lot of money, and the city added some more, and a botanical garden was born. Most of the planting and design from the '70s to the mid-'90s was done by the curator, Roy Forester.

I did many stories about Roy Forester, who told me about shrubs and trees and flowers. But what I remember most about him was he could not touch a slug. He was close to everything growing, except snails without shells.

"Oh, God," he said one day when we were out poking through the leaves and a slimy slug crawled out.

"You don't like them?" I asked with disbelief. He was the main designer of the garden. He knew everything. And most of all, I loved slugs.

I picked it up.

"Oh, lord," he said.

I could see him holding his stomach. At last I had the upmanship on someone. This is not a frequent occurrence on my part.

"I just can't," he said.

I fondled it, sort of, as it crawled over my fingers.

Okay, enough of that. Never gloat. Roy Forester designed VanDusen Garden and the work is amazing.

But equally so is Jason Traversy, the gardener under the Burrard Street Bridge.

Initials for places are currently in, like DUMBO, down under the Manhattan Bridge overpass in New York, and SoHo, South of Houston, in New York, and SoMa, south of Main, in Vancouver. Well, Jason is GUBB, Garden Under the Burrard Bridge.

Two years ago when we met him he was working in the shadows of the bridge on Pacific Avenue. He was sweating and lifting and shovelling and moving, hauling rocks of rubble one way and peat moss the other.

"What you doing?"

"Making a garden," he said.

"But you don't get any rain under here, and no sun," I said.

He picked up his three-hundred-foot hose, which he bought himself, and said, "I supply the water. And enough light slips under to make some plants grow." The hose was attached to the outside of the Aquatic Centre, which allowed him to use the water.

Jason was lean and smiling and working hard. He had cleaned out the rubble of mattresses and broken bottles and some broken souls who were sleeping under there.

"The kids in the daycare next door would not walk this way," he said.

Then he got used coffee grinds from Starbucks and mixed them with the peat moss and dug it all into the soil. He spent about a thousand dollars of his own money on the peat moss. Then he went back and did more, and more until the soil under the bridge was as rich as the parks at the ends.

He put in plants and flowers and at the edges, corn, where enough sun reached to grow such things.

"The kids in the daycare come out now and ask me about the plants," he said.

The second year I stopped by again.

"You're not quitting," I said.

"No," with a big smile. "This makes me feel good."

He was building rock statues out of the broken bits of concrete that he dug out from the dusty soil. They looked like garden gnomes in the shadows. Then he watered the dry dirt until he was able to grow ground cover around the statues.

"I just want to make it look better," he said.

"Have you always been so nice?" I asked.

"No. I used to drink four or five bottles of wine a night."

"You're kidding."

"No. I weighed two hundred and thirty flabby pounds."

I was looking at a lean gardener with a shovel.

He said he works nights as the host in a large restaurant.

"In that job, everyone buys you drinks. And I drank them."

He had wine and whisky and more whisky and wine. And when he looked in a mirror one soggy morning there was a lot more to him than when he first got the job.

He decided that was not good. It does not take much to change your life, just looking reality in the face and shaking your head.

He quit drinking, that day, and on his way to work he walked under the bridge.

"It is darn ugly under here," he said.

He decided to fix it, along with himself.

When I met him he weighed one hundred and eighty pounds. That is fifty less than when he started gardening.

His flowers are blooming, his statutes are standing and his health is growing.

Butchart, Queen Elizabeth, VanDusen and GUBB. They all ended the ugly.

THE DAY DAVID INGRAM LOST
HIS (SKY TRAIN) VIRGINITY

David Ingram lost his transit virginity last week. David is a Global editor. That means he lives his working life inside a small, dark room looking at multiple TV monitors and putting unconnected pictures together to make sense.

Outside of work he is the single most-travelled person in the newsroom, perhaps in the province, and could be in the country. He has been to virtually all the Third and Fourth World countries as well as most of the First and Second World places that you could find on Google.

In short, you name it and he's been there and when he is there he travels by bus, or rickety old trains, or mules.

"How do they compare to the Sky Train?" asked Brian Coxford, who is Global TV's most versatile and longest serving reporter.

"Sky Train?" said David.

"You know, that thing that rides above the ground and passes in front of the TV station," said Brian.

"I've seen it," said David.

"Ever been on it?"

David did not answer. Brian rolled his eyes.

That was when Brian went around the newsroom taking up donations in a cup on which he wrote: Send David Away on the Sky Train.

He raised $8.63.

Brian called everyone he could get to squeeze into David's edit room and made the formal presentation.

The next day David was standing at a bus stop. It was not just the Sky Train that was new to him.

"Someone said hello to me. I was just minding my own business and he said 'hello.'"

David said he thought he was going to ask for money, but no. He was just a friendly fellow bus rider waiting in the early morning for a bus.

"More than thirty years I've driven to work, and no one ever said hello," he said. "A hello was nice."

But he said the bus had a bell that went *ding, dong, ding*. That was not so nice. Every time the door opened. No variety. No change in tune. Just *ding, dong, ding*. And that was every time the door opened.

David plays guitar in a band, and now sitting in his edit room he was muttering *ding, dong, ding*, like if he heard someone playing that same riff over and over in his band he would put his foot through the guitar.

He transferred from the bus to the Sky Train.

"It was amazing," he said. "Such a beautiful view of rooftops. You can't see rooftops in a car. There were flat rooftops and pointed rooftops, and then more rooftops."

He took a picture out the front window of the train he was riding in. It shows rooftops.

"From up there you can see this was a beautiful city once," he said. "Then they filled it with rooftops."

He got off at work, an hour and fifteen minutes after he left home. It takes forty minutes to drive.

Then he rode home. No one said hello, but it was the same rooftops, same *ding, dong, ding*, followed by *ding, dong, ding*.

"But," said David proudly, "I am no longer a Sky Train virgin." He smiled, as only someone can smile when they know what it feels like and what they've been missing.

"And thanks to Brian, I had $1.13 left over." Which made his loss also his gain.

It's sort of like the mile high club, except it was only thirty feet up.

"But it was good, the first time always is," he said.

DUMBER THAN DUMB

If you are going to be a thief try not to be an idiot also. The gang had a good plan. At the beginning of a three-day holiday weekend they would break into the building next door to the building that had the name on the front: Vancouver Vault and Safety Box.

It was at Cambie and Hastings and inside in a deep basement were a thousand safety boxes, from cigar box-size to large drawers. It was a private depository for those who did not want to use a bank. Some customers did not want to wait until a bank vault became available. Others did not want to use their real names for storing whatever it was they wanted to store.

There was a great deal of cash and jewelry and gold in those boxes, and on that long weekend the gang of idiots broke in and moved their way through several locked doors into the basement of the building next door.

Then they spent the next ten hours with power drills and crowbars and sledge hammers hacking through the foundation walls that separated the two buildings. That meant these guys had to plough, punch and gouge their way through nearly four feet of reinforced concrete. They were paying gallons in sweat, curses, blood and dust-covered scratched fingers to find their way to wealth.

Finally, they crawled into the dark basement of the safety vault. Can you imagine a bunch of kids stepping into a candy store after closing hours? Or better yet, imagine a bunch of criminals stepping into a vault after closing hours? No one around to tell them to stop because stealing is wrong, and no curious eyes poking into their business. This was in the mid '70s and security cameras had not yet been invented. The only alarms were on the upstairs doors to the vault.

Throughout all of Saturday and Saturday night they worked, probably harder than they ever did in their lives. They lit the room with flashlights and used crowbars to rip open box after box. They scooped out gold and jewelry and cash. Gold bars, gold coins, diamonds, and stacks of bills were being stuffed into suitcases they had brought.

There was so much they had trouble lifting the cases. They barely slept that night, just dozing from exhaustion for a few minutes, but then dreams of gold snapped them back to work.

By Sunday afternoon they were pooped and hungry and rich. The sandwiches and beer they had brought were long gone. There was still a hill of gold on the floor, but they had no more suitcases. They thought it would be a good haul, but never imagined it would carry them for the rest of their lives. There were millions in their bags.

They could even afford to give up crime.

Monday morning those of us covering police news wandered into the tiny office where the deputy chiefs had their press conferences. Back then the force was smaller, crime was less and the deputy chiefs met with reporters each morning around a table with coffee cups. It was extremely informal. There was no speech by a special media liaison cop standing behind a podium.

There were usually two or three break-ins, a few accidents and some fights. It was hard to be a police reporter then. Politics had more devious characters.

"We would like to report the arrest of four suspects in the largest break-in and theft in the history of the city," said the deputy chief.

"What break-in?" we said.

The deputy smiled. "The largest break-in ever in the city, didn't I say that?"

"What break-in? What arrests?" How could we be crime reporters if we didn't even know there was a crime?

"To be honest," said the deputy chief, "we didn't know about the crime either until we caught them."

"Caught who?"

"The suspects, I know I said that part."

As it turned out, the crooks took all the gold and cash and jewelry they could and crawled back out through the hole in the wall, struggling to pull the suitcases with them. They dragged the suitcases up the stairs of their escape building, cursing the weight but joking about how they were going to spend the money. Then they checked that the sidewalk was clear, and hauled the cases out to two cars they left parked in front and with a good deal of grunting loaded them in the trunks and back seats. The cars groaned and the exhaust pipes scrapped the ground.

And then they drove to the airport and bought tickets to the eastern US and put the cases up on the scale to check them in.

The needle shot up like a bare foot stepping on a thumb tack.

"Wow," said the check-in woman.

"Don't worry, we'll pay for the extra weight," said one of the crooks.

"What do you have in there, lead?" asked the clerk.

"No, gold, no, not really," joked the crook, and he laughed as though to say, 'have you ever heard anything so silly?'

The clerk put tags on the cases, got another clerk to help her move them to the conveyer belt, gave the men their tickets and after the men walked away she called security who called the police. The men were arrested before they finished their coffee in the waiting area.

All the loot was recovered, the men were booked into the jail at 312 Main Street and then after a little questioning the police went to the scene of the crime. It was all backwards and the story was fantastic.

Imagine, they could have simply driven east, or north, or even south. There was very little security at the border then, and none if you went to Calgary. There were virtually no clues left behind. They could have been rich in Canada. They could have quietly moved to southern California and bought trendy houses overlooking the ocean. Instead, they bought airline tickets.

Dumb doesn't begin to describe them.

Then came page two, and this is the story called, "How could some dumb thieves cause me this much of a problem?"

We took pictures of the gold and diamonds and stacks of cash. We put them on television with the encouragement of the police because they wanted to return the stolen property to its owners.

Some came to claim what was theirs, but the largest bulk of it just sat and waited in the police property office. The safe crackers were not the only crooks in town. Although there was little violent street crime back then, there was a good deal of illegal prostitution, gambling and stock manipulation. I knew one of the people involved in prostitution, although he said he was just helping the women do their business and keeping them safe.

He looked at the pictures of the gold bars and stacks of cash and his eyes got wet. He had put them into the vault because it was too much to keep in a bank; after all, how many boxes can you rent without raising suspicion, and he couldn't keep it at home because you can't trust anybody these days, he said.

But he couldn't go to the police and say that was his because how could a guy who sold a little whisky quite legitimately make a million dollars on the side? And he wasn't the only one.

After a year of not being claimed, a forklift was used to move the heavy metal to a vault where it was absorbed into the city's budget and evaporated in road salt and sewer repairs and even the building of a new jail on a vacant lot at Gore and Powell Streets, which would hold some future bank robbers.

That jail was built behind the new provincial courthouse at 222 Main Street, which would hold some future bank robbers who might be inept, but could never be as stupid as the ones who paid for the jail.

A REALLY STUPID LAW BREAKER

Now if you were going to drop off a large piece of unwanted goods, like for instance an old bath tub, and you did not want to take the time and expense to go to the dump, where would you go?

Of course you would not do anything like that because you care about your fellow citizen and you would not want to leave your garbage on someone else's property. But if you did do such a thoughtless, inconsiderate and nasty deed it would be done somewhere in which no one could see you doing such a mean and selfish and hard-to-forgive act, unless you were really stupid.

"If you have a moment would you come over here and I'll show you someone who is really stupid," said Ozzie Kaban.

I cannot turn down such an offer as that, not when it comes from a very powerful man who is as large as a football player and who runs his own protection agency. Ozzie has pictures on his walls of guarding many famous people. He is a private investigator. He is a bodyguard, a private eye and he has fought and beat cancer. Don't mess with Ozzie.

I parked at his office at Nanaimo and First Avenue in Vancouver. I had to squeeze in alongside a junky old bathtub that looked out of place in his parking lot.

Ozzie asked how stupid can a person be when they do something that they do not want to be seen doing but do it under a sign that says: Kaban

Protective Agency, which is under not one, not two, "but count them," says Ozzie, pointing up at his security cameras.

There are fourteen of them surrounding the building. They are intended to be obvious so that they will deter crime and stupid people. You cannot help seeing them.

A row of cameras was looking down at Mr. Stupid when he parked his pickup truck alongside the sign which should hint that he should not be doing something such as he is about to do.

Inside his office Ozzie ran the tape. There was the man opening the back of his pickup truck. And there he was unloading the bathtub. And there was a picture of his face. And there was a picture of his licence plate.

"But this we didn't see until this morning," Ozzie said.

While Mr. Minus IQ was struggling to haul the tub off the truck he dropped a small roll of bills, which probably fell out of his shirt pocket.

Ozzie's assistant found the $35, which Ozzie told her was her bonus for having sharp eyes.

And then Ozzie said he had already put the tub up for sale on the Internet and someone had bought it for $50.

His next step would be a visit to the Mr. Dumber-Than-Dumb and when you get a visit from Ozzie he can leave you feeling somewhat troubled.

Ozzie has done this work all his life. "They all think they are so smart," he said.

He smiled. He shook his head. He looked up at the camera. He did not have to add anything else.

BATHROOMS

Vancouver is a great city. What makes a city great? Lots of people. Lots of parks. Lots of coffee houses. Lots of bathrooms.

Wait a minute. Vancouver is a terrible city. There are two public bathrooms in town. One of them is on the most infamous corner of the city where drugs are sold openly and you would have to push your way through ten dealers to get to a urinal. And the other is on a corner where depending on the time of day there are either drug dealers or it is so desolate and empty that you suspect someone will pop out of nowhere and scare you out of your need for a bathroom.

The first, first. Main and Hastings in 1902 was the site of Vancouver's first city hall. It was an elegant building of carved stone filled with city clerks with starched collars. It was the first public building in the city to be lit by gas flames, and the local folks would come down at night to stand outside and look at the lights inside. It was like English Bay now with the fireworks, except this was more exciting. Imagine, lights at night.

But there was no indoor plumbing. First install the lights, then put in the relief. So an outdoor, underground toilet was dug and decorated for the citizenry. It was located just a little ways away from City Hall, a few steps toward Hastings Street where livestock was auctioned off on the corner.

Later the Carnegie Foundation said it would build a library next to City Hall, because, after all, that was the centre of town. The library went up where the flimsy livestock building was, and the lawmakers agreed to share their toilet with the book readers, especially since the new library was built right alongside the toilet.

"I'm glad it's there and not here," probably said the politicians.

The Carnegie home for books and improvement of the mind looked as elegant and beautiful as the City Hall next door. It remains one of the most classic buildings in the city and it was a gift from a man who wanted to spread literacy to the world.

When Andrew Carnegie was a boy he worked fifteen hours a day in a factory and there was little hope anything would ever change in his life. Then he met a man who allowed him to read in his private library. First the fifteen hours, then the books, and what he learned in those books, he said, taught him how to become the richest man in the world.

He wanted to do the same for others. He built 2,500 libraries, more than 150 in Canada. Everything was free, the only obligation on the contract was that the cities that got the gifts maintain the buildings. Everyone happily signed.

"You mean it costs us nothing? Give me the pen."

Thirty years later the city fathers got tired of the old City Hall. "It's so old-fashioned," they said. "Let's build a new City Hall." They also needed more space because Point Grey and South Vancouver had joined with the old city to make one mega city, which needed a mega building to house the mega number of bureaucrats, administrators and politicians who were running the city. So they built a big building up at Twelfth and Cambie, big, in the classic style of big. During World War II, City Hall looked bigger than the city.

But what do we do with the old City Hall? Well eventually it started falling apart. Apparently the bricks that it was made of were not baked very well. They came from Mayor David Oppenheimer's brick company on Bowen Island.

When the building was under construction the builders found that the bricks on the first floor did not have enough strength to hold a second floor, so the architect had to add some buttresses around the outside to keep it all together. Eventually it became easier just to knock it down.

Now the same spot that held the beautiful City Hall has a beautifully classic dollar store, one storey high with tar roof and glass front, which sells ashtrays and mops. It is another example of forward thinking.

After City Hall was demolished came the thought: "We should get rid of that old library too. It looks so old-fashioned."

Up comes the wrecking ball. But whoops, the Carnegie Foundation keeps track of such things. They like their libraries.

"Just a second, before you send that iron ball into the walls, look at this contract your forefathers signed," said the Carnegie people. "It says you will maintain the building."

"So?" said the city fathers, "we kept it clean."

But the definition of maintaining does not include reducing it to rubble and dust. That means it could not be knocked down, and those few words agreed to on paper are the only reason the Carnegie Centre survived. And outside it, underneath the sidewalk, is the old toilet.

It is maintained extremely well, and is clean and has attendants in both the men's and women's side. If you can ignore the drug dealers, visit the toilets. Once you are inside you will feel safe and comfortable. And it is too bad the drug addicts did not take Andrew Carnegie's advice.

But my favourite toilet is at Victory Square. That was the site of the city's first courthouse. It went up in 1891, a beautiful granite exterior of carved stones and Greek columns. It had a long, powerful staircase, twenty-six steps high so that when you climbed up you felt like you were going to an important place, which was true. You were going into the court of law. If you had to go to the bathroom you went down the steps and out on the sidewalk onto Hamilton Street, then down more steps into an underground biffy.

The building looked like it could last forever. Fourteen years later it was abandoned. Too small, they said. Soon afterwards it was demolished and the land used for revival meetings and later the Cenotaph was built there. A few of the lower steps of the courthouse were incorporated into the park, which became home for drug dealers and the homeless.

Ten years ago a movie was being shot in the park. It was a perfect setting, the producers said. The movie had a scene in it about homeless people living in the shadow of the monument to those who gave their lives in defence of a free way of life. The only problem was the park was filled with homeless people, real homeless people.

The movie company had to pay them to leave so that actors could dress up like homeless people and huddle on the same ground under the same monument.

But the toilet survived the courthouse, the revival meetings, the drug dealers and the movie. I did a story down there and met two of the most delightful bathroom attendants you could ever hope to find. A man on one side, a woman on the other and they kept the place sparkling, free of drugs and loiterers. You should visit that toilet. It's safe, warm and cozy. Walk down the stairs and go into the distant past in the city where you know the judge, the accused, and the lawyers once all stood at the same lowly level when it came to easing their discomfort.

ABBY'S STORY

It is the most powerful story of my life, and I did not cover it. And I have written about it before, and I will tell it over and over because some stories are more than inspiration and more than life-affirming. And some let you know just how truly strong a person, even a child, can be.

The difference is between all the times I wrote this story and this time, I met her. And she is everything I have ever thought, and more.

September 7, 1976. It was my first day at the TV station. I walked into the basement newsroom and the assignment editor, Keith Bradbury, was wild.

"They discovered Abby Drover. In Port Moody, get going." A reporter, Alyn Edwards, and cameraman Grant Faint were already there. Maybe I could help, he said.

Abby Drover was starting to fade from the news. Six month earlier she had disappeared on her way to school. A twelve-year-old girl suddenly was not seen again. Searches day after day near her home had turned up nothing, not a hair, not a shoelace, not a disturbed leaf.

She was gone, obviously kidnapped, although officially no one could say that, but where in the world would a twelve-year-old girl with no problems at home and no reason to run away go? She was kidnapped.

After a week the searchers said there was nothing more they could do.

After a month the police said the same. After two months her parents had cried so much there was nothing left to come out.

Time passed and the stories about Abby Drover went from page one to page two to the back of the paper and then fell into the pile that never make the news. Everyone knew her name, no one knew her fate. Everyone imagined she had been killed by some sick, disgusting man who ravaged her and then hid her body.

And then came September 1976, and the news that she had been found, alive.

Unbelievable. Totally without any possibility of truth, she was alive.

It was on Gore Street in Port Moody. It was just off the Barnet Highway. I found the address and walked around to the garage. There was one policeman still guarding it. Alyn and Grant had already been there and gone.

"What happened?" I asked the policeman.

"She was down there and they found her. That's all. It was incredible how it happened.

"They went to check on the husband, they thought he was going to kill himself. They saw his foot disappear under the counter."

It was a jumble of words and I remember them exactly. Those are things that get sealed in your brain and you never forget how they sound and the order they came in and the amazement of them.

I asked where and he pointed inside the garage to a trap door under a workbench.

"Could I go down there?"

He said yes.

This was before there were police spokespeople and before the areas would have been sealed off and the only information that would have been revealed would have been that a woman who may or may not be the subject of a previous investigation has been found and a press release revealing nothing more will be issued the next day. Public information has not benefited with the advent of public information spokespeople.

I opened the trap door under the workbench and climbed down a ladder in a shaft about fifteen feet deep. At the bottom was a heavy wooden door. I opened it and saw padding on the inside of the door.

Then I stepped into a room that was about the size of a one-man cell in a cruel maximum security prison. It was small. There was a bed on one side with coiled steel springs under the torn, filthy mattress. There were handcuffs attached to the bed.

I gagged from the smell.

A young girl had been kept caged down here with no water, other than what her captor brought in, no toilet, other than what her captor took away, no air, other than what seeped in under the door, no food other than what he brought, when and if he felt like it.

Five minutes in it was terrifying. It was the dungeon of Abby Drover for one hundred and eighty days and nights.

It was built as a bomb shelter during the nuclear scares of the 1950s and '60s. It was supposed to keep a family alive for a week or two after the atomic bombs fell, before they were able to crawl out and take on life in the shattered world. It was not supposed to be the room for torture of a terrified little girl.

As I heard the story, Donald Hay had planned the kidnapping of another girl. He plotted and watched her, but unknown to him she was sick the day he put his plan into action. Abby was walking down the path to the sick girl's house to get her homework and take it to school. Hay grabbed her as she rounded a hedgerow.

He realized immediately he had the wrong girl, but he could not just let her go. He put his hand over her mouth. She fought and kicked with all the strength of a twelve-year-old, but he was a large man in his forties.

He carried her into his garage, in which he had painted all the windows black. Then he pulled open the doors of the cabinet under his workbench, yanked open the hidden trap door and forced Abby down the shaft.

At the bottom he opened the heavy wooden door and pushed her inside. There he did unspeakable, unthinkable things to a little girl.

I covered the trial and the most heart-wrenching thing I remember was the prayers Abby wrote on the white edges of newspapers. She would tear off the edges and then tie them up with strands of her hair.

The worst thing I remember was that Hay took his family to Disneyland while she was down there and he left her some chocolate bars and water. He often told her to be good to him or he would not bring her any more food.

The best thing, the most amazing thing was how the cop on that morning after her release told me how she was saved.

Hay's wife had heard again another tirade from him as he stormed out of the house saying he was going to kill himself. He went into the garage. His wife called the police. They checked the garage door, but it was locked. His wife did not have a key, but they could see the entire inside of the garage through cracks in the paint on the windows and there was no one in there.

They told his wife that he was not there and they would keep a lookout for him. She insisted that he went into the garage and begged them to check again. Presumably more to placate her than anything else, one of the cops went back to look through the cracks.

At that same moment Donald Hay was coming up from the bomb shelter. He saw the shadow of the figure approaching the window. He turned and dove back under the workbench.

The cop peeked through the crack in the paint and saw a foot disappear under the workbench. The door was pounded open and they grabbed Hay halfway down the shaft.

After they had him in handcuffs one of the cops went back down the shaft and opened the door.

"Oh, my God," he said.

Thirty years later at one of the endless hearings that Donald Hay requests to get out of jail, I met Abby Drover. She is a mother of five. She had a smile. She is the strongest woman I have ever known.

P.S.

Imagine if the police had spotted him two seconds sooner, before he was able to open the doors under the cabinet. He would have been taken away to Riverview, where it is doubtful that he would have said anything about someone he had trapped below ground.

Or imagine if they had been two seconds later and he had pulled in his foot. In that case they would have walked away convinced he was not in the garage.

Two seconds, maybe less, on either side was the window that saved Abby. It is hard, at least for me, not to think that someone was keeping that window open.

MAYBE TOO BRAVE

Sometimes you hear a story and it sets you free.

I did a series on old bank robberies and I learned about one in a building I never knew was a bank. On the corner of Victoria and Powell, across the street from the Princeton Hotel, is a grey three-storey rooming house with some stores on the first floor. Its back is against the railroad tracks. It does not look like a bank now.

But in 1950 two robbers went in with guns out. One of them shot and killed a teller. A few days later one of the robbers was shot to death in a gunfight with police. Then police surrounded the hideout of the other robber who knew what the penalty would be. He would hang by a rope until he was dead. So he shot himself.

It was a brief story in a series on crime. But the next day I got a call from a man in his sixties who was almost in tears. I could hear that over the phone. And with the tears there was also relief in his voice. You can hear that when someone wants to talk and it comes flooding out because it is something that has to be said.

He thanked me for the story because he grew up knowing only that something had happened one day in the bank where his father worked. It was something terrible, something that changed his father's life, but the son never knew what that horrible thing was. The result was he and his sister suffered for a lifetime because of the ignorance.

"My father was in the bank that day. He was a teller," he said. "Only now I know what happened."

After that day his father was withdrawn. He never again played with his children.

"My father would only say that he would not tell us about it because it was so awful. He always said he wanted to spare us."

"And he told us never to ask about it."

The man on the phone was almost crying. He said his father spent a lifetime being distant and cold.

The father was trying to be brave and protect his children. He kept the burden on himself. He thought he would be a good father that way. Silence was his mandate.

I cannot argue with anyone's choice of how to live his life. That is his business, not mine. But if his kids had known what he went through they would have spent a childhood in awe of their father, the man who was in an actual bank robbery. They would have told stories that made the other kids envious. They would have waited for their father at the end of the banking day and hugged their hero dad, glad that he had come through another dangerous day at the bank. They would have told their own children and the next generation would have grown up bragging of their brave grandfather, possibly the most significant incident in his life.

Instead they had nothing.

The last thing the man on the phone said was, "now I understand my father."

Stories are like genies. If you keep them locked up they can't work their magic.

ORIGINAL SIN

On the Pope's last visit to the US he talked a lot about sin. There are new sins now, many of them having to do with saving the planet.

He reminded me of a sin my friends and I committed once. It was back in the 1950s and Buddy Knox had just recorded "Party Doll." It was a cool song. It was number one on the hit parade, but the Pope said anyone who listened to it would go to hell.

That was because there was one line in it that was sinful, and if we listened to that line it would corrupt us. So we all wanted to hear it.

But every mother said if the Pope said it was a sin you can't listen. That applied to the Jewish mothers also who did not want their children going to hell with the Christian kids.

And we were told we could not listen to just part of the song because we might slip and hear the whole thing.

Buddy Knox had come from a town in Texas called Happy. It had only 690 people.

How could anything sinful come from there?

And he formed a band with two other guys and they paid $60 to record the song he wrote. They had no drums so the drummer used a cardboard box which they stuffed some cotton in to make it sound like a drum.

How could anything sinful come from that?

And they had to record the music at midnight because the traffic in the street outside was too noisy to do it in the daytime.

How could anything sinful come from so much dedication?

Buddy's sister sent the record to a music producer in New York who put it on the air and it sold a million copies in 1957.

But we couldn't hear it.

So we chipped in together and bought a record. A 45 rpm, which had a fat hole in the middle and one song on each side. And we sneaked into a basement and put it on a record player and listened. Then came the sinful line: *Come along and be my party doll and I'll make love to you.*

Holy mackerel, we couldn't believe it. We had sinned, and we were still alive.

"What are you kids listening to?" One kid's mother came down the stairs.

"Nothing, nothing, just some cowboy music," we lied. Now we were in deep trouble, lying about sinning.

We ripped the record off the player and stood on it. By the time she left it was too scratched to play again.

The Pope was right. Sin had cost us the price of a record. And we weren't sure about our future. But we all left that basement feeling very grown up. We had learned sin could indeed come from a place called Happy.

THE HOMELESS BOOKWORM

There are so many stories of homeless people that have nothing to do with pain, suffering or poverty that they could make a Broadway comedy called: Roofless, Success Without A Ceiling.

There are the growing numbers of school experiments with mannequins dressed with a coat and pulled-down hat who get coins dropped in a cup in front of them. And there is the woman, often at Thurlow and Albernie Streets in Vancouver, who a cameraman I work with insists on giving money to because she is "so sweet" who goes home at night to a condo in Yaletown. And there was the elderly gentleman immigrant who brought his newspaper to a corner on Lonsdale in North Vancouver most mornings, sat on a stool, read his paper and watched people drop coins in a spare hat he put on the sidewalk. His other hat he kept on his head. I wish I could have asked him what he thought of this quaint custom of ours, but he did not speak English.

But as for beating the system, there is a homeless guy I see nearly every day who has aced everyone.

He is at Grandview Highway and Boundry Road, just at the entrance to the Trans-Canada. At a red light he walks along the median holding a sign saying: Homeless, Hungry, God Bless. He often gets a few coins.

When the light turns green he turns around, puts the sign under his arm and pulls out a book that he was holding there. And then he reads on the walk back.

He reads novels mostly. I can see just close enough to get a glimpse at the titles if he is opening it as I pass by. But a few times I have seen him with textbooks and self-help books. I see when he starts one, and in two or three days he is finishing it. He is a fast reader. The next day he starts a new book.

I am not criticizing, I am complimenting. I admire anyone who can get paid while going to school. He has turned homelessness into a study hall.

I have watched this guy read at least fifty books since he started being homeless a few years ago. Rain and winter are difficult times, but in truth I seldom see him there when the weather is bad.

But can you imagine if he ever gets a job? "Hey, you, put down that book and get to work. We're not paying you to read."

No point in that, not when he already has a system that he could write a book about and get rich enough so that he would never have to work again.

NO JOY IN MUDVILLE

I'll tell you why sports can rip the soul out of you.

Yesterday, briefly, it stopped raining and I went out into the parking lot at the Global Television station and did what I have done virtually every day of my life when it has not rained too heavily or snowed.

I threw a rubber ball against a wall. It is my only sport. I do not play golf or tennis or hockey. I simply throw a ball against a wall and catch it and throw it again. It is not yet an Olympic sport.

Just as most kids in Canada grew up playing road hockey I grew up playing stickball. That is baseball played on the street with a rubber ball and a broomstick. We played it every day when it was not raining too heavily or snowing.

When I was not playing I was practising by throwing a rubber ball against a wall.

I remember being in Grade Two in a schoolyard pretending I was a big league pitcher. I hit that one brick over and over. Strike two, strike three. You're out! Next batter.

That game is cemented in my memory like cotton candy stuck in your hair because it started to rain. It rains a lot during baseball games, but there were more batters coming to the plate.

I could not quit now. Hit the brick and it was a strike, miss and it was a ball. The count was building against me. Rain could wait. The game was in the balance, and if we lost this the whole season would be a washout.

Three balls and one strike. The score was suddenly tied, and the bases were full. The other team was still at bat and I was on the mound.

Now the rain was running down my face and my shirt was soaked but I knew I couldn't quit. My team depended on me. We could not stop because of something as silly as rain.

It was a full count. The next pitch decided everything.

"Mikey, come in out of the rain!"

My babysitter. I don't need a babysitter, I'm seven years old, but my mother had to work and my father was in a bar, so someone should take care of me, my mother decided.

My care watcher was my aunt and she was very spooky. I thought she was a witch. But she let me wander the streets so long as I came home before my mother got there.

"Come home NOW!"

She did not want to get reprimanded by my mother for me being soaked. Probably my mother would not pay her then. Sports has so many backroom deals and most of them wind up interfering with the outcome of the game.

"One more pitch."

"No. Now!"

I turned to throw, in defiance and to win the World Series.

The ball slipped off my wet fingers. I had not concentrated.

"Wild pitch!"

I could hear them yelling in the stands. "Wild pitch!"

All the runners scored and we lost. Like cotton candy in my hair, it is still there.

More than half a century later was that day with the break in the weather. I was in the parking lot of the TV station throwing a ball against a wall.

I have probably thrown a million pitches since that day in the school-yard. If I had any stress, this would be my stress reliever. It is my exercise. After thirty-three years of throwing at that same wall I can hit pretty darn near any spot on it.

Some video editors come out to get some sunshine between the rains. One of them for a joke sticks a piece of plastic on a rough spot on the wall.

"Can you hit it?"

I say nothing. Silence and action is the only way to impress others. I wind up. They are watching, and I almost hit it.

They boo.

I throw again. And miss. And again. And again.

More people come out for the sunshine, which is quickly vanishing.

They watched, and I missed again.

He used to be good, someone says. In his younger days.

Again I miss. I look up at the sky. Not a single cloud around.

Hurry up and hit it, one editor says. We have to go back to work.

I try again, but even if my life were at stake along with my job, I swear that darn piece of plastic had a force field protecting it.

If only it would rain, I think.

"Let me try," says Ian Haysom. He is the news director, the boss. He is English. He grew up with soccer. He can't throw. He has no form in his wind up. He lets go, and nails that sucker dead centre. First pitch. He gives me back the ball.

They all go inside. I throw again.

No one saw it.

STICK BALL FOR SALE

You can't buy a memory, although they are often for sale.

"You lived for stickball, right, Dad?" my daughter said. "You've got to see this."

We went into Restoration Hardware, which does not sell hardware. But they do sell stuff that you say, oh man, I gotta have that, followed by, oh boy, I can't afford that.

She took me past the silver candlesticks and the gold picture frames to a pile of stickball bats, on sale.

Each was in a box and each had written on it: "From the Bronx and Brooklyn the asphalt field of dreams spreads out to the world."

Inside each was a handcrafted maplewood stick with electric tape wrapped at one end. The tape was to make it look authentic. Sticker price, $29.

My baseball goodness god. Stickball to me was street hockey to you. You needed nothing but a stick, a ball and kids. But you never paid for it. The hockey sticks were held together by glue and tape.

The sticks in stickball came when your mother turned her back and you unscrewed it from the broom.

Now they are maplewood handcrafted in a box.

It was 75 percent off because, get real, nobody in Vancouver grew up playing stickball. This is a street hockey town. But can you recall your busted-up, ripped-up street hockey stick that had survived a hundred games? And then can you see a prim and polished stick being sold in a fancy box which said that you could relive the days of your youth just by owning this?

I picked up a box with the stickball bat inside. At 75 percent off they were almost giving it away.

I stood in line. I thought of the games I had as a kid. My friends. The thrill of being ten years old.

"Will that be cash or charge, sir?"

Never mind, I said. I put it back. Things are not as real as memories, and fancy things that pretend they are something they are not are like people who do that. I walked down the sidewalk holding my granddaughter's hand. "Someday," I told her, "I'll teach you to play stickball, with a broom stick we swipe from your mother."

MEN AND WOMEN ARE DIFFERENT

My wife screamed a few nights ago, and I went to her rescue.

"I'm in the garage, help," she yelled.

I rushed. The garage is attached to the house.

She shrieked again as I bolted through the door.

"It's a mouse," she said.

I know this is a cliché. I know everywhere in the world there are man-woman jokes that begin with, "it's a mouse."

But she told me this was not just any mouse, but an actual living mouse.

Well, that's different.

And this one was probably "that big."

She spread out her fingers.

"Maybe even this big."

She spread them further.

Holy mackerel, I thought, a mouse that big is probably a tough guy and best left alone.

"Get rid of it," she said.

I told her it would probably go away on its own, since there was a large gap under the garage door.

"But it might not," she said.

So the next day I went to the store and bought a mousetrap.

The grey-haired woman clerk told me to be careful. "These things can get you into trouble."

"Small problem," I said. "I can handle it."

I set out the trap with cheese. The next morning the trap was sprung, the cheese was gone, but there was no mouse.

Okay, smart guy, I said. This is not the way it is supposed to work. I went back to the store, got two more traps. The old clerk saw me, but I went to a different check-out aisle.

Following morning, three sprung traps and no mouse. This is war, I said. I hate to kill, but if I'm going to try to kill you I expect you to do your part and die.

I buy two more traps. I had to go back to the old clerk.

"Be careful," she said. "The problem may be bigger than you think."

At home I opened a can of smoked oysters, ate some and baited five traps. My theory was if he jumped away from one he might get confused and jump into another one.

Bingo, the theory worked. Or maybe it was the oysters. The mouse stayed to lick his lips. I felt like a victorious warrior.

"Oh," said my wife, "you didn't kill it, did you? I just wanted you to get rid of it. Not hurt it."

We had a little funeral. One person at the burial site in the frozen ground was not speaking to the other person. Between the two persons was air colder above than the ground below.

The next time I was in the store the grey-haired clerk asked me if it worked.

"Yes, fine," I said, with a tone in my voice that was more telling than a lie detector.

"And did you say you were sorry?"

"To the mouse?"

"No, to your wife?"

"How did you know I have a wife?"

"Because you were not thrilled with your hunting."

I told her the "sorry" part was not included in the instructions with the mousetraps.

She said men have so much to learn.

The sad part about all this is it is true.

VARIETY CLUB ANGEL

It was like the angels were pointing the way.

The morning of the big fundraising campaign for Children's Hospital and Clive Jackson asked me to do a story about it.

"Do anything. We have the inside covered, the doctors, the kids, the government. But maybe you can find something else," he said.

Clive is passionate about the hospital. News should not only be news, but it should help the community too, he believes. It was his idea to start the fund drive.

I was standing outside the hospital. I remembered the old Children's Hospital when a cameraman and I did a Christmas story. We followed doctors from room to room who were painting Christmas angels on windows and doors and the kids were laughing and there was brightness even if the windows were leaking cold air.

The cameraman was Ross Willows, a guy who lived in a cold-water flat on East Hastings and spent his non-working hours in the bars of skid row. He was friendly, and bright, but going nowhere in life, at least nowhere anyone except himself thought he should be going.

Children's Hospital was falling apart. It was beyond fixing. It was the early 1980s.

I smiled when I remembered because Ross disappeared shortly after that. At the time, I thought he had died.

But what would the story for tonight be? I had no idea. Start by walking in the front door. That might lead to something.

A few steps before the entrance I saw a rock, a small boulder about big enough for a kid to climb on, and it had a plaque.

"Read it, you idiot," I said to myself. You never know what you are going to find by reading something.

"Dedicated to Agnes Watts, 1982, who funded . . ." It did not matter what the rest said.

I remembered Agnes. I remembered the angel. That wonderful woman with the incredible story.

The Variety Telethon was struggling and entering its twentieth hour when a spry old lady walked onto the stage of the Queen Elizabeth Theatre where the show used to be held and calmly donated a quarter million dollars. The money was to go to Children's Hospital.

A quarter million dollars in 1982 was like the heavens opening. The fundraisers were happy to break one million for the whole weekend.

The previously unknown little old lady became a local star overnight. The hospital people were jumping.

I met Agnes the next day. What a story.

She was married to a backwoods loser who beat her. She and her daughters often had no shoes in the winter, in northern BC. She said her husband would pull food away from her at the table, then throw the plate at her.

How do people like that get married? Even God probably shakes his head.

She left him in 1923 and took her children with her. They went to Vancouver and with pitiful little money that she had hoarded she made a down payment on a small rooming house.

For the next fifty years she scrubbed the floors of the house, and scrubbed the clothes of the men who lived there, and worked in a paper mill to feed her children, and then her children left home and she was an old lady in her eighties with nothing.

Then something happened. Someone wanted to build a towering apartment house on her tiny rooming house. It was in the West End.

She sold it for more than $100,000. Someone else advised her to put her money in the stock market, just as it was going into its gigantic, feverish uphill run and in half a dozen years she had a quarter million dollars.

By this time her daughters were elderly and they left no grandchildren for Agnes.

"I could do nothing but give the money to the government in taxes or give it away," she told me in 1982. "So, I gave it away."

Then came the night at the telethon.

Twenty-six years later I was staring at the rock that has her name on it. A small child ran over to it and started climbing it.

The cameraman was taking pictures of the child and I was looking at the clouds. The child was called Phoebe. She has diabetes. Her parents have to carry a syringe of insulin. They said they weigh every bit of carbohydrates that she eats. She has spent much time in the hospital.

But today it was not her turn. They were waiting for her brother to have an operation. He had a cleft palate.

Despite all that, this family was laughing while their daughter was playing on a rock with a plaque on it.

I told them about Agnes. They said she must have been wonderful.

Yes, beyond measure.

At Agnes's funeral the priest called her the Variety Club Angel.

There was the story for the television and the telethon in 2008, given by an angel who returned from 1982.

A week later I was having coffee with another old friend who is a cameraman.

"You ever know what happened to what's his name who used to live on East Hastings and was pretty wild?" I asked.

I could not remember his name.

"Ross Willows," he said.

"Yeah, is he still alive?"

"Don't you know?" he said.

"No."

"His sister had cancer while she was living in New York. Ross went to take care of her. He tried everything to help, but she died."

"Sad," I said.

"But she had married well," my friend said. "And had a lot of money. And was a widow when she passed away. And what she did not leave to her children she left to Ross."

Ross Willows has spent the last twenty years living in a fancy condo in Manhattan, raising his sister's children, and vacationing in the Bahamas.

That rock was a blessing.

THE DARN MEDIA

I want to tell you about the Darn Media. How they slant stories and leave things out.

There was a bad accident. A Friday night on 176th Street, just off Highway 1, a teenager went into the back of a semi.

The seventeen-year-old kid driving was dumb as can be. No seat belt. His head smashed into the windshield and the steering wheel crushed into his chest.

But he was alive. A good Samaritan was right behind him. He stopped, ran over to the accident and called 911. Then he pulled open the door and with all the blood and glass, a horrible sight, he made sure the boy was still breathing.

You didn't see that part on television, did you? The next day there were pictures of the accident and the head smashed into the windshield, but you didn't see the guy who helped.

Before the pictures were taken this good Samaritan was comforting the driver. The injured kid wanted to talk to his mother. So this guy who came out of the rainy darkness to help, got the phone number from the kid and called his mother on his cell phone.

He told her that her son had been in an accident, but he was okay. He was praying that was true.

Then he held the phone against the kid's ear so he could whisper to his mother.

And then the firemen came and this good Samaritan disappeared without leaving his name, without saying a word. He was gone.

Darn media. You only saw the firemen lifting this kid out of the car, and the screams when his broken legs were moved. Sensationalism. A terrible thing.

Of course you didn't see the good Samaritan because his name was Steve Lyon, a news cameraman from Global TV who has seen and photographed scores of accidents. He stopped and helped the kid and made the phone calls and held the phone against the kid's ear, and only when the firemen came did he stop helping and get his camera. Not before then.

Darn media. They leave out so much of the story.

THE ARCHERS

I was editing with Simon Bonaface recently when he said, "Whoops, wait a minute. 'The Archers' are on."

If you are English, like Simon, you know "The Archers." If you are not, you should not know because it could hurt your brain.

"The Archers" is a radio program on the BBC that has run 15,397 episodes without anything actually happening.

"It's great," says Simon. "Just listen."

So on the radio, thanks to the computer, I listen to Ruth who must leave work early to take care of Meriel who has a stomach ache caused by cake and fizzy drinks.

"That's it?" I ask.

"That's it!" says Simon.

"Is there sex in it?"

"Noooo, no sex," says Simon.

"Violence?"

"Noooo, no violence," says Simon, although sometimes they get annoyed at each other, but they never yell.

It all takes place in a small village, and it is about simple country folks. They talk about the weather and bunions and how the crops are doing.

"Anything else?"

"No, not much ever happens there," Simon says in a way that lets me know nothing else is ever expected to happen.

Simon said his grandmother used to listen to it. It has been on the air without a break since 1950. It is the world's longest-running radio soap opera and is an institution, a religion, in Britain.

"Can we start working now?" I ask.

"Wait, just wait," he said. "I have to find out if Ruth gives Meriel some tea for her stomach."

"How can you have a story without sex and violence and intrigue and murder and tax evasion?" I asked.

"You'd have to be British to understand," he said.

I leave the edit room shaking my head and ask Ian Haysom, the news director, if he ever heard of "The Archers."

"Heard of it? It's great. You should listen to it between now and Christmas. It really gets good."

I said this is only July. Christmas is a long time off.

"It takes some time to get into it," he said.

"So, if this is so wonderful why did you ever leave England?" I asked.

"No parking spaces," he said

Sort of like the Archers, in real life.

THE REAL STORY

It is like fishing. They are never there until you don't have a hook in the water. I am speaking, of course, about stories, which are like fish because they nourish our lives and equally important they keep me employed, which I like very much.

Cameraman Geoff Fontes and I are in our fishing boat with rubber tires cruising the back alleys and main streets with the camera ready and we ain't finding nothin'.

Wait, there's potential. A guy in his van is trying to get into an underground parking lot but the van is just a smidge too high. Maybe he's going to try to squeeze in. I jump out. Geoff parks and gets the camera.

We know great stories can start with a tiny incident. Maybe the driver has measured the opening and knows he can do it even though it looks like he can't. Then he will tell us "where there's a will there is a way." I will ignore his cliché and he will be an inspiration.

I am thinking that maybe he has no choice and will do it somehow. I am hoping something amazing is going to happen.

Then he backs up and drives away.

I will be strong. We will fish somewhere else.

Two hours later we still have found nothing. I am getting weak. I pray the phone does not ring from the office saying they need the camera somewhere else.

We see little kids watching a construction site. No. They are in a daycare and we cannot take their pictures. We see guys moving a dock around Granville Island. No, "we are just moving a dock, and besides, we're finished."

All the while Geoff is getting pages about buildings burning in Tennessee and police stand-offs in California. He belongs to some kind of emergency notification network that tells you about disasters of the world. He has even modified it so that he hears only of fatalities where at least two are deceased. Except for that, he is a cheerful guy.

We see a city worker standing by a front-end loader with a flat tire. Have you ever seen a front-end loader with a flat? Fascinating. The city repair truck comes and two guys get out to fix it.

There must be something interesting about changing tires on front-end loaders, I say.

"Nope," they say. "We just change it."

At last we see some kids throwing rocks on Trout Lake, which is frozen. The rocks make tweeting and chirping sounds. That is wonderful. And then we meet a grandfather who is willing to carry home a chunk of ice for his grandson whose little hands are cold. That is beautiful. And the grandfather says it is his job to make the impossible become real for his grandson. That is even more beautiful. I am happy. We have caught a prize.

Then I go to edit with Jamie Forsythe who works in one of the microwave trucks, which is really a mobile broadcast centre where he is able to edit and send live reports to the newsroom.

He is parked next to Science World. When I get there we both see a homeless man nearby who has piled up his blankets over his shopping carts and crawled inside his flimsy shelter right next to the giant shinny silver ball that contains the wonders of the world. His tiny home looks so out of place.

We go to work and Jamie edits, meaning he puts the pictures together that makes the story look good, and I write about the frozen pond. We finish and it is nearly 6 p.m. and we get out of the truck. And there, surrounding the homeless man's shelter, a group of young women are exercising.

They have put their exercise mats on the ground in a circle around his cart and they are skipping ropes, and then doing push-ups and sit-ups. The women all look healthy and fit and are under the guidance of a trainer who is telling them how to get more reps and hops and how to build their abs while the homeless man is peeking out through the blankets. The women are close enough so that when they stretch out their legs some of them touch the cart.

It is a living story of contrasts, of rich and poor, of separate worlds and of oblivion to one of those worlds. Jamie has an emergency camera, but as he gets it out the women are just finishing their body building. They roll up their mats, tuck away their water bottles, and jog away. The cart covered with blankets remains alone.

It would have been a beautiful story of how we actually live. But it got away.

Then again, there's always tomorrow.

YOLA IS FEELING MUCH BETTER NOW

It was magic. Dog poop cleaned the snow off my driveway.

When I drove home last night and got to the block before my house I was worried. The nice operator of the city snowplow had made a wall down the curb three feet high. No one could get in or out of their houses, or driveways or front yards.

My house was around the corner.

Then I turned the wheel and what the heck is that? My driveway was completely cleared. It was shovelled. It had no snow.

I pulled in happy as a guy with a shovelled driveway could be and looked across the street. My neighbours were waving to me through their window.

I have very nice neighbours, the kind of neighbours you would pray for. I wrote about them in my latest book, which if you got a copy of you would learn that they have birthday parties for the garbage men, which of course makes them very special. And if you bought a copy of my book I would be happy.

They invited me over for wine and food. They are celebrating. Why are they celebrating?

Because Yola pooped.

Yola is a dog, a dachshund. And Yola had been sick for a while, very sick, and getting worse. She was not pooping. She was near dying.

Caroline, who is Yola's main guardian, had been to several vets. The bottom bid was $900, the top, $1,200, to cut her open and say: "This seems to be a case of post medical-octavial-sinoposis-hieroglyphics." Which sounds very bad no matter how you say it.

And then they add, "For another $500 we will runs more tests, unless of course you do not care about Yola." And of course you do care about Yola.

Yesterday, right before going for the operation, Caroline took Yola for one last walk.

Two minutes later you could hear Caroline's voice at the end of the street.

"Yola pooped! YOLA POOPED!!"

And not just poop, but Yola pooped a large piece of the blanket that had been in Caroline's daughter's room. It was a very large, amazingly large piece of blanket poop. A piece so large it would be hard to believe it could fit inside such a small dachshund.

From almost dying Yola started jumping off the curbs. She raced in circles. She barked. She was a happy Yola.

"Here is a $1,000 bag of poop," said Caroline, showing off a plastic bag filled with darkly stained former blanket.

The neighbours wanted to celebrate. But wait a minute. How do you celebrate poop when the garbage police are coming down the block?

A city truck with a sinister guy getting out, opening garbage cans and looking in.

Can you imagine:

"Excuse me, ma'am, no need to get excited. I'm the garbage sheriff hunting for illegal, criminal, immoral and unethically overfilled cans."

This on the street where they bake cakes for the garbage men. (Story in the last book.)

"We're not going to bake YOU a birthday cake," one neighbour said to the garbage inspector.

Meanwhile Yola is still jumping off the curbs. Yola is feeling very good.

Then all the neighbours decided to celebrate the passing of the poop by building a snowman. All of them? Yes, all are home today. Bruce is a high school teacher. The schools are closed. Jim drives trains for CN. He rests at home between trips. Perry is a set designer for TV shows. The writers are on strike.

Caroline is a TV director. Same strike. Beth is a court reporter. Court's cancelled because of snow. Barb is a full-time stay-at-home mother, but today the schools are closed so her kids, Isobel and Jimmy, are staying home so she is staying home making hot chocolate for stay-at-home kids, like Kate and Alice, who are also home playing in the snow.

Then they build the snowman, and Beth has a snowman kit. A snowman kit? What's a snowman kit?

"I got it in a thrift store for 90 percent off," she said. "Who could resist?"

They made a seven-foot-tall snowman and put in the felt eyes that looked like pieces of coal and the plastic nose that looked like a carrot and Perry made one of the eyes wink at Yola because that is what he does when the writers are not on strike.

Then they ran out of things to do and said, "Let's celebrate the poop by cleaning Mike's driveway." That is the magical part.

And then I came home to the surprise and they invited me to visit.

"We toast to Yola, and her blanket," they said.

And I toast to my neighbours who cleaned my driveway. And to a pint-sized dog, who if she did not poop there would have been much worry, possibly a tragic outcome, a large bill to pay, no snowman with a winking eye, and no shovelled-out driveway.

It was a very good poop.